Infection Control in the
Child Care Center and Preschool

Third Edition

Infection Control in the Child Care Center and Preschool

Third Edition

Edited by

Leigh G. Donowitz, M.D.

Professor of Pediatrics
Division of Infectious Diseases
University of Virginia Health Sciences Center
Charlottesville, Virginia

Williams & Wilkins
A WAVERLY COMPANY

BALTIMORE • PHILADELPHIA • LONDON • PARIS • BANGKOK
BUENOS AIRES • HONG KONG • MUNICH • SYDNEY • TOKYO • WROCLAW

1996

Editor: Kathleen Courtney Millet
Managing Editor: Joyce Murphy
Production Coordinator: Barbara J. Felton
Designer: Wilma E. Rosenberger
Typesetter: Peirce Graphic Services, Inc.
Printer/Binder: Vicks Lithograph

ISBN 0-683-18041-X

90000

9 780683 180411

351 West Camden Street
Baltimore, Maryland 21201-2436 USA

Rose Tree Corporate Center
1400 North Providerce Road
Building II, Suite 5025
Media, Pennsylvania 19063-2043 USA

Accurate indications, adverse reactions, and dosage schedules for drugs are provided in this book, but it is possible that they may change. The reader is urged to review the package information data of the manufacturers of the medications mentioned.

Printed in the United States of America

First Edition, 1991
Second Edition, 1993

Library of Congress Cataloging-in-Publication Data

Infection control in the child care center and preschool / edited by
   Leigh G. Donowitz.—3rd ed.
      p.   cm.
   Includes bibliographical references and index.
   ISBN 0-683-18041-X
   1. Communicable diseases in children—Prevention.   2. Day care centers—
Health aspects.   I. Donowitz, Leigh G.
   [DNLM: 1. Communicable Diseases—in infancy & childhood. 2. Communicable
Disease Control.   3. Child Day Care Centers. WC 100 I385 1996]
RJ401.I528   1996
614.4'4—dc20
DNLM/DLC
for Library of Congress   96-30380
                                                                                            CIP

The publishers have made every effort to trace the copyright holders for borrowed material. If they have inadvertently overlooked any, they will be pleased to make the necessary arrangements at the first opportunity.

To purchase additional copies of this book, call our Customer Service department at **(800) 638-0672** or fax orders to **(800) 447-8438.** For other book services, including chapter reprints and large quantity sales, ask for the Special Sales department.

Canadian customers should call **(800) 268-4178,** or fax **(905) 470-6780.** For all other calls originating outside of the United States, please call **(410) 528-4223** or fax us at **(410) 528-8550.**

Visit Williams & Wilkins on the Internet: **http://www.wwilkins.com** or contact our Customer Service department at **custserv@wwilkins.com**. Williams & Wilkins customer service representatives are available from 8:30 am to 6:00 pm, EST, Monday through Friday, for telephone access.

97 98 99 00
2 3 4 5 6 7 8 9 10

To my children
Nick and Jeff
and to healthy child care
for all children

Preface

The rapid increase in the number of women in the work force over the past 40 years has created the need for child day care centers and preschools. More than 15 million children under 5 years of age spend all or part of their day in care outside their home, and it is anticipated that by the year 2000, 80% of children under 1 year of age will have a mother working outside the home.

The prevention of the spread of infectious diseases in the child care and preschool setting has been addressed by attempting to exclude sick children from attending child care during their illness. However, experience has shown that these exclusionary rules do not prevent isolated cases and outbreaks of infection that then extend beyond the child care and preschool attendees to their families and the surrounding community. One of the reasons for the very high rate of infectious disease amongst child care and preschool attendees is that this is our most infection-susceptible age group. Infants and children under the age of 5 lack prior exposure to most infectious pathogens, and thus there is rapid spread of infection in this susceptible population. Their close contact, care, and play coupled with their lack of hygienic practice further facilitate transmission of infectious agents. Isolation of infected cases is further hampered in that many children are infectious before they become symptomatic, are chronic carriers of pathogens, or have mild to asymptomatic infections that go undiagnosed but can spread to other children or adults.

The goal of this book is to provide child care and preschool providers, pediatricians, family practitioners, and public health officials with a current and easy to read reference on infections and infection control for children in day care. This book provides:

- An overview of how infections are spread.

- Suggested policies for enrollment requirements, staff education, and employee health.

- Guidelines for children at greater risk of infection (e.g., infants, immune-compromised children, and children with chronic diseases).

- Guidelines for investigation and management of outbreaks.

- Information on specific pathogens with information on the reservoir, transmission, incubation, infectious periods, and suggested management of each infection in this unique setting.

In conclusion, I wish to thank my secretary, Linda Bryant, who single-handedly organizes, edits, and provides the secretarial assistance that makes each edition of this book better than the last. I also would like to acknowledge the authors of this text who not only provide their expertise, time, and scholarship in writing this book but who, as respected colleagues and pediatricians, have spent their lives treating and preventing the spread of infection in children.

Leigh Grossman Donowitz, M.D.

Contributors

Stuart P. Adler, M.D.

Professor and Division Chairman,
  Pediatric Infectious Diseases
Medical College of Virginia
Richmond, Virginia

Susan M. Anderson, M.D.

Associate Professor
Department of Pediatrics
Kluge Children's Rehabilitation Center
Charlottesville, Virginia

James W. Bass, M.D.

Colonel, Medical Corps
Senior Clinical Consultant in Pediatrics and
  Pediatric Infectious Diseases
Department of Pediatrics
Tripler AMC, Hawaii

Thomas A. Bell, M.D., M.P.H.

Health Officer, Cowlitz County and Lewis County
Longview, Washington

Leigh G. Donowitz, M.D.

Professor of Pediatrics
Department of Pediatrics
University of Virginia Health Sciences Center
Charlottesville, Virginia

E. Lee Ford-Jones, M.D.

Project Director, Quality Out of Home Child Care
Canadian Paediatric Society
Department of Paediatrics
Division of Infectious Disease
The Hospital for Sick Children
Toronto, Ontario
CANADA

Anne A. Gershon, M.D.

Professor of Pediatrics
Director, Division of Infectious Disease
Department of Pediatrics
Columbia University College of Physicians and Surgeons
New York, New York

Charles M. Ginsburg, M.D.

Professor and Chairman of Pediatrics
Department of Pediatrics
University of Texas Southwestern Medical Center
Dallas, Texas

Kenneth E. Greer, M.D.

Professor and Chair
Department of Dermatology
Charlottesville, Virginia

Moses Grossman, M.D.

Professor Emeritus, Pediatrics
University of California, San Francisco
Department of Pediatrics
San Francisco General Hospital
San Francisco, California

Caroline Breese Hall, M.D.

Professor of Pediatrics and Medicine
  in Infectious Diseases
University of Rochester Medical Center
Rochester, New York

Scott A. Halperin, M.D.

Professor of Pediatrics
Dalhousie University
Izaak Walton Killam Hospital for Children
Halifax, Nova Scotia
CANADA

Margaret R. Hammerschlag, M.D.

Professor of Pediatrics and Medicine
Division of Pediatric Infectious Diseases
State University of New York
Health Science Center at Brooklyn
Brooklyn, New York

Gregory R. Hayden, M.D.

Professor of Pediatrics
Department of Pediatrics
University of Virginia Health Sciences Center
Charlottesville, Virginia

J. Owen Hendley, M.D.

Professor of Pediatrics
Head, Pediatric Infectious Diseases
Department of Pediatrics
University of Virginia Health Sciences Center
Charlottesville, Virginia

Mary Anne Jackson, M.D.

Associate Professor of Pediatrics
The Children's Mercy Hospital
University of Missouri School of Medicine
Kansas City, Missouri

Richard F. Jacobs, M.D., F.A.A.P.

Horace C. Cabe Professor of Pediatrics
Chief, Pediatric Infectious Diseases
University of Arkansas for Medical Sciences
Arkansas Children's Hospital
Little Rock, Arkansas

Barbara A. Jantausch, M.D.

Assistant Professor of Pediatrics
The George Washington University School of
   Medicine and Health Sciences
Children's National Medical Center
Washington, D.C.

Deborah L. Kernested, R.N.

Project Co-ordinator, Quality Out of
   Home Child Care
Canadian Paediatric Society (CSP)
Department of Paediatrics
Division of Infectious Disease
The Hospital for Sick Children
Toronto, Ontario
CANADA

William C. Koch, M.D.

Assistant Professor of Pediatrics
Medical College of Virginia
Richmond, Virginia

Sandra M. Landry, R.N., M.S.

Nurse Epidemiologist
Thomas Jefferson Health District
Charlottesville, Virginia

Andrew D. Lynk, M.D., M.S.C., C.T.M., F.R.C.P.(C)

Chief of Pediatrics
The Cape Breton Regional Hospital
Sydney, Nova Scotia
CANADA

Marian G. Michaels, M.D., M.P.H.

Assistant Professor of Pediatrics and Surgery
Division of Allergy/Immunology and
   Infectious Diseases
Department of Pediatrics
University of Pittsburgh School of Medicine

Children's Hospital of Pittsburgh
Pittsburgh, Pennsylvania

Trudy V. Murphy, M.D.

Associate Professor of Pediatrics
University of Texas Southwestern Medical Center
Dallas, Texas

John D. Nelson, M.D.

Professor of Pediatrics
The University of Texas Southwestern Medical Center
Dallas, Texas

Ross A. Pennie, M.D., F.R.C.P.C.

Associate Professor of Pathology and Pediatrics
Infectious Disease Service
Chedoke-McMaster Hospitals
Hamilton, Ontario
CANADA

Philip A. Pizzo, M.D.

Acting Director, Division of Clinical Sciences
Chief of Pediatrics
Head, Infectious Disease Section
National Cancer Institute
Bethesda, Maryland

Keith R. Powell, M.D.

Professor of Pediatrics
Associate Chair for Clinical Affairs
University of Rochester Medical Center
Rochester, New York

Karen S. Rheuban, M.D.

Associate Dean for Continuing Medical Education
Professor of Pediatrics
Department of Pediatrics
University of Virginia Health Sciences Center
Charlottesville, Virginia

William J. Rodriguez, M.D., Ph.D.

Chairman, Department of Infectious Diseases and
   Microbiology Research
Professor of Pediatrics
The George Washington University School of Medicine
   and Health Sciences
Children's National Medical Center
Washington, D.C.

Andrea J. Ruff, M.D.

Associate Professor
Department of International Health
Johns Hopkins University
School of Hygiene and Public Health
Baltimore, Maryland

Theresa A. Schlager, M.D.

Assistant Professor of Pediatrics
Department of Pediatrics
University of Virginia Health Sciences Center
Charlottesville, Virginia

Gwendolyn B. Scott, M.D.

Professor of Pediatrics
Director, Division of Pediatric Infectious Disease and Immunology
University of Miami School of Medicine
Miami, Florida

Eugene D. Shapiro, M.D.

Professor of Pediatrics and Epidemiology
Department of Pediatrics
Yale University School of Medicine
New Haven, Connecticut

Ziad M. Shehab, M.D.

Professor of Clinical Pediatrics & Pathology
Pediatrics Infectious Diseases Section
Department of Pediatrics

The University of Arizona Health Sciences Center
Tucson, Arizona

Jane D. Siegel, M.D.

Professor of Pediatrics
Department of Pediatrics
Division of Infectious Disease
The University of Texas Southwestern Medical Center
Dallas, Texas

Ciro V. Sumaya, M.D.

Administrator, Health Resources and Services Administration
Rockville, Maryland

Timothy R. Townsend, M.D.

Associate Professor of Pediatrics
Johns Hopkins Hospital
Baltimore, Maryland

Ronald B. Turner, M.D.

Associate Professor of Pediatrics and Laboratory Medicine
Director, Pediatric Infectious Diseases
Children's Hospital
Medical University of South Carolina
Charleston, South Carolina

David A. Whiting, M.D.

Clinical Professor of Dermatology and Pediatrics
University of Texas Southwestern Medical Center
Dallas Associated Dermatologists
Dallas, Texas

Richard J. Whitley, M.D.

Professor of Pediatrics
University of Alabama at Birmingham
Department of Pediatrics
Children's Hospital
Birmingham, Alabama

Terry Yamauchi, M.D.

Professor and Vice-Chairman
Department of Pediatrics
Arkansas Children's Hospital
Little Rock, Arkansas

Contents

Section I

Transmission

How Germs Are Spread

J. OWEN HENDLEY, M.D.

Child day care centers provide a unique setting conducive to transmission of infectious agents. Preschool-aged children who are susceptible to virtually every infection congregate daily with their peers. Each child brings viruses, bacteria, and parasites from his or her own family to share. The gathered children have habits of personal hygiene that are either questionable (at best) or deplorable (on the average). A child who acquires an infection may generously share these germs with adult workers in the child care center, with his or her own parents and siblings, and with peers at the center.

This book would not be needed if we had an easy and practical method to prevent transmission of pathogens in the child care or preschool environment. Since we do not have such a method, I will highlight what we know about transmission of infectious agents as a basis for at least limiting spread.

Three steps are required for transmission of an infectious agent from an infected individual to an uninfected person (Table 1–1). First, the pathogen must be excreted by the infected person from a site such as the nose or the mouth or in the feces. Excretion does not occur through the skin (except from boils, impetigo, or varicella) or through clothes. Second, the excreted pathogen must be transferred to the well person. Transfer could be through the air (aerosol spread), or by direct contact (hand-holding), or by way of an intermediary surface (door knobs). Finally, the infecting agent must reach a susceptible site (usually the mouth, the nose, or the eye) to infect the well person. A pathogen on the skin of a well person does not infect that person unless it is inoculated onto a susceptible mucosa.

Table 1.1.   Pathogens Transmitted in the Child Care Center

	Bacteria	Viruses	Parasites
Direct	Group A streptococci Staphylococcus aureus	Herpes simplex Herpes zoster	Pediculosis Scabies
Respiratory	Bordetella pertussis Group A streptococci Haemophilus influenzae Neisseria meningitidis Mycobacterium tuberculosis	Adenovirus Influenza Measles Parainfluenza Respiratory syncytial virus Rhinovirus Varicella	
Fecal-oral	Campylobacter Escherichia coli Salmonella Shigella	Enteroviruses Hepatitis A Hepatitis E Rotavirus	Cryptosporidium Giardia lamblia Pinworms
Contact with infected blood and secretions (urine, saliva)		Cytomegalovirus Hepatitis B Hepatitis C Herpes simplex Human immuno-deficiency virus	

The sites from which organisms are excreted by an infected child are known. Agents (viruses, bacteria, and parasites) that infect the gastrointestinal tract are excreted in the feces. Viruses and bacteria that infect the respiratory tract are excreted in respiratory tract secretions (nasal mucus, droplets in cough or sneezes) and not in feces. Cytomegalovirus is excreted in both saliva and urine (Table 1–1).

The three transmission steps (Table 1–2) may be illustrated with two examples. In the first, transmission of a virus causing gastroenteritis (such as rotavirus) would begin with excretion of the virus in the diarrheal stool of the sick child. Transfer to a well person would result from contamination of the hands of the person with stool, while changing

Table 1.2.   Three Steps Required for Transmission of an Infectious Agent[a] from an Infected to an Uninfected Person

Excretion	Pathogen must be excreted from site(s) by infected person
Transfer	Pathogen must be transferred to well person
Inoculation	Pathogen must reach susceptible site in well person

[a]Infectious agent could be bacteria, viruses, or parasites.

the diaper of the infant. The final step, inoculation of a susceptible site, requires that the well individual put his or her hands or contaminated articles into his or her mouth. The virus, after being swallowed, then would infect the lower gastrointestinal tract. Transmission by this fecal-oral route could be interrupted by removing the contaminating virus from the hands of the individual by the use of soap and water.

A second example is provided by transmission of respiratory viruses (rhinovirus, respiratory syncytial virus), which are excreted in nasal secretions and may be in droplets expelled during coughing. These viruses in droplets may be transferred to the well person by way of the air. Susceptible mucosal sites would be inoculated as the well person breathes the droplet-contaminated air. The frequency of transmission of agents through the air is probably small, although this is not known for certain. On the other hand, viruses in nasal secretions may contaminate the hands of the sick person and articles in the environment by way of the hands. Transfer to the hands of the well person occurs during contact with contaminated articles or the hands and nasal secretions of the sick child. Inoculation, the final step in transmission, requires that the hands of the well person contact the lining of his or her nose or eye so as to deposit the virus on the mucosa. This self-inoculation step could be interrupted by rinsing the virus off the hands before mucosal contact, such as occurs from nose or eye rubbing.

What can be done to prevent transfer of infectious pathogens in the child care setting? Constant cleaning of the diaper changing area is an obvious means of reducing environmental contamination with fecal material. Frequent handwashing by adults working in the child care center is one control measure that all could agree is needed to prevent both self-inoculation and transfer of pathogens contaminating hands to other children. The availability of handwashing facilities and the importance of the repetitive use of these facilities by children and personnel cannot be overemphasized.

Section II

Policies

2

Guidelines for Attendees and Personnel

TERRY YAMAUCHI, M.D.

With the steady increase in the numbers of children attending child care centers and preschools, the need for infection control guidelines for this special population also has increased.

GENERAL POLICIES OF THE CENTER

Liaison with Parents and Physicians.   Child care and preschool staff are potentially a very valuable resource in health promotion and maintenance. They should maintain a close working relationship with parents and physicians to ensure that vaccinations are up to date and health problems are promptly identified and adequately managed. Transition times with parents at the beginning and end of the day should be used thoughtfully. Parents should be asked to identify symptoms of any infection in the child or household members at drop-off time.

Liaison with Public Health.   Child care and preschool staff should maintain a close working relationship with their local public health departments. Personnel should appreciate the public health care provider's responsibility for all children as opposed to the parents' primary concern for their own child and the private physician's primary concern for his or her patient.

Physical Organization.   There should be separate rooms and caregivers for diapered and nondiapered children. Food preparation areas must be separate from diaper change areas; each should have handwashing facilities. Bathrooms must include handwashing facilities. Cribs should be separated by at least 3 feet to decrease the

9

transmission of airborne pathogens, and bedding and mattresses should not be shared unless thoroughly cleaned between users.

Staffing Issues.   A staff:child ratio of 1:3 or 1:4 and a small group size (8 to 12 infants maximum) are required. Staff require training and ongoing supervision of their work. Assignment of a primary caregiver will reduce exposures and thus the risk of infection. Responsibilities for diaper changing and food and formula preparation should be assigned to different staff as much as possible. Infants should also be protected from other children and caregivers who are ill with colds or other infections.

ATTENDEE POLICIES

Children attending day care or preschool should be free of known infectious disease unless the center has specific facilities for care of the sick child. Behavioral characteristics of the preschool child attendee make for easy transmission of infectious agents. Because of the difficulty in identifying contagious illnesses during the incubation period and the well-known fact that contagium may be present well before symptoms develop, it is imperative that when an infection is recognized, alternative child care be arranged. Parents or guardians should be carefully questioned as to symptoms of infection in the attendee as well as other family members (siblings and parents). Symptoms such as fever, lethargy, poor feeding, decreased activity, or unusual behavior should be a warning that prodrome to illness may be occurring. Although these symptoms do not necessarily warrant exclusion from the child care facility, close observation for further developing illness is indicated.

Alternate Care for the Sick Child.   Symptoms such as diarrhea, vomiting, rash, skin lesions, wound infections, cough, or runny nose should alert personnel to the strong likelihood of an infectious disease (Table 2–1). The symptoms listed above may also be the result of other conditions not related to infectious agents; however, most often they are associated with transmissible microbial organisms, and whenever possible another care source for these children should be sought. On enrollment, the parent needs to provide the alternate arrangements to be made when a child is identified as ill during the day. Parents must understand the center's policies on ill children and the exclusion guidelines set out by public health authorities.

Table 2.1.   Common Signs and Symptoms of Childhood Infection

Coughing	• Respiratory infections, bronchiolitis, sinusitis, pneumonia caused by respiratory syncytial virus, parainfluenza, influenza, adenovirus, pertussis, *Haemophilus influenzae*, pneumococcus, and others
Diarrhea	• Multiple infectious agents including *Salmonella, Shigella, Campylobacter*, rotavirus, enterovirus, and parasites
Fever	• May be a general symptom of viral or bacterial diseases
Headache and/or stiff neck	• May be a symptom of many illnesses but with fever may represent bacterial or viral meningitis
Infected skin or sores	• May represent impetigo or wound infection, and child should not be allowed in day care without physician consent
Irritability that is unusual or unexplained crying	• May be a symptom of many illnesses but with fever may represent bacterial or viral meningitis
Itching of body or scalp	• Close observation for lesions or agents such as scabies
Lethargy	• May be a general symptom of viral or bacterial diseases
Pink eye	• Tearing, itching of eye, swelling and tenderness, along with redness to eye represents conjunctivitis, either viral or bacterial in nature
Rapid or altered breathing	• Respiratory infections as above
Rash	• Generally must be evaluated on a case-by-case basis; whenever there is a question of etiology, physician should be consulted
Sore throat	• Respiratory infections, pharyngitis, tonsillitis, viruses and group A streptococcus (strep throat)
Stomatitis	• May be a symptom of viral gingivostomatitis (Coxsackie, herpes)
Vomiting	• May be a general symptom of viral or bacterial diseases
Yellow skin and/or eyes	• May be a symptom of hepatitis, and child should not be allowed in day care without physician consent

Table 2.2. Recommended Vaccines for Child Care Center and Preschool Attendees

Vaccine	Comment
Diphtheria-tetanus-pertussis (killed)	• Immunization at 2, 4, 6, and 18 months of age and to be repeated at school entry and every 10 years throughout life
Haemophilus influenzae type b conjugate (killed)	• Immunization at 2, 4, 6, and 15 months of age
Hepatitis B (killed)	• Immunization at birth, 1 and 6 months
Influenzae (killed)	• Yearly vaccine
Mumps (live, attenuated)	• One dose at 15 months of age
Polio (live, attenuated)	• Immunization at 2, 4, and 18 months, repeated at 4 to 6 years of age
Rubella (live, attenuated)	• One dose at 15 months of age
Rubeola (live, attenuated)	• One dose at 15 months of age (may be desirable to give earlier if there is an epidemic), repeated at entry to middle school
Varicella (live, attentuated)	• Immunization at 12 to 18 months

Attendee Immunizations.   Child care and preschool attendees should be up-to-date on their immunizations. The following vaccines should be required for children attendees to day care and preschool facilities: diphtheria-tetanus-pertussis, *Haemophilus influenzae* type b, hepatitis B, mumps, polio, rubella (German measles), rubeola (measles), and varicella (chickenpox) (Table 2–2). The hepatitis A and influenzae vaccines are safe and effective and should be encouraged for all day care children.

Attendee Medical History.   Every effort should be made to acquire an adequate medical history on all attendees. Essential medical information should include immunization records, known allergies, past illnesses, infections, trauma, and medications.

PERSONNEL POLICIES

Child care and preschool personnel should be free of known infections and maintain high standards of personal hygiene. A medical history should be obtained from the day care employee. The history should recognize employee susceptibility by documenting previous infections, immunizations, and medications. Especially important is the history of childhood illnesses such as measles, mumps, rubella, and chickenpox to determine the child care workers' current immune status to the vaccine-preventable diseases. This information takes on added importance in that the immunity induced by some vaccines appears to lessen over a period of time (pertussis and measles vaccines); other vaccines do confer lifelong protection, and the protected and unprotected employee should be identified. Specific immunization recommendations for child care and preschool personnel are outlined below.

Personnel taking medications that may suppress the immune response are at increased risk for infections. Although corticosteroids are the medications more frequently associated with decreasing the immune response, the usual dosage for acute treatment (i.e., allergic reactions) is not enough to compromise the normal host response. Even long-term corticosteroid therapy for such diseases as asthma or systemic lupus erythematosus does not suppress the normal host response enough to cause concern. Higher doses of corticosteroid or chemotherapeutic agents used in hematology/oncology and/or transplantation individuals are the only conditions that place the child care worker at increased risk of infection. If there is any question regarding the employee's immune status, a statement clarifying the current status from his or her prescribing physician is suggested. As stated above, the employee should be free of known infections and maintain high standards of personal hygiene.

Preemployment Physical Examination.   A physical examination should be obtained to ensure that personnel are physically able to carry out the tasks assigned for the area of employment. Obvious physical disorders that may be conducive to transmission of infectious diseases, such as dermatitis, must be cleared by a physician before the employee is allowed to work in areas of child contact.

Preemployment Culturing of Personnel.   Culturing for enteric pathogens is still required in some states, and individual state health regulations should be reviewed. In general, culturing of child care personnel before employment is of little value and should not be necessary. However, personnel should be informed that culturing may be required if surveillance data so indicate during an outbreak investigation.

Personnel Immunizations.   The following vaccines are highly recommended for day care and preschool employees: diphtheria-tetanus, hepatitis A, hepatitis B, influenza, mumps, polio, rubella (German measles), rubeola (measles), and varicella (chickenpox) (Table 2–3).

Diphtheria-tetanus toxoid vaccines have been widely used in the United States and have markedly decreased the incidence of these diseases. Because of the seriousness of these two diseases and the fact that child care workers may be at higher risk, diphtheria-tetanus toxoid vaccination should be carried out every 10 years. It may be necessary to reimmunize personnel who have encountered wounds thought to be contaminated and if more than 5 years have lapsed since the vaccines were last administered.

Rubeola (measles), mumps, rubella (German measles), and varicella (chickenpox) vaccines are live, attenuated viruses. They are available as combination or single vaccines. Each vaccine should be considered separately in regard to its efficacy and use by child care personnel.

Table 2.3.   Immunization Recommendations for Child Care Center and Preschool Personnel

Vaccine	Comment
Diphtheria-tetanus (killed)	• Booster if none in past 10 years
Hepatitis A (killed)	• Proof of immunization or disease in the past
Hepatitis B (killed)	• Proof of immunization or disease in the past
Influenza (killed)	• Yearly
Mumps (live, attenuated)	• Proof of immunization or disease in the past
Polio (inactivated)	• If no immunization in past or booster is found to be needed
Rubella (live, attenuated)	• Proof of immunization or disease in the past
Rubeola (live, attenuated)	• Proof of immunization or disease in the past
Varicella (live, attenuated)	• Proof of immunization or disease in the past

Child care personnel lacking a history of disease or immunity (antibody) by laboratory testing (if available) should receive the vaccines.

Remember that although the attenuated measles, mumps, and rubella virus vaccines have not demonstrated disease and/or transmission, the potential for infection in a compromised child must be considered. Personnel receiving these vaccines can excrete the attenuated viruses for several weeks. Therefore, it seems prudent to limit exposure of newly vaccinated employees, especially to the immunocompromised child, while vaccinees are shedding the attenuated virus.

Poliomyelitis is a disease that has almost disappeared in the United States, and this accurately reflects the efficacy of the poliovirus vaccines. Currently, two types of poliovirus vaccine are available: inactivated poliovirus vaccine (IPV) and live, attenuated oral poliovirus vaccines (OPV). Controversy exists as to which vaccine should be used in this country. As a general rule, persons 18 years or older are at little risk of acquiring wild poliovirus infections and do not require vaccine. However, it is advised that child care and preschool personnel be fully immunized against poliovirus. Inactivated poliovirus vaccine is the vaccine of choice for the unvaccinated child care worker.

The current drop-off in use of the pertussis vaccine for infants has resulted in an increase in whooping cough in infants and children. Speculation has also been raised as to the increased susceptibility of previously immunized adults. In 1994, adolescents and older individuals were found to be the second largest group (after infants) to contract pertussis. Pertussis in these older persons is atypical, with protracted cough, mild illness, but continued infections. Transmission of whooping cough from infants and children to adult caretakers has been demonstrated. Of perhaps greater concern is the transmission of this bacteria from the adult caretaker to the unprotected infant or child. Reimmunization with pertussis vaccine is not recommended because of the increased risk of adverse reactions. Currently, protection of the exposed caretaker consists of administration of oral erythromycin for 14 days.

Influenza virus infections are well-known in the child care facility. The influenza vaccine is a killed virus vaccine and is recommended for all child care personnel. Unfortunately, the influenza virus undergoes periodic changes, and if those changes occur after the vaccine strains have been selected, the vaccine may not be protective. Since the influenza virus vaccine induces protective antibody with a relatively short life, annual immunization is necessary for maximum protection. Because the immune response to the vaccine requires about 2 weeks for antibody levels to become protective, in times of epidemics it may be necessary to administer prophylactically the antiviral agent amantadine (Symmetrel).

Hepatitis B virus vaccine is recommended for all child care workers, but, most importantly, for staff of institutions for the mentally retarded and staff who care for children from high-risk families.

The newly licensed varicella vaccine should be administered to all nonimmune child care workers. This is a live, attenuated vaccine that may produce a few atypical pox lesions but is effective and safe in immunocompetent adults who we know will be exposed to this pathogen in the child care setting.

The newly licensed hepatitis A vaccine is effective and safe and should be used for all child care workers. Although this illness is generally mild or even asymptomatic in children, it can easily spread in this setting and the adult disease can be severe, debilitating, and prolonged.

PET AND ANIMAL POLICIES

Pets and animals may be advocated for use in some day care settings. The benefit of these programs remains to be demonstrated. In many states, it is illegal to bring animals other than Seeing Eye dogs into facilities involved in child care. It is advisable that the child care facility remain in compliance with federal and state licensure regulations.

Remember that pets may be vehicles for diseases. They may initiate allergic reactions in some children, they may cause accidents, unpleasant odors may result, and they may infringe on other children's rights. Animals brought into a strange new environment may not act as they normally do in more familiar surroundings.

The list of diseases associated with pets and animals is extensive. There are many microorganisms, including bacteria, viruses, fungi, and parasites, associated with animals commonly used as pets. With this background information, child care centers and preschools considering the use of pets or other animals within the facility must carefully weigh the potential benefits against the potential risks of exposure of each and every individual (child and staff) within the facility. Until further information is available, it seems prudent to limit the area and exposure in which pets and animals can be used in a center.

RECOMMENDED CLEANING AND DISINFECTION

The child in day care is frequently one who crawls and explores the environment with his or her mouth. Likewise, many day care children are incontinent of urine and feces. For these reasons it is important that the environment be kept as clean as possible. Because of the increased numbers of children and the usual higher ratio of children to adults in the child care setting than in the home, it may be more difficult to maintain cleanliness.

Regularly scheduled environmental cleaning, such as vacuuming, sweeping, dusting, and washing, is an essential element of preventing spread of infectious agents. Standard household cleaning materials are adequate for most environmental surfaces. Care should be taken to ensure proper dilutions and removal after use because of the potential toxicity of many standard products.

Special care may be needed in certain locations such as food preparation and consumption, diaper changing, toilets, and sleep areas, as these are higher in risk for transmission of infectious agents.

Contaminated Surfaces.   Special cleaning of contaminated surfaces requires removal of organic material, followed by application of a commercial cleansing agent. With the growing concern over acquired immune deficiency disease caused by the human immune deficiency virus, additional precautions are indicated. Blood and body fluids contaminated with blood (blood is visible) should be flooded with a bleach solution diluted 1 part bleach to 10 parts water. Many commercial cleansing agents are also acceptable for this purpose, but the label should be carefully reviewed for this use. After thorough soaking, the mixture (contaminated material plus cleansing agent or bleach solution) should be carefully removed, and the area cleaned with the routine product.

Bedding.   Individual bedding should not be shared and must be washed at least weekly.

Carpets.   Carpets are a special surface that are extremely difficult to maintain. In general, the same principles apply, but because carpets may remain wet for long periods of time and thus retain infectious material, the drying of the carpet following clean up, as for other surfaces described above, is imperative. I would consider previously contaminated carpets to be of high risk for transmitting infectious agents, even if cleaned, until they have dried.

Toys and Play Equipment.   In the child care setting, toys and play equipment may be shared by many children, and the potential for transmitting infections is obvious. Toys are especially challenging because of the varying materials and textures involved. In general, soft, cuddly toys should be discouraged, as they require washing and drying, which may be much more difficult than toys of impervious materials. Infants may play with washable toys that are disinfected before and after use by another infant. (To clean, wash toys with dishwashing detergent and water, then rinse in a dilute (1:10 to 1:100 bleach solution.) Infants should not be given shared, nonwashable soft toys that may be contaminated with infectious secretions.

HANDWASHING PROCEDURES

The importance of handwashing cannot be taken lightly. Hand transmission of infectious agents has been recognized for more than 100 years. Handwashing is the single most important procedure for preventing the transmission of infections in the child care and preschool setting. For example, 50% reduction rates in diarrhea were observed in centers adopting a careful handwashing regimen.

Handwashing is the mechanical removal of infectious agents. In the child care center, soap and water are all that is needed to carry out this procedure. What must be taught and reinforced is the importance of performing handwashing correctly and frequently.

Day care employees should be taught that handwashing prevents the employees from infecting themselves or their family members, as well as protects the children in their care.

For routine handwashing, the hands should be wet, and soap applied with vigorous rubbing together to lather on all surfaces for at least 10 seconds, followed by thorough rinsing under running water and drying. Bar soap is acceptable but should be kept in a manner to allow drainage of water.

Handwashing should be carried out when visible contamination or soiling occurs, after use of the toilet, following diaper changes, after handling any body fluids, before eating or feeding, and after tending children with known infections.

To facilitate correct, frequent handwashing, a sink, running water, soap, and clean, preferably disposable, dry towels are necessary.

DIAPERING PROCEDURES

Since so many children in the child care setting are not toilet-trained, diaper changes are necessary. Correct changing of diapers is required to prevent the spread of infectious agents in the fecal material. Even asymptomatic children may harbor infectious microorganisms in their stools. Spread of diseases via the fecal-oral route is well documented but can be prevented if proper procedure is followed.

It is essential that the diapering area is separated from areas of food preparation and feeding. Paper diapers are the preferred materials. Cloth diapers may be stored with the paper diapers, but both should be kept far from the area of the soiled diapers to prevent contamination. The changing surface should be away from other child activities and covered with a smooth, moisture-resistant, cleanable cover.

A tightly covered container with a foot-operated lid is preferred for the soiled diapers. A plastic trash bag or disposable container should be placed into the plastic container. This must be emptied daily, or more frequently as needed.

When changing the soiled diaper, disposable gloves may be used if so desired or available. The removed soiled diaper should be folded inward, to cover fecal material. The child's skin is then cleansed to remove stool. Soap and water may be needed to remove visible soiling. After the clean diaper has been applied and the child has been removed from the changing area, the soiled diaper is placed in the covered container. The changing surface is cleansed with a detergent spray or soap and water and allowed to dry. Hands should be carefully washed whether gloves are used or not.

FOOD PREPARATION

Food preparation areas require sinks and towel supplies separate from diaper change facilities. Hands must be washed before food and formula preparation *and* before feeding an infant. Food should be refrigerated, and any unused food or formula discarded within 24 hours.

Section III

Care of High-Risk Children

3

Young Infants

ANDREW D. LYNK, M.D.,
DEBORAH L. KERNESTED, R.N.,
AND E. LEE FORD-JONES, M.D.

When compared with infants cared for at home, young infants in child care centers are more likely to develop both minor (nuisance) and serious (life-threatening) infections. In addition, signs of serious infection may be subtle. Child care centers are not appropriate for infants unless staff are active in health promotion and infection control activities. A young infant should be cared for by a trained, primary (regularly assigned) caregiver within a safe and stimulating environment. The total group size should be small, and the staff:child ratio less than or equal to 1:4. We have known for a number of years that these same measures, which reduce the risk of infection, also are important to a child's healthy emotional development.

INFECTIOUS RISKS

Young infants in child care centers are uniquely prone to potentially more frequent and severe infections for several reasons.

Increased Susceptibility. An infant's immune system (natural bodily defense against infection) is less developed and capable than that of an older child's. This results in more difficulty fighting an initial infection as well as repeated illnesses with the same infectious agent.

Infants Lack Complete Immunization.   Infants who have not received their initial three diphtheria-pertussis-tetanus-polio vaccinations (2, 4, and 6 months) are more susceptible to infections such as whooping cough.

While not all mothers want to or really need to breast-feed, it should be noted that electing not to breast-feed may deprive infants of the protective benefits of breast milk against infections.

Increased Exposure.   It is normal for any child entering a group situation where exposure is increased (e.g., public school) to have more infections. Infants in group care face such increased exposure from staff, other children, and even other parents. This results in ample opportunity for transmission of infectious agents, primarily via unwashed hands (very common) but also through contaminated objects and surfaces.

Infants, in general, require more handling by caregivers for changing diapers, cuddling, feeding, and cleaning of facial secretions. Without proper preventive measures (e.g., handwashing), caregivers and other children may easily transmit high doses and wide varieties of infectious agents from one infant to another.

Infants also have frequent hand-to-mouth contact. This increases their exposure to any infectious agents in their surrounding environment, which may have been contaminated by sick staff or children or by apparently healthy children or staff who are at the beginning or end of an infectious disease. Respiratory viruses, for example, will persist for hours on surfaces. Other common infectious agents causing diarrheal illness (rotavirus, *Giardia*), hepatitis (HAV), and cytomegalovirus (CMV) diseases may live for days to weeks on toys and play mats.

Tendency to Complications.   While some infectious agents, such as respiratory viruses, are a nuisance when they occur in the older child, in the young infant they may lead to complications such as ear or lung infections.

COMMON INFECTIONS

Infections in infants attending child care centers can be broken down into (a) those causing illness in infants and adults (staff, parents), such as respiratory and diarrheal infections, (b) those causing illness only in the infants (e.g., *Haemophilus influenzae* meningitis), (c) those causing illness only in adults (e.g., hepatitis A), and (d) those causing illness only in special situations (e.g., cytomegalovirus affecting the fetus of a pregnant staff member or parent).

Infants are commonly and repeatedly infected with seasonal viruses, which may cause colds, diarrhea, rashes, and fevers. Colds in infants are commonly complicated by ear or eye infections and sometimes by pneumonia. Although hepatitis A may be a common and mild infection in infants in child care, it may cause more serious disease in susceptible adults (caregivers, parents) who are secondarily exposed at work or at home. Although it is much less common, infants in larger child care settings are more likely to be exposed to bacteria such as *H. influenzae,* which may cause serious infections such as pneumonia, bacteremia, and meningitis.

INFECTION CONTROL

Special Infection Control Needs.   Infants do require special infection control procedures. Pediatric infection control experts now recommend the same things psychologists have known for years to be important to an infant's well-being: a primary caregiver who is trained and motivated, a small group size, and a good staff:infant ratio of less than or equal to 1:4.

Physical Organization.   There should be separate rooms and caregivers for diapered and nondiapered children. Food preparation areas must be separate from diaper change areas; each should have handwashing facilities. Bathrooms must include handwashing facilities. Cribs should be separated by at least 3 feet to decrease the transmission of airborne pathogens, and bedding and mattresses should not be shared unless thoroughly cleaned first.

Staffing.   A staff:child ratio of 1:3 or 1:4 and a small group size (8 to 12 infants maximum) are required. Staff require training and ongoing supervision of their work. Assignment of a primary caregiver will reduce exposures and thus the risk of infection. Responsibilities for diaper changing and food and formula preparation should be assigned to different staff as much as possible. Infants should also be protected from other children and caregivers who are ill with colds or other infections.

Handwashing.   Handwashing is a crucial infection control measure. Careful handwashing reduces transmission of infections dramatically. For example, 50 percent reduction rates in diarrhea were observed in centers adopting a careful handwashing regimen.

Diapering.   Hygienic precautions, especially handwashing and surface cleansing, must be ensured during the changing and disposing of diapers. Disposable diapers are recommended. Handwashing facilities including clean towels must be available.

Food Preparation.   Food preparation areas require sinks and towel supplies separate from diaper change facilities. Hands must be washed before food and formula preparation *and* before feeding an infant. Food should be refrigerated, and any unused food or formula discarded within 24 hours.

Toys.   Infants may play with washable toys that are disinfected before and after use by another infant. (To clean, wash toys with dishwashing detergent and water, then rinse in a dilute 1:10 to 1:100 bleach solution.) Infants should not be given shared, nonwashable soft toys that may be contaminated with infectious secretions.

Environmental Cleaning.   Individual bedding must be washed at least weekly. Other surfaces should be cleaned between use or daily, depending on the item.

Surveillance of Infants for Symptoms of Infection.   Primary caregivers must be watchful for subtle signs of infection in young infants, such as changes in feeding or behavioral patterns. These may be the only manifestations of serious infections in young infants.

Risks to Healthy Children.   Healthy children exposed to infants at child care centers do have an increased risk of infection. Staff working with diapered infants may directly (via hands) or indirectly (via food, mats, or toys) infect other healthy children if hygienic precautions (separate staff, separate areas, handwashing) are not maintained. Note that infected infants may appear well if they are just starting or ending an illness or have mild or clinically undetectable infections such as is the case with hepatitis A. It is therefore crucial to maintain hygienic precautions at *all times.* Allowing infants and older mobile children to play together increases everyone's exposure to infectious agents.

Infants who have acquired infections such as diarrhea or head and chest colds at the child care center are likely to infect 20 percent to

100 percent of their own healthy family members. In most cases the healthy child, if older, will have milder disease, and the reason for separation of infants from healthy children is primarily to protect the infant. In the case of hepatitis A, infection is usually more severe in the older child or adult.

Exclusion from Child Care Center Attendance.   As with older children, infants should be screened daily and excluded when they have signs and symptoms of illness that require a degree of care or manpower beyond the staff's abilities and available time. The following is a list of signs and symptoms of infection in infants that should serve as attendance exclusion criteria:

- Fever (rectal temperature is greater than 101° Fahrenheit or 38.3° Centigrade)
- Rash with fever
- Diarrhea (loose stools that cannot be contained with a diaper)
- Vomiting
- Unusual tiredness
- Poor feeding
- Persistent crying or irritability
- Breathing difficulties or persistent coughing
- Yellow skin or eyes (jaundice)

When child care staff notice any of the symptoms above, the parents should be contacted, and medical attention sought.

Recommendations for Personnel.   All personnel caring for young infants should receive specific training and ongoing supervision regarding:

- Disease transmission and prevention
- Principles and practice of hygiene
  - (a) Handwashing
  - (b) Diapering procedures
  - (c) Food handling, preparation, and feeding
  - (d) Environmental cleanliness
- First aid and cardiopulmonary resuscitation

- Recognition of behavioral variations in both healthy and ill infants
- Maintenance of daily records on each infant, based on information from staff and parents

Signs of illness in young infants may be subtle. Caregivers should consistently look after the same infants and communicate closely with their parents on a daily basis so that they may recognize which behaviors (e.g., feeding, temperament, stooling) are normal and which are not.

Caregivers should have written policies and procedures to deal with infant illnesses and emergencies. Ideally, child care centers should have access to a nurse and/or physician consultant and to copies of relevant aspects of each child's current health records.

Caregivers should not look after more than three or four infants, nor should they work concurrently with toddlers and older children.

Staff who are sick with the following illnesses should not take care of infants:

- Diarrhea and/or vomiting
- Measles, mumps, or rubella
- Chickenpox or shingles
- Skin infections
- Pulmonary tuberculosis
- Hepatitis
- Head colds and coughs
- Cold sores on lips

Parental Advice. Young infants at child care centers are prone to more frequent minor and serious infections than are infants cared for at home and older children.

Exposure to infectious agents at any child care center is dependent on several factors:

- The total number of children at the center
- Infant group size (ideally, not more than 8 to 12)
- The ratio of staff to infants (ideally, less than 1:4)

- Whether or not each small group of infants has an exclusive, skilled, primary caregiver
- The training and supervision of the staff in standard environmental hygiene practices (e.g., proper handwashing after diaper changing and before food preparation and feeding)
- The floor design and availability of proper equipment to ensure safe hygienic practices (e.g., number of sinks, separate diaper and kitchen facilities, 3-foot space between cribs, physical separation of infants and their caregivers from older children)
- The enforcement of specific, written exclusion policies for children and staff
- Liaison with the local department of public health

Parents must have prearranged alternative care plans for their infants in the event of illness. They should appreciate the importance and benefits of well-supervised health procedures and exclusion policies. They should always advise the child care center of the cause of any illness necessitating their child's absence.

Parents should get to know and maintain daily communications with their child's primary caregiver.

Parents should be aware that young infants, even in excellent centers, will probably have more frequent colds and febrile illnesses, most of which will be minor. However, it may be difficult for caregivers to distinguish minor from serious febrile illnesses in infants less than 3 to 6 months of age.

4

Children with Immunodeficiencies

PHILIP A. PIZZO, M.D.

INFECTIOUS RISKS

Protection of a child's body against infection includes the cooperative activity and interaction of physical barriers (e.g., lining of intestinal and respiratory tracts), cellular and soluble factors produced by blood cells and the immune system to help fight invading microorganisms, in concert with the protective effects that come from the organisms that normally colonize various body surface areas. When any one of these components becomes impaired by either a disease or its treatment, an immune deficiency and increased susceptibility to infection can occur. Unfortunately, in a number of immunodeficiencies, more than one component is adversely affected, rendering the body at risk for a wide array of potential infectious complications.

Immunodeficiencies have traditionally been divided into either those that are congenital or those that are acquired. Congenital immunodeficiencies are uncommon and can affect one or more components of the immune system. These deficiencies often become manifest shortly after birth but may sometimes become apparent only during the early years of life. An acquired immunodeficiency refers to a deficit of the immune system that is the consequence of a disease or treatment occurring after birth. Of the acquired immunodeficiencies, the abnormalities consequent to cancer and its treatment and the severe sequelae of infection with the human immunodeficiency virus (HIV) represent the major causes of acquired immunodeficiency in childhood.

Regardless of whether the immune impairment is a defect with which the child was born or whether it occurs after birth as a consequence of disease or its treatment or a new infection such as HIV, the end result is the inability to fight off germs that either are newly acquired or have already been part of the normal microbial flora.

COMMON INFECTIONS

Immunocompromised children are subject to infection with virtually all classes of microorganisms. These include the bacteria, fungi, viruses, and protozoans. However, the risk for infection to any one or more of these microorganisms can be related to the specific immune defect or constellation of immune impairments that have occurred. Accordingly, there are both similarities and differences in the types of infections that occur in children who are immunocompromised as a consequence of cancer or HIV infection.

The child with cancer is at highest risk for infection when receiving more intensive courses of cytotoxic chemotherapy. This is the period when neutropenia is most common and when infection with various members of the indigenous microflora are most likely to occur. Gram-positive and Gram-negative aerobic bacteria are the major causes of infection during the early stages of neutropenia. In most centers around the country, Gram-positive organisms (particularly staphylococci and streptococci) now predominate. In some cases, such as with the coagulase-negative staphylococci, infections are related to the presence of indwelling Hickman-Broviac catheters or abnormalities of the gastrointestinal mucosal integrity. In other cases, the streptococci (such as the alpha viridans streptococci) can cause serious infection as a consequence of certain types of chemotherapy (cytarabine) or ulcerations in the oral cavity sometimes associated with the herpes simplex virus. In addition to Gram-positive bacteria, Gram-negative organisms, especially *Escherichia coli*, *Klebsiella*, and *Pseudomonas aeruginosa*, can also lead to serious infection during periods of neutropenia. Although fungi have become increasingly important as a cause of infection in the neutropenic cancer patient, these infections occur predominantly in patients who have more prolonged periods of neutropenia. The child with cancer is also at risk for infection with certain parasites, the most notable of which is *Pneumocystis carinii*. Reactivation infections can occur with viruses, particularly in the herpes group. The most notable pathogens are herpes simplex and cytomegalovirus. Varicella-zoster virus also represents a very notable threat. Indeed, without treatment, the occurrence of varicella-zoster virus in a seronegative child who is undergoing immunosuppressive therapy can be associated with significant morbidity and even mortality. Also, the respiratory viruses (especially respiratory syncytial virus, parainfluenza, and adenovirus) can cause serious respiratory and systemic infections in immunocompromised cancer patients. Because of its increasing frequency and the occurrence of outbreaks in recent years, measles virus must now once again be added to the list of potential pathogens for the cancer patient.

For the child who has undergone a bone marrow or organ transplant and who is receiving immunosuppressive therapy to maintain the graft, the predominant infections that occur are a consequence of depressed cellular immunity. These include, therefore, reactivation infections with *P. carinii* or with the herpes viruses or adenovirus. Of the herpes viruses, herpes simplex virus and cytomegalovirus are again most notable, and if the child has not previously been infected or immunized, exposure to varicella or measles can also result in significant morbidity. For those children who have had chickenpox and who have undergone bone marrow transplantation or who have received intensive chemotherapy, there is an increased risk for developing reactivation infection with varicella-zoster virus, which is manifested as dermatomal lesions. Depending upon the intensity of the chemotherapy, children who are significantly immunosuppressed and who develop dermatomal zoster are at heightened risk for developing cutaneous or visceral dissemination with this virus.

Children with HIV infection, like those with cancer, can develop infection with virtually all the classes of microorganisms. Although the immune abnormalities in children with cancer can be severe, they are generally intermittent and may abate when chemotherapy is not being given. In contrast, the immune deterioration associated with HIV infection tends to be progressive and unrelenting. Accordingly, the actual pathogens and patterns of infection can vary between children with cancer versus those with HIV infection. For example, the child with HIV infection is at increased risk for developing bacterial infections with encapsulated organisms such as *Streptococcus pneumoniae* or *Haemophilus influenzae*. This is most

likely consequent to the antibody dysfunction and defective neutrophil chemotaxis that occur in children with HIV infection. Unless
they have indwelling catheters in place or are hospitalized, children
with HIV infection are less commonly infected with the Gram-negative or Gram-positive bacteria that predominate in pediatric cancer
patients. Fungi also can cause significant infections in children with
HIV disease; the major pathogen is *Candida*, and the major site of infection tends to be mucosal, particularly the oral cavity (manifested
as thrush) or the esophagus (manifested as an esophagitis with re-
trosternal burning pain). It is rare for the child with HIV infection to
develop invasive fungal disease because quantitative impairments
of neutrophils are much less common in these children than in children with cancer. Parasitic infections do occur in children with HIV
disease, most notably *P. carinii,* although this again represents a reactivation infection consequent to the degree of immunosuppression that has occurred in the child with HIV. In infants, however,
pneumocystis pneumonia can occur as a primary infection and is associated with considerable morbidity and mortality. This underscores the importance for early diagnosis and for surveillance to define high-risk children. To date, it has been infrequent for children
with HIV infection to develop some of the other opportunistic infections that have been so common in adults, such as toxoplasmosis or
cryptococcosis. However, children with HIV disease are subject to
viral infections including the respiratory viruses (which can be associated with chronic shedding of RSV or parainfluenza), the herpes
virus, cytomegalovirus, and, of course, the varicella-zoster virus.
These are the same organisms that can infect normal healthy children, but for the child with HIV disease, the consequences of infection can be considerably greater. Indeed, children with HIV can develop chronic infection, with varicella-zoster virus, and severe
infections, including blindness, with cytomegalovirus. Children
with HIV infection can also develop chronic infections with organisms such as cryptosporidia, salmonellae, or mycobacteria. Although the atypical mycobacteria (e.g., mycobacteria avium-intra-
cellulare) predominate in children, like adults with HIV disease,
Mycobacterium tuberculosis is another likely cause of infection and the
increased frequency of this infection in high-risk children, along
with the burgeoning problem of drug-resistant strains, is of considerable concern.

In summary, children with immunodeficiencies are subject to a wide array of pathogens. Many of these organisms are part of the normal flora of patients and do not cause infection when the immune system is intact. Thus, for example, the child with cancer is more susceptible to infections that arise from within his or her own body than from those that occur as a consequence of exposure to others. To a large degree this is also true of children with HIV infection, although they have a heightened susceptibility to the common bacterial organisms that occur throughout childhood, particularly *S. pneumoniae* and *H. influenzae*. Although children with immunodeficiency are more vulnerable to these infections, were they to share these same organisms with children who were immunocompetent, either no infection would occur, or if infection did occur, it would be no more serious than had it been acquired from a child who had no known immunodeficiency state.

INFECTION CONTROL

There are both similarities and differences in the infection control measures that should be considered and applied to children with cancer, AIDS, or other immunodeficiency states. Because they will represent the majority of the children at risk, the recommendations that follow will be categorized according to (a) whether the underlying disease is cancer and treatment is with immunosuppressive therapies and (b) whether these children have AIDS. The single overriding principle that applies to the care of immunocompromised children (as well as healthy children) is careful handwashing, especially following diaper changes or assisting with toileting procedures. Second, adherence to the principles of universal precautions when handling blood should always be followed. It is more likely that a child (or staff member) in a child care center or preschool will not be diagnosed or recognized as being immunocompromised. Thus, staff education and adherence to simple infection control principles and procedures should be followed at all times and by everyone to keep the child care center or preschool safe for both children and staff members.

Special Infection Control Needs.

Children with Cancer or Those Receiving Immunosuppressive Therapy. Since the majority of infections that arise in children who are immunocompromised because of cancer or its therapy arise from organisms that are already part of the patient's own microbial flora, they generally do not require special infection control procedures. Indeed, the majority of these organisms (Gram-positive and Gram-negative bacteria, *Candida, P. carinii,* and even herpes viruses) are ubiquitous and generally are not causes of infection in immunocompetent individuals. Thus, these patients are at risk for infection from microorganisms that they already carry within them rather than from organisms that they might acquire from other children or from their environment. At the same time, the microorganisms responsible for causing infection in neutropenic children or in children who are receiving immunosuppressive therapy do not represent a particular hazard for children who are immunocompetent. There are, however, some exceptions, the most notable of which are viruses such as the varicella-zoster virus and measles. Children with cancer or those receiving immunosuppressive therapy who have not had a prior history of chickenpox and are exposed to an individual with chickenpox or with dermatomal zoster are at risk to develop primary varicella. Untreated, this infection can be extremely serious in the immunosuppressed child and carries a significant degree of morbidity or even mortality. Fortunately, the advent of antiviral therapy with acyclovir has significantly reduced the serious morbidity and mortality associated with primary varicella in an immunosuppressed individual. The recent approval of the varicella-zoster vaccine, if widely used, also may decrease the risk for infection. Although the varicella-zoster vaccine is NOT recommended for use in immunocompromised, it is anticipated that herd immunity could decrease the overall risk for this infection. Nonetheless, the major current objective is to attempt to prevent varicella by recognizing when an exposure has occurred and administering immunoprophylaxis to the immunosuppressed child. Thus, if there are active cases of chickenpox in the child care center, children who are immunosuppressed should not be in attendance, since it is unlikely to expect that they would be able to remain separated enough to offer protection. Chickenpox is, of course, one of the most contagious illnesses, and individuals who are seronegative are at high risk for developing infection through close contact with an infected individual. Should an exposure occur in the child care center, it is imperative that the physician of the child with cancer or those receiving immunosuppressive therapy be notified immediately. In almost all instances the recommendation will be for the child to receive varicella-zoster immunoglobulin, as this has been shown to either attenuate or prevent entirely the risk for developing an infection following exposure. However, to be successful, varicella-zoster immunoglobulin must be administered within 72 hours from the time of exposure. If an immune-compromised child has received intravenous immunoglobulin (IVIG) within 2 weeks of the exposure it is not necessary to administer zoster immune globulin. Similarly, children who are immunosuppressed and who are exposed to a youngster who has developed measles should also receive immunoprophylaxis with gamma globulin in order to attempt to attenuate or prevent infection.

For the child with cancer, two additional infection control issues apply. First, although it is acceptable for children with low blood counts to attend child care or preschool, it must be noted that when their neutrophil count is low, they are at risk for developing an infectious complication, primarily with organisms that arise from within their own body. Fever is the major predictor of infection in patients with neutropenia. Consequently, if a child with cancer who is neutropenic becomes flushed and appears febrile or has lethargy or lassitude, his or her temperature should be taken. This should be done by the oral or axillary route but never with a rectal thermometer. This is because the use of a rectal thermometer in a child who is neutropenic can lead to erosions around the anus that could become a site of serious infection. If the temperature is elevated above 38° C, the child's parents or caretakers should be notified, and most likely, the child will need to be admitted to the hospital to receive antibiotic therapy until the source of the fever is determined or the period of risk (low neutrophil count) has passed. The second specific consideration applies to children who have indwelling Hickman-Broviac-type catheters. Of course, these catheters should not be manipulated in the child care or preschool environment, but if the child complains of tenderness around the skin or on the chest wall or along the abdomen where the catheter is placed, visual inspection to determine whether there is redness or tenderness should be undertaken. If this is the case, immediate medical attention is necessary, since an infection along the catheter tunnel is likely. Similarly, if the child develops a fever, even in the absence of low blood counts, and has an indwelling catheter, it is important that the child's parents and physician be notified, since, again, antibiotic therapy is likely to be necessary. In neither of these cases, however, do the infections that arise represent hazards for other children.

Children with HIV Infection.   Children with HIV infection also are at risk for infections that arise from both their own indigenous flora and those that can be acquired from sources outside their own body. Since the predominant bacterial infections that occur in children with HIV infection are due to encapsulated bacteria such as *S. pneumoniae* or *H. influenzae*, it is quite possible that these organisms might be acquired from other children in a child care setting. However, since these organisms are ubiquitous, it is not reasonable to impose any particular isolation or restriction that would exclude children with HIV disease. Even if they were immunized in the past, children with HIV may develop pertussis, making it important to consider this possibility in a child with a persistent or whooping-like cough. As with a child with cancer, the predominate opportunistic infections (oral pharyngeal or esophageal candidiasis, *P. carinii* pneumonia) represent reactivation infections and are not ones that could be altered by special isolation or protection systems. Also similar to the child with cancer or to those receiving immunosuppressive therapy, children with HIV infection are at heightened risk for complications related to varicella-zoster virus or measles virus. Consequently, the same isolation and immunoprophylactic procedures described above for children with cancer should be applied to those with HIV infection. Although data are anecdotal, there is the suggestion that certain respiratory viral infections such as those due to the respiratory syncytial virus may be more serious in children with HIV infection or that symptoms and virus excretion may be more prolonged. However, because this organism is also ubiquitous and because it could not be easily differentiated on clinical grounds from other upper or even lower respiratory tract infections occurring in immunocompetent children, it is not possible to recommend specific preventive strategies that might protect the child from acquiring this particular organism.

For both children with cancer and children with HIV infection, there are few data regarding the hazards of exposure to immunocompetent individuals who have been recently vaccinated. Although it appears likely that most vaccinations with attenuated or killed viruses or organisms are not likely to cause problems, it is possible that excretion of certain viruses such as oral poliovirus might represent a hazard for the child who is severely immunosuppressed. There is at least the theoretical possibility that excretion of poliovirus following administration of the live oral polio vaccine in an immunocompetent child might contribute to transmissibility. The live varicella vaccine has recently been approved for normal healthy children and since a small percentage of children who receive this viral vaccine may develop a rash with vesicles that contain virus, it is possible that contact with these children may represent a hazard. However, since this same live vaccine has been tested in children undergoing cancer therapy and has not been associated with significant morbidity, the severity of infection associated with such contacts is likely to be minimal.

Risks to Healthy Children.
Children with Cancer or Those Receiving Immunosuppressive Therapy.   Since the vast majority of infections that occur in children undergoing cancer therapy are with organisms that are not likely to be pathogenic to an immunocompetent child, normal healthy children are not at increased risk for infectious complications simply by having close contact with children with cancer. Moreover, those organisms that are potential infectious hazards are not associated with any increase in morbidity because they were acquired from a child who had cancer or who was receiving immunosuppressive therapy. Again, the major organisms of concern are likely to be viral and include in particular the varicella-zoster virus. It should be noted that children receiving immunosuppressive therapy may have a longer incubation period for varicella-zoster virus than do immunocompetent children, and rather than considering their period at risk as being from days 10 to 21 after exposure, most authorities would recommend that they be considered at risk for infection from days 10 to 28 after exposure to a child who had active varicella. There are no data to support that children with cancer have an increased likelihood for transmitting other common viral or bacterial pathogens as compared with those who are immunocompetent, and, therefore, no special precautions or recommendations are necessary.

Children with HIV Infection.   Although children with HIV infection do have an increased rate of infection with common bacterial organisms such as *S. pneumoniae* and *H. influenzae*, they are as likely to acquire as to transmit these organisms, and there are no data to support that children with HIV infection are more contagious or that the organisms are more virulent. However, it must be noted that among the bacteria are two organisms that could represent infectious hazards in healthy children. The first is *Salmonella*, since children with HIV infection can develop chronic infections with this organism. It has been generally recommended that HIV-infected children who are not toilet-trained be excluded from the child care settings. While on the surface this advice seems reasonable, it is still possible for fecal-oral transmission to occur. Of course, the most important infection control measure that can be executed in any setting is careful handwashing. If both children and staff are instructed about the importance of this practice, especially after toileting or changing diapers, it seems likely that the risks for infection transmission can be well controlled. The second bacterial infection that deserves mentioning is mycobacteria. Although the majority of mycobacterial infections that occur in children and adults with HIV infection are due to atypical organisms, there has been an increase in the incidence of tuberculosis in urban areas, particularly with drug-resistant strains, that has been particularly associated with individuals infected with HIV. Although children who develop primary tuberculosis infections are usually not contagious, if a child with HIV disease has active tuberculosis, the child could pose a hazard to other children and would need to be excluded until the infection was cleared. Importantly, parents of children with HIV are vulnerable to acquisition or reactivation of tuberculosis and, if they are infected and contagious, they pose a threat to both other children as well as personnel.

Most of the fungal organisms that occur in children with HIV do not represent infectious hazards for healthy children. *Candida* is a ubiquitous organism and most immunocompetent children are already colonized with it. *Cryptococcus* occurs only rarely in children with HIV infection, and person-to-person spread with this organism does not occur. Although *Histoplasma* can occur in children with HIV infection, in endemic areas this organism is ubiquitous, children are at risk for acquiring it in their home and environment, and the risk would not be increased by contact with children with HIV infection. Similarly, most of the parasitic infections that might occur in children with HIV disease are not likely to represent infectious hazards to immunocompetent or healthy children. *P. carinii* represents a reactivation infection, and virtually 100% of children who are immunocompetent have already acquired this organism by the time they are 2 years of age. Thus, exposure to a child with *P. carinii* pneumonia does not represent a hazard to the healthy child. Infants less than 2 years of age with HIV infection are susceptible to *P. carinii* pneumonia if their CD4 count declines and they are not receiving prophylaxis. Gastrointestinal infections associated with cryptosporidia or *Isospora belli* can be a significant cause of diarrhea in the HIV-infected child. These organisms can cause transient infection in other immunosuppressed children as well as in immunocompetent individuals. However, in healthy children, symptoms are transient and chronic infection does not occur. Thus, exposure to an HIV-infected child with cryptosporidia diarrhea does not represent a hazard to the healthy child in the child care or preschool setting.

Similar to children with cancer or those receiving immunosuppressive therapy, varicella can be a more significant infection in children with HIV disease. In addition, chronic or persistent cutaneous infections with the varicella-zoster virus can occur in HIV-infected children. Of course, if the HIV-infected child does develop active varicella, he or she should not be in a child care or preschool setting until the infection is resolved. Should a healthy child acquire the varicella-zoster virus from an HIV-infected child, there is no likelihood that the infection will be more serious than if it had been acquired from another healthy individual. Children with chronic skin lesions, whether due to the varicella-zoster virus or bacteria or other organisms, represent a risk when those lesions are active or draining. In general, if lesions are draining and cannot otherwise be covered, it is recommended that the HIV-infected child not have contact with other children in the child care or preschool setting.

The major concern, of course, centers around the possible transmission of HIV itself within the child care or preschool setting. Fortunately, this is an extremely difficult virus to transmit, and transmission can only occur by direct contact with blood or through sexual activities. Casual contact such as is incurred by playing or interacting in a normal family setting is not associated with the transmission of HIV infection. Indeed, a number of studies have demonstrated that even close contacts, including kissing, sharing of food and eating utensils, toothbrushes, and other supplies, do not contribute to a risk for transmission of this virus. Much has been made about the possibility of transmission of HIV by biting. However, there is no proof that HIV has ever been transmitted by biting, and the likelihood for this route of transmission is remote. At this time, the American Academy of Pediatrics recommends that only children who engage in repetitive biting behavior be excluded from child care or school. Thus, the only concerns that require attention for transmission of HIV should center on either blood transmission or sexual activity. Should the child with HIV infection have an injury that bleeds, or have a bloody nose, or have a cutaneous lesion that is oozing blood, care should be taken in assisting or helping the child. The use of universal precautions is recommended because in many settings it is possible that a child may be unrecognized as being infected with the virus. Accordingly, children and staff should be educated that whenever there is a youngster or an individual who has a bleeding lesion, gloves should be worn when offering assistance, and bloody fluids that may have spilled onto the floor, toys, or surfaces should be cleaned with a dilute (1:10) solution of bleach and water. Of course, such a solution should *not* be used to clean the child, since it can be caustic to body surfaces. Should there be a question of sexual abuse within the child care or preschool setting, the possibility for HIV transmission must be considered, and testing may be appropriate and necessary.

Hepatitis B virus is transmitted in a similar way to HIV but is far more contagious, presumably because the inoculum size in blood or body fluids is much higher for hepatitis B virus than for HIV. The most effective precautions that could be used to curtail transmission of hepatitis B are those of universal precautions and universal immunization. Thus, if universal precautions are exercised, they will be effective against both the hepatitis B virus and the HIV. While hepatitis B is not found in the stool, hepatitis A can be transmitted by the fecal-oral route and underscores the importance of handwashing. Cytomegalovirus is also a ubiquitous organism in immunocompromised children and can be acquired by seronegative women. Urine or secretions are the likely sources for infection and again focus on the need for handwashing when bodily excrements are handled.

While precautions are easier to employ when the child is known to be infected or immunodeficient, it must be underscored that within a child care center, it is likely that the diagnosis will be unrecognized or that information may be withheld. Thus, especially in areas of the country where the rate of HIV is highest (i.e., large urban areas), it is likely that children with HIV will be found in child care centers and preschools.

Exclusion from Child Care or Preschool Attendance.

Children with Cancer or Those Receiving Immunosuppressive Therapy.   The major reasons for exclusion are when the child requires medical care or has an infection that is clearly transmissible to healthy children or staff members. As noted above, if the child with cancer has a low neutrophil count and develops a fever, he or she should be referred to a medical care system for antibiotic therapy. Similarly, if the child has an infection around an indwelling catheter or develops a fever and has a catheter, he or she must be referred to medical care for immediate intervention. Relatively few infections that occur in the child with cancer or those receiving immunosuppressive therapy represent hazards to other children and thus criteria for exclusion from the child care center. Those that would include infections with varicella-zoster virus manifested either as chickenpox or dermatomal zoster or as infection with the measles virus. Although the immunocompetent child who has a negative history for varicella and who has contact and exposure with an infected child is at risk to develop chickenpox 10 to 21 days after the exposure, the child with cancer or who is receiving immunosuppressive therapy has a somewhat longer period of risk that might extend up to 28 days after the infectious exposure. Thus, a child with cancer may need to be excluded from the child care center or preschool from day 10 to 28 after an exposure if he or she is at risk to develop primary varicella. Risk is defined as a negative history of infection or a negative antibody titer against the varicella-zoster virus. Should the child have another potentially communicable disease, such as tuberculosis, exclusion from the center is necessary until adequate therapy has been delivered. It should be noted, however, that similar precautions would pertain to immunocompetent children who might acquire a similar infection.

Children with HIV Infection.   Similar to the child with cancer, only rarely is it necessary to exclude the child with HIV infection from the care center. Indeed, the major infectious hazards that would represent a source of concern would be if the child had an infection with tuberculosis, varicella, or measles. Similar guidelines and durations of exclusion would be followed for the child with HIV infection, as was noted for children with cancer or who were immunocompetent.

Recommendations for Personnel.   The most important practice that personnel can follow in caring for any child is careful handwashing. Indeed, whether the child is immunocompetent or immunosuppressed, the transmission of a variety of common infections, including respiratory viruses and gastrointestinal viruses (including hepatitis), could be reduced if careful handwashing is practiced. Furthermore, staff members should instruct children to wash their hands, particularly after toileting. Staff, of course, should always wash their hands between diaper changes or when assisting children with their toileting activities. When there is a known infectious hazard and staff must come in contact with soiled diapers, disposable gloves should be worn by the staff member. It must be underscored that wearing gloves is not a substitute for careful handwashing, since this practice must still be followed and adhered to as carefully as possible.

In urban areas where the risk for having a child with either HIV disease, tuberculosis, or hepatitis B is higher than in rural areas, staff should be informed about the potential infectious hazards as well as their routes of transmission. To that regard, staff must also be comfortable with the reality that the transmission of HIV virus by the kinds of contact that take place in a care setting are virtually impossible. Nonetheless, staff should exercise the principles of universal precautions when handling bloody secretions or a bleeding lesion. As noted above, spilled blood should be cleaned with a dilute solution of bleach and water.

Parental Advice.   Parents should be reassured that the presence of a child who has cancer, who is receiving immunosuppressive therapy, or who has HIV does not represent a threat to the health of their child. Education is the best way to provide assurance. The now vast experience of household contacts, as well as those in various school settings, should provide reassurance that contact with children with AIDS or those who are severely immunosuppressed because of cancer treatment will not result in transmission of diseases beyond those that could be acquired from otherwise healthy children. Any time children are in a closed setting, the likelihood for transmission of a variety of common infectious diseases is increased. However, children with AIDS or those receiving immunosuppressive therapy are not more likely to transmit infection but indeed are, in turn, more likely to acquire certain of these infections. Thus, the parent of the healthy child can be reassured that his or her child will not be exposed to undue hazard by having contact with a child with cancer or with a child who is immunosuppressed because of a variety of therapies or because of the HIV.

5

Children with Chronic Lung Disease

LEIGH G. DONOWITZ, M.D.

INFECTIOUS RISKS

Children with cystic fibrosis, asthma, bronchopulmonary dysplasia, or other chronic pulmonary disease are not at increased risk of acquiring infection. However, they are at marked risk of developing severe and life-threatening infection with pathogens that ordinarily cause mild upper respiratory infection, bronchitis, flu, and pneumonia in the healthy child.

COMMON INFECTIONS

Unless there are other aspects to their disease that make them immunocompromised (e.g., corticosteroid therapy, asplenia, transplantation or cancer therapy), the infections in children with chronic lung disease do not differ from those of their family or other children in the child care center or preschool.

INFECTION CONTROL

Special Infection Control Needs.   Preventing infection is the hallmark of effective infection control in this population. Vaccine prevention of preventable causes of infection is imperative, and this specifically includes pneumococcal vaccine, *Haemophilus influenzae* type B vaccine, and yearly immunization with influenza vaccine. If possible, the infant with chronic lung disease should have a limited number of caretakers who thus minimize the child's exposure to a large number of pathogens. Consideration should be given to avoiding group child care during the times when many children at the center or school have upper respiratory illness (e.g., influenza season).

Risks to Healthy Children.   There are no unusual infectious risks caused by children with chronic pulmonary disease. These children may have unusual pulmonary and upper respiratory flora, but these organisms are not causative of disease in healthy children.

Exclusion from Child Care or Preschool Attendance.   Children with pulmonary disease who have worsening of their pulmonary symptoms (cyanosis, grunting, altered breathing, increase in cough, vomiting) should be evaluated promptly by their physician. They should not be monitored in the child care or preschool setting.

Exclusion for infectious diseases should be guided by the recommendations for all children (note Section IV and the specific pathogen in Section V), realizing that children with chronic pulmonary problems may have a prolonged and more serious course.

Recommendations for Personnel.   Personnel should be extremely cautious in caring for the child with chronic lung disease to ensure that mild infection in themselves or other attendees is not spread to these children. This is best effected through careful handwashing, particularly after handling children with other viral respiratory illnesses.

Parental Advice.   Parents of healthy children should be told that children with chronic lung disease pose no unusual infectious risks to healthy children.

Parents of a child with chronic pulmonary disease should monitor their child for signs and symptoms of increased respiratory distress, particularly during seasons of increased viral respiratory illnesses. Parents should consider alternate child care situations where their child avoids group child care during times when many children at the center have upper respiratory illnesses. Parents should ideally have their child with chronic pulmonary disease cared for by a limited number of caregivers.

6

Children with Cardiac Disease

KAREN S. RHEUBAN, M.D.

INFECTIOUS RISKS

Children with congenital heart disease do not tolerate significant lower respiratory tract illness. The mortality rate of patients with respiratory syncytial virus and coexisting congenital heart disease approaches 50% in some studies. Because their pulmonary compliance is already reduced in the baseline state, patients with large left-to-right shunts and pulmonary edema do not tolerate acute pneumonitis.

COMMON INFECTIONS

The infections of children with heart disease do not differ from those of the surrounding family members. The exceptions are the child known to have asplenia, in which case overwhelming bacterial infection may occur (bacteremia and meningitis) or if they have been immunosuppressed following heart transplantation.

INFECTION CONTROL

Special Infection Control Needs. Preventing infection is the hallmark of effective infection control in this population. Vaccine prevention of preventable causes of infection is imperative and this specifically includes *Haemophilus influenzae* type B vaccine and yearly immunization with the influenza vaccine. Children with asplenia also should be immunized with the pneumococcal vaccine. Careful handwashing should be exemplary when a viral illness is in the child care center or preschool. If at all possible, the infant with significant congestive heart failure should receive care from a limited number of caretakers during outbreaks of upper and lower respiratory viral infections, specifically respiratory syncytial virus.

Risks to Healthy Children.   There are no unusual infectious risks caused by children with congenital cardiac disease.

Exclusion from Child Care or Preschool Attendance.   Although children with congenital cardiac disease do not have altered immunity (except in the case of infants and children with asplenia), viral respiratory illnesses may exacerbate the respiratory symptoms of congenital heart disease.

Infants with fever and changing respiratory symptoms (faster respirations, grunting, poor color) should be promptly evaluated by their physician and not left in the child care setting or preschool.

Recommendations for Personnel.   Careful handwashing should be exercised after handling children with obvious viral illnesses.

Parental Advice.   Parents of healthy children should be told that children with congenital cardiac disease pose no unusual infectious risks to healthy children.

Parents of children with congenital cardiac disease should monitor for signs and symptoms of increasing respiratory distress particularly during seasons of increased viral respiratory illness. They should consider avoiding child care during times when many children at the center have upper respiratory illness symptoms. Parents should ideally have the child cared for by a limited number of caregivers.

7

The Child with Disabilities

SUSAN M. ANDERSON, M.D.

Children with physical disabilities, cognitive disabilities, or sensory impairments all may be provided care within a child care or preschool setting.

The etiology of motor impairment in children with physical disabilities is varied; the majority are children with encephalopathies. Children with static encephalopathies include those with cerebral palsy, a nonprogressive disorder of movement, tone, and posture, and those with Down syndrome who have hypotonia and motor delays. Children may have progressive encephalopathies from either infectious etiologies such as acquired immunodeficiency syndrome (AIDS) or metabolic disease such as nonketotic hyperglycinemia. Children with static encephalopathy have a nonprogressive disorder and will continue to gain skills but at a slower-than-expected pace; in contrast, children with progressive encephalopathies will continue to have motor deterioration and lose previously acquired abilities. Children who have an acquired physical disability secondary to a closed head injury may have an evolving motor exam with improvement noted over time. Children with spinal cord injuries or myelomeningocele have paralysis below the motor level of the lesion. Children with neuromuscular disease include children with anterior horn cell disease (e.g., Werdnig-Hoffmann), myopathies, and Duchenne's muscular dystrophy. Children with physical disabilities may also include children with congenital or acquired amputations and children with burn injuries.

Children with static or progressive encephalopathies may also have cognitive impairments. Children with static encephalopathies include those with mental retardation, developmental delay, and Down syndrome. Children with cognitive disabilities secondary to progressive encephalopathies will have deterioration of their language and problem-solving abilities, whereas children with closed head injuries may have an evolving picture with improvement noted over time. Children with learning disabilities are rarely identified before school age; however, the hallmark of the learning disabled child is discrepancy between language-based and problem-solving abilities. Children with minimal brain dysfunction, attention deficit disorder, or communication disorders (e.g., infantile autism) may be included among those with cognitive disabilities.

Children with sensory impairments include those who are blind or deaf.

INFECTIOUS RISKS

Children with disabilities are at increased risk of infection for several reasons. Children with severe motor impairment may be at increased risk secondary to both immobility and ineffective neurologic control of critical musculature. A child who is both immobile and has impaired control of pharyngeal musculature may be less able to clear respiratory secretions and thus be at risk of pulmonary infection. Children with severe immobility may be more prone to otitis media, particularly if their head is frequently in a dependent position and they are not able to clear oral secretions. Children with spinal cord injuries or myelomeningocele, because they have neurogenic bladders, are at increased risk of bladder colonization and symptomatic urinary tract infection.

Children with disabilities may also have reduced ability to manifest their symptoms. Some children may be unable to communicate symptoms effectively because of oral motor dysfunction or language delay. In addition, there may be the loss of physical ability to demonstrate specific symptoms. Children with neurogenic bladders, despite having an increased incidence of urinary tract infections, often do not have classic symptoms of urinary tract infection, such as frequency, urgency, and dysuria. Children with specific brain injury or cervical level spinal cord injury may have ineffective temperature control and may not demonstrate fever. In addition, children with disabilities may be less likely to receive well child care or be completely immunized.

COMMON INFECTIONS

There is no increased incidence of upper respiratory infections in children with disabilities. The occurrence of an upper respiratory infection in a child with oral motor dysfunction may compound the difficulty the child already has in handling secretions. There is an increased incidence of otitis media in children with cleft palate, secondary to palatal insufficiency. There is an increased incidence of otitis media in children with Down syndrome, secondary to shortened and relatively horizontal eustachian tubes. There is an increased incidence of otitis media in children with oral motor dysfunction related to the inability to handle oral secretions.

As for lower respiratory infections, there is an increased incidence of aspiration pneumonia in children with disabilities, secondary to both oral motor dysfunction and the increased incidence of gastroesophageal reflux. Many of these children have a disordered swallow secondary to oral motor dysfunction and are unable to protect their airway. Children with oral motor dysfunction may include children with motor disability such as cerebral palsy, myopathy, or anterior horn cell disease and children with Arnold-Chiari malformation, which may be seen as a single malformation or in combination with myelomeningocele. Children with neuromuscular disease or cervical-thoracic spinal cord injury are more likely to develop pneumonia and debilitating lung disease if they acquire influenza.

Children with disabilities are just as likely as other children to get viral gastroenteritis, but they are more likely than other children to have complications such as dehydration secondary to inadequate oral intake.

In children with neurogenic bladders (commonly seen with myelomeningocele or spinal cord injury), there is an increased incidence of significant bacterial colonization of the urinary tract. Due to lack of sensation, children with neurogenic bladders are often not symptomatic with lower urinary tract disease in terms of classic symptoms of dysuria, frequency, and urgency but may present with the history of a change in color or odor of their urine or symptoms of fever or abdominal pain. There is an increased incidence of urinary tract infection with significant immobility, as might be seen with severe cerebral palsy or prolonged casting for immobility (e.g., spica cast).

Children with disabilities are just as likely as other children to have childhood meningitis. Children with shunted hydrocephalus have an increased incidence of meningitis or ventriculitis secondary to the presence of the foreign body.

Skin infections may be more common in certain subgroups of disabled children. Decubitus ulcers may develop in children with spinal cord injury or myelomeningocele secondary to the loss of sensation. Cellulitis and impetigo may be more likely in children who are mentally retarded, because of repeated self-stimulatory or self-injurious behavior.

INFECTION CONTROL

Special Infection Control Needs.   For children who have disabilities, the most important infection control procedures are those that apply to any child, such as good handwashing. In addition, there should be appropriate education of all child care providers regarding those signs and symptoms of infection to which any particular child in their care is prone. For example, those who are caring for a child with myelomeningocele should be aware of the signs of urinary tract infection and shunt infection and should provide vigilant skin care, particularly in the diaper region.

Children with AIDS may have cognitive or motor disabilities, which are most often progressive in nature. The child with AIDS, because he or she is immunocompromised, is at risk of acquiring infection from other children in the child care setting. There is no risk to other children or child care providers who have casual contact with the child with AIDS. As with all children, handwashing is recommended after diaper changes. It has been suggested that children with AIDS who are frequent biters of other children or those who may have open or oozing sores may put others in the child care setting at risk; however, this has not been proven.

Children with congenital cytomegalovirus (CMV) may have motor, cognitive, or sensory disabilities. Because CMV is such a ubiquitous virus, 1% of all infants are infected in utero. However, only 5% of these have severe manifestations of prenatal infection. Children with congenital CMV may excrete virus for some time following their birth. However, the majority of children in child care settings who excrete CMV are those who acquire the infection postnatally. For this reason, children with congenital CMV should not be singled out for isolation or exclusion. No special measures are indicated except good handwashing.

Children with congenital rubella most commonly have visual, hearing, or cognitive impairments. Children with congenital rubella are able to transmit the disease to susceptible contacts until they are 12 months of age or until they have documented negative nasopharyngeal and urine cultures after 3 months of age. Although other infants in a child care environment may have acquired passive immunity from their mother, older infants, unimmunized children, children of unimmunized mothers, and child care providers may be included among susceptible contacts. Because 10 to 15% of the adult population is rubella-susceptible, susceptible child care providers and preschool staffs should be immunized.

Children with congenital herpes may have recurrent cutaneous or oral herpes lesions but do not need to be excluded from child care or preschool settings. Cutaneous herpetic lesions should be covered with a dressing. Because oral herpes is extremely common and those who are infected may shed between recurrence of their fever blisters, there is no need to exclude these children.

Risks to Healthy Children.   Healthy children are only at risk of acquiring infection from children with disabilities in those special circumstances that have been described where the disability is of infectious etiology. Be careful, however, not to assume that all children whose disability is of infectious etiology necessarily put other children at risk. For example, a child who has cerebral palsy resulting from an episode of *Haemophilus influenzae* meningitis at 9 months of age does not impart any increased infectious risk to healthy children.

Exclusion from Child Care or Preschool Attendance.   A child should be excluded from a child care center or preschool if the treatment of the disease is not consistent with normal setting functioning. For example, a child with pyelonephritis may require hospitalization and intravenous antibiotic therapy. If a child care center or preschool is unable to provide the environment and resources to maintain this intravenous access, then this child should be excluded from the child care setting until this special medical treatment is no longer needed.

Second, a child should be excluded from a child care or preschool setting if that individual child's health is at significant risk secondary to his or her presence in that setting. For example, a child with AIDS who is immunocompromised may himself be at risk by being in close proximity to other children.

Third, a child should be excluded from attendance at a child care center or preschool if the child's presence in the center places other children at risk for infection. A child who both is a chronic biter and has hepatitis B may infect other children through biting. Children who are actively shedding rubella virus in an environment where there are many susceptible individuals may infect others through secretion exposure; however, susceptible individuals may protect themselves through immunization.

Recommendations for Personnel.   Routine health care maintenance is of primary importance in a child care center or preschool that provides care to disabled children. Personnel should ascertain for each child all pertinent diagnoses in language understandable to all caretakers.

Child care providers should have an understanding of each disability and all associated complications such that the signs and symptoms of infection in each individual child will be recognized. Emergency phone numbers should be maintained for primary physicians and other physicians, if appropriate, for all children in a child care and preschool setting. As with all children, the immunization status of each child with disabilities should be determined.

Personnel in the child care or preschool setting should monitor routine safety. Play areas, both inside and outside, should be accessible and safe for all children in the care of that center. The surfaces should be appropriate for mobility. If the center will be transporting children, car seats and child restraints should be available and adapted for all children in the care of that center.

The most important factor in the prevention of infection in children both with and without disabilities is good handwashing.

Parental Advice.   Children with disabilities are no more likely to transmit infections to other children than are children without disabilities; a child cannot catch a disability from another child. Parents should be aware of the health, safety, and illness policies of the center and should make certain that their own child and all children in the center are fully immunized.

8

Children with Chronic Skin Disease (Eczema)

KENNETH E. GREER, M.D.

INFECTIOUS RISKS

Although the cause of atopic eczema is unknown, there are several important known factors that probably account for the increased risk for cutaneous infection. These patients have deficiencies in their immune system. Most notable is the deficient chemotactic responsiveness of white blood cells, making these children unusually susceptible to viral, bacterial, and certain fungal cutaneous infections. In addition, eczematous skin appears to be especially prone to colonization with certain infectious organisms.

COMMON INFECTIONS

Atopic eczema patients are markedly susceptible to cutaneous infections with viruses, such as herpes simplex (eczema herpeticum or Kaposi's varicelliform eruption when it becomes widespread), molluscum contagiosum, warts, and vaccinia (eczema vaccinatum). Eczema vaccinatum occurred when children or their families were vaccinated for smallpox, but it may still occur in children of military personnel who receive smallpox vaccination. Eczema patients also are unusually susceptible to bacterial infection or colonization with *Staphylococcus aureus*, and they may be more prone to develop superficial fungal infections with *Trichophyton rubrum*.

INFECTION CONTROL

Special Infection Control Needs. When the child with chronic skin disease is infected with certain organisms, special precautions may be necessary to prevent the spread to other children. Conversely, when nonatopic children or other personnel in the center have certain cutaneous infections, especially fever blisters (herpes simplex, cold sores), the child with atopic eczema should be protected from close contact with individuals who are infected. Medical treatment is available for these infections, but in specific instances, such as with eczema herpeticum, the child with chronic skin disease may have to be excluded from the center temporarily. The primary physician would be the best person to make this decision.

Risks to Healthy Children.   If the viral infection is widespread and unprotected (molluscum contagiosum, herpes simplex, etc.), there is a potential risk of spread. However, these situations have not been reported and are more theoretical than real. Atopic children who are being medically treated for heavy bacterial colonization or infection present no significant risk for infection to the other children.

Exclusion from Child Care or Preschool Attendance.   Children are excluded from the center or preschool only when they are considered to be contagious. This is usually the case when they have herpes simplex infection. In addition, if the child has serious bacterial infection with *S. aureus* and the child is not being adequately treated, temporary removal from the child care or preschool setting would be appropriate. In general, atopic children should be treated as are other children at the center.

Recommendations for Personnel.   The personnel need to be aware of the special needs of the atopic child, which often include needs not necessarily related to infection (dietary, exercise, clothing) but which may exacerbate the skin condition, allowing for an increased risk of infection. In addition, the personnel need to be aware of what type of infections these children may develop.

Parental Advice.   Advise parents of well children that eczema in and of itself is not contagious. If the atopic eczema child requires therapy for an intercurrent infection, like any other child at the center or school, the child will receive treatment and return only when there is no longer an infection risk to the other children.

9

Children from Developing Nations

ROSS A. PENNIE, M.D., F.R.C.P.C.

INFECTIOUS RISKS

Children from developing nations often come from regions where sanitation is poor and diseases are transmitted by food and drink contaminated by pathogenic organisms. Overcrowding and malnutrition may lead to increased incidence of other diseases, such as tuberculosis.

There are several organisms that a previously infected child can continue to carry and excrete for prolonged periods after the acute symptoms have resolved. In a child care center or preschool, it is these organisms, excreted for prolonged periods, that pose a risk of child-to-child transmission.

COMMON INFECTIONS

Pathogenic organisms potentially carried for prolonged periods by children from developing nations are:

Bacteria
Salmonella
Shigella
Campylobacter jejuni
Mycobacterium tuberculosis
Viruses
Hepatitis A virus
Hepatitis B virus
Hepatitis C virus
Cytomegalovirus
Human immunodeficiency virus

Parasites
  Protozoa
    Cryptosporidium
    Giardia lamblia
    Entamoeba histolytica
    Dientamoeba fragilis
    Plasmodia (malaria)
  Worms
    Hymenolepis nana (dwarf tapeworm)
    Trichuris trichiura
    Hookworm
    Ascaris lumbricoides
    Strongyloides stercoralis
    Schistosoma
    Taenia solium (cysticercosis agent)

However, most of the organisms listed above are *not* transmissible directly from one child to another. The reason varies with the organism but may be because the life cycle requires an intermediate animal host, the eggs must mature in the soil before they are contagious, or the organism must be transferred very directly through sexual activity or infected blood or needles.

Therefore, common tropical organisms readily transmissible in a child care center or preschool are:

Bacteria
  Salmonella
  Shigella
  C. jejuni
  Mycobacterium tuberculosis
Parasites
  Protozoa
    Giardia lamblia
    Entamoeba histolytica
  Worms
    Hymenolepis nana (dwarf tapeworm)
    Taenia solium (cysticercosis)
Viruses
  Cytomegalovirus
  Hepatitis A

INFECTION CONTROL

Special Infection Control Needs.   The organisms of concern are all transmissible by the fecal-oral route (except for cytomegalovirus and *M. tuberculosis*). Therefore, infection control should focus on good personal hygiene, good handwashing, the preparation of food by staff who do not care for children in diapers, and the exclusion of children with diarrhea. These measures are not special and are recommended for every child care center or preschool, regardless of whether it is attended by children from developing nations.

Children with tuberculosis are not contagious unless they are obviously ill with symptoms such as chronic cough and weight loss. A chronically ill child from a developing country should therefore be evaluated by a physician before the child enters the care center or school.

Risks to Healthy Children.   Healthy children are at theoretical risk of infection from the short list of enteric pathogens listed above. Practically speaking, the organisms most commonly transmitted are *Salmonella, Shigella,* and *Giardia lamblia.* The risk of infection can be reduced by the routine use of good personal hygiene as discussed above.

Exclusion from Child Care or Preschool Attendance.   Children from developing nations should be excluded from child care or preschool attendance when they have an unexplained chronic illness or when they have acute diarrhea. A child who repeatedly bites should be excluded until it is certain that he or she carries neither hepatitis B virus nor human immunodeficiency virus.

Recommendations for Personnel.   Child care and preschool personnel should understand that there is little likelihood that a child from a developing country will pass along a dangerous disease to other children. Routines of good personal hygiene and the exclusion of children with diarrhea should be established to minimize the transmission of gastrointestinal disease.

Any child who appears to be chronically unwell should be evaluated by a doctor who has been informed that the child may have a disease endemic to the tropics and be investigated accordingly.

Parental Advice.   Parents may find the following information helpful:

- Children get diarrhea in child care centers and preschools regardless of whether there are children there from developing nations.

- Parents should make certain that there is good personal hygiene practiced in the child care center or preschool before enrolling their child.

- Foreign children in the child care or preschool setting are at minimal risk of spreading serious disease to other children.

Section IV

Guidelines

10

Control of Isolated and Epidemic Infection

SANDRA M. LANDRY, R.N., M.S.

An estimated 13 million children in the United States are enrolled in child care programs, either part-time or full-time. These infants and young children are particularly susceptible to many infectious agents, due to their limited immunity, the degree of close contact between children and staff, and the lack of hygienic practices. Infectious diseases readily spread among the children, staff, family members, and community. The child care setting carries a great potential for infectious disease outbreaks.

An outbreak or epidemic is defined as a recent or sudden excess of cases (three or more) of a specific disease or clinical symptom. Individual cases of certain diseases, such as measles, constitute an outbreak. A foodborne outbreak occurs when two or more persons experience gastrointestinal tract disease after ingesting a common food or water.

The investigation of an outbreak or suspected outbreak of a disease may not be required for every infectious problem you identify. In some situations, the factors associated with the problem may be apparent, and you can implement control measures without conducting an investigation. But if you do not know the factors (causative agent, source, and/or mode of transmission) associated with the problem, a systematic investigation of the outbreak should be conducted (Table 10–1).

Table 10.1.   Systematic Approach to Outbreak Investigation

1. Verify the diagnosis of the reported or suspected case (illness).
2. Implement interim infection control measures.
3. Develop a case definition.
4. Search for existing and new cases.
5. Characterize the cause by person, place, time, and risk factors.
6. Formulate a tentative hypothesis.
7. Update infection control measures.
8. Test the hypothesis. (In most child care centers or preschools, this step may be eliminated unless resources are available to conduct the necessary studies.)
9. Write a report summarizing the results of the investigation.

EPIDEMIC INVESTIGATION

To verify a reported or suspected infectious disease in a child, contact the child's physician. The local health department may be contacted to assist in the investigation as well as follow-up of exposed persons. After the diagnosis is confirmed, a decision to proceed with the investigation depends on multiple factors such as causative agent, immune status of the children exposed, mode of transmission and incubation period of the infectious disease, and the time interval between onset of the illness in the index case and notification of the center.

If high morbidity or mortality is occurring, the problem is unique or unusual, or there is a possibility of litigation or political pressure, the problem should be investigated. But if the problem has occurred previously or you know the contributing factors, implement infection control measures without an investigation.

After the diagnosis is confirmed, interim infection control measures to contain or interrupt the transmission of the infectious disease should be implemented. All members of the child care setting should be informed of the implementation of the control measures (Table 10–2). More specific control measures may be necessary as more information becomes available during the investigation.

The nature of the case or infectious problem that is occurring should be defined in order to recognize existing or new cases. The definition should be based on the causative agent, site of infection and/or clinical

Table 10.2.   Examples of Interim Epidemic Control Measures

---

1. Wash hands with soap and water immediately after handling infants, blowing noses, changing diapers or using toilet facilities, and before handling food. The use of disposable gloves is helpful but not a substitute for good handwashing.

2. Discourage sharing of personal articles and toys.

3. Clean soiled surfaces with a disinfectant, such as household bleach diluted 1 part bleach to 10 parts water.

4. Change clothing as soon as it is soiled; place in a plastic bag to be sent home.

5. Use disposable diapers; discard into a covered container.

6. Cohort infected or exposed children with personnel who are not caring for noninfected or unexposed children.

7. Assess staff's risk and need for intervention to ensure that all employees are protected.

8. Exclude new admissions to the child care center or preschool during the outbreak.

9. Notify families of the involved children; instruct them to keep the sick child or children at home (Appendix 10.1).

---

signs and symptoms. As the investigation proceeds, further information may be obtained that will require the case definition to be revised.

The search for existing and new cases is necessary in order to estimate the magnitude of the problem. The staff should be educated regarding signs and symptoms of the illness so they can monitor exposed children and staff for the onset of the illness. Families should be asked to notify the center if their child becomes ill. To complete case findings, absences from the center should be contacted.

Characterize the data collected by person, place, time, and risk factors. The interrelationship of these factors will help formulate a valid hypothesis of the cause of the outbreak, the population at risk, and the incubation period of the infectious disease should be revealed.

EPIDEMIC HYPOTHESIS

Based on the data collected, formulate a tentative hypothesis regarding the causative agent, source of infection and mode of transmission of the infectious disease. The hypothesis should explain the majority of cases and permit intervention and control measures. Case control study, cohort study, and prospective intervention study are epidemiologic approaches to test the hypothesis.

Unless an outbreak is associated with a commercial product, considerable morbidity, or mortality, hypothesis testing is usually aborted, particularly if the outbreak clears with coincident infection control measures.

The final step in the investigation of an outbreak is a written summary of the findings and recommendations to prevent a similar occurrence in the future. The report should include facts only—no explanations. The completed report should be disseminated to management and the individuals involved in the investigation.

EPIDEMIC PREVENTION

To prevent the spread of communicable illness among children and staff, health policies must be designed to reduce the risks associated with infections in the child care setting. Employee health guidelines should define health maintenance for personnel, including immune status and requirements for updating immunizations, disease history, tuberculosis screening, and work restrictions if an employee has or is exposed to a communicable disease. The staff should be required to participate in educational programs regarding hygienic practices, modes of transmission, and signs and symptoms of infectious diseases.

Requirements for program participants should include specific preadmission requirements for physical examination and current immunization status; children must receive additional immunizations as necessary. Recommendations for exclusion of sick children from the child care or preschool setting should include specific communicable diseases as well as criteria for return to the center following an illness (Table 10–3).

The child care or preschool administrator should be observant of illnesses occurring in staff and participants to determine whether patterns of infections occur. If a pattern is detected, prompt intervention is necessary. A resource consultant (e.g., public health provider, pediatrician) should be available to assist the child care center or preschool in determining appropriate preventive measures to prevent the spread of infectious diseases.

Table 10.3.   Communicable Diseases in Child Care Centers and Preschools

Infection	Infective Material	Incubation Period	Comments
Amebiasis (*Entamoeba histolytica*)	Feces	2–4 weeks	*Case:* Exclude during acute illness, until treated and until stools are free of oocysts. *Contacts:* Symptomatic contacts should be excluded until stools are screened for oocysts.
Campylobacter enteritis	Feces Contaminated food or water	1–7 days	*Case:* Exclude until 48 hours of effective therapy or until asymptomatic, whichever is shorter. *Contacts:* Exclusion not required.
Chickenpox (varicella)	Infected exudate Respiratory secretions	10–21 days	*Case:* Exclude until lesions are dry and crusted. *Contacts:* Exclude immunosuppressed children during outbreak.
Conjunctivitis Bacterial	Purulent exudate	24–72 hours	*Case:* Exclude until 24 hours of effective therapy. *Contacts:* Exclusion not required.
Viral (adenovirus, etc.)	Purulent exudate	12–72 hours	*Case:* Exclude until symptoms resolve. *Contacts:* Exclusion not required.
Cytomegalovirus	Infected urine and saliva	1 month	*Case:* Exclusion not required. *Contacts:* Exclusion not required.

(continued)

Table 10.3. Communicable Diseases in Child Care Centers and Preschools (*continued*)

Infection	Infective Material	Incubation Period	Comments
Diarrhea	Feces	1–3 days	*Case:* Exclude until symptoms resolve. *Contacts:* Exclusion not required.
Fifth disease (erythema infectiosum)	Respiratory secretions	4–14 days (usually 12–14 days)	*Case:* Exclusion not required. *Contacts:* Exclusion not required.
German measles (rubella)	Respiratory secretions	14–21 days (usually 16–18 days)	*Case:* Exclude for 7 days after onset of rash. *Contacts:* Those who are pregnant and not immunized should seek medical advice.
Giardia lamblia	Feces Contaminated food or water	1–4 weeks	*Case:* Exclude until asymptomatic. *Contacts:* No exclusion required.
Gingivostomatitis (herpes simplex virus)	Infected secretions	3–5 days	*Case:* Exclude until cutaneous lesions are dry and crusted. *Contacts:* Exclusion not required.
Hand-foot-mouth disease (Coxsackie A16)	Feces Respiratory secretions	4–6 days	*Case:* Exclusion not required. *Contacts:* Exclusion not required.
Hepatitis A	Feces	15–50 days (usually 25–30 days)	*Case:* Exclude until 10 days after onset of symptoms and symptomatically able to participate in general activity. *Contacts:* Prophylaxis should be considered for staff and children.

Hepatitis B	Infected saliva or blood	6 weeks–6 months	Case: Exclude during acute illness and children with chronic hepatitis B surface antigen who bite or cannot contain secretions. Contacts: No exclusion required.
Impetigo contagiosa (Staphylococcus)	Lesion secretions	7–10 days	Case: Exclude for 48 hours of effective therapy. Contacts: Exclusion not required.
Infectious mononucleosis	Saliva	5–7 weeks	Case: Exclude until symptomatically able to tolerate general activity. Contacts: No exclusion required.
Influenza	Respiratory secretions	1–3 days	Case: Exclude until symptomatically able to tolerate general activity. Contacts: No exclusion required. Monitor for symptoms.
Lice (pediculosis)	Infested area	Approximately 7–10 days after eggs hatch	Case: Exclude until treated. Contacts: Examine for infestation and recommend treatment if needed.
Measles (rubeola)	Respiratory secretions	6–21 days, (usually 10–12 days)	Case: Exclude until 5 days after appearance of rash. Contacts: Check immunization status. Exclude immediately on signs of prodrome.

(continued)

Table 10.3. Communicable Diseases in Child Care Centers and Preschools (*continued*)

Infection	Infective Material	Incubation Period	Comments
Meningitis Meningococcal	Respiratory secretions	2–10 days	*Case:* Exclude during acute illness and until treated. *Contacts:* Seek physician's advice concerning prophylaxis.
Haemophilus influenzae	Respiratory secretions	2–14 days	*Case:* Exclude during acute illness and until treated. *Contacts:* Seek physician's advice concerning prophylaxis.
Mumps (infectious parotitis)	Respiratory secretions	12–25 days	*Case:* Exclude for 9 days from onset of swelling; less if swelling subsides. *Contacts:* Susceptible contacts should seek physician's advice.
Pharyngitis Nonspecific	Respiratory secretions	12–72 hours	*Case:* Exclude only if child has fever or is unable to participate in general activities. *Contacts:* Exclusion not required.
Streptococcal	Respiratory secretions	1–4 days	*Case:* Exclude for 24 hours of effective therapy. *Contacts:* Exclusion not required.
Pinworms (*Enterobius vermicularis*)	Feces, contaminated fomites, clothing, house dust, etc.	2 weeks– 2 months	*Case:* Exclude until treated. *Contacts:* Exclusion not required.

Respiratory infections (upper respiratory infections, colds, bronchitis)	Respiratory secretions	12–72 hours	*Case:* Exclude only if child has fever or is unable to participate in general activities. *Contacts:* Exclusion not required.
Roseola	Probably respiratory secretions	5–15 days	*Case:* Exclude until rash has disappeared. *Contacts:* No exclusion required.
Rotavirus	Feces	1–3 days	*Case:* Exclude until asymptomatic. *Contacts:* No exclusion required.
Salmonellosis	Feces Contaminated food	6–72 hours	*Case:* Exclude during acute illness, usually 5–7 days. *Contacts:* Stool cultures not indicated in absence of symptoms.
Scabies	Infested areas	2–6 weeks; 1–4 days after repeat exposure	*Case:* Exclude until treated. *Contacts:* Direct inspection of body.
Scarlet fever (*Streptococcus*)	Respiratory secretions	1–4 days	*Case:* Exclude for 24 hours of effective therapy. *Contacts:* Exclusion not required.
Shigellosis	Feces	1–7 days (usually 1–2 days)	*Case:* Exclude for 5 days of antibiotics or until stool cultures are negative. *Contacts:* Stool cultures indicated only in suspected outbreak.

(continued)

Table 10.3. Communicable Diseases in Child Care Centers and Preschools (*continued*)

Infection	Infective Material	Incubation Period	Comments
Tuberculosis	Respiratory secretions	2–10 weeks	*Case:* Exclude until physician advises return. *Contacts:* Seek physician's advice concerning prophylactic treatment.
Whooping cough (pertussis)	Respiratory secretions	7–21 days (usually 7–10 days)	*Case:* Exclude until 5–7 days of effective therapy and physician advises return. *Contacts:* Seek physician's advice concerning prophylactic treatment.
Yersiniosis	Feces Contaminated food or water	2–11 days (usually 3–7 days)	*Case:* Exclude during acute illness. *Contacts:* Exclusion not required.

Sample Information That May Be Sent Home to Parents or Guardians[a]

The disease(s) checked below are now occurring in your child's day care center or preschool, and your child may have been exposed. You may want to call your physician if any of the symptoms listed here appear. Better protection for all results when ill children are kept home until they have recovered.

—**Amebiasis (*Entamoeba histolytica*):**

Usually asymptomatic but occasionally varies from acute diarrhea with fever, chills, and bloody or mucoid diarrhea to mild abdominal discomfort with diarrhea containing blood or mucus, alternating with periods of constipation or remission. The incubation period is 2 to 4 weeks. The child will not be allowed to attend if the diarrhea contains blood or pus or is accompanied by fever. The child may return following treatment for the acute illness, and stools are free of oocysts.

—**Chickenpox (varicella):**

Small water blisters on the scalp, neck, and covered parts of the body are usually the first signs noted. The blisters break easily. The child may become cross, tire easily, and have a fever during the first few days of disease. The incubation period is 10 to 21 days; commonly, 13 to 17 days. Sick children must be kept at home until all lesions are dry and crusted.

—**Conjunctivitis:**

Inflammation of the eye, causing redness, tearing, and occasionally formation of pus. The incubation period is 12 to 72 hours for viral

---

[a]*Adapted from the Child Care Center, University of Virginia Health Sciences Center.*

infection and 24 to 72 hours for bacterial infection. Children with conjunctivitis must be kept at home until 24 hours after initiation of effective bacterial therapy or, in viral disease, until symptoms disappear.

—Cytomegalovirus:
Rarely produces symptomatic disease; when it does, it is characterized by fever, sore throat, and swollen lymph nodes (glands). The incubation period is 1 month. Children will be allowed to attend as long as they are able to function within the normal activities of their class.

—Diarrhea:
Increase of frequency and change of consistency in bowel movements from the child's normal pattern; fever may or may not be present. The incubation period depends on the causative agent (salmonellosis—6 to 72 hours; shigellosis—1 to 7 days; yersiniosis—2 to 11 days; *Campylobacter*—1 to 7 days; viral—24 to 48 hours). The child will not be allowed to attend if diarrhea is accompanied by fever or other symptoms, such as vomiting, irritability, dehydration, lethargy, blood, or pus. The child may return once the diarrhea is manageable and/or symptomatic infection has been treated.

—Fifth disease (erythema infectiosum):
A rose-red rash (slapped-face appearance) on the face, which fades and recurs and may spread to the limbs and trunk. By the time the rash appears, the child is no longer contagious and may return to child care or preschool.

—German measles (rubella):
A light rash, mild symptoms, with glands behind the ears and neck enlarged. The incubation period usually is 14 to 21 days. Sick children must be kept at home for a minimum of 7 days after the onset of rash and until all symptoms have disappeared.

—*Giardia lamblia*:
May be associated with a variety of intestinal symptoms, such as chronic diarrhea, abdominal cramps, bloating, frequent loose and pale greasy stools, fatigue, and weight loss. The incubation period is 1 to 4 weeks. Sick children must be kept at home until symptoms have resolved.

—Gingivostomatitis (herpes simplex virus):

Infection may be mild to severe and is marked by fever and malaise lasting a week, accompanied by vesicular lesions in and around the mouth and nose. The incubation period is 3 to 5 days. Children must remain at home until the lesions are dry and crusted.

—Hand-foot-mouth disease (Coxsackie A16):

Characterized by sudden onset, fever, sore throat, and lesions that may occur on the inside of the mouth (cheeks, gums, and sides of tongue) as well as on the palms, fingers, and soles. Occasionally, lesions appear on the buttocks. The incubation period is 4 to 6 days. Children will be allowed to attend, as long as they are able to function within the normal activities of their class, including outdoor activities.

—Hepatitis A:

Sudden onset of fever, malaise, loss of appetite, nausea, and abdominal discomfort followed by jaundice. The incubation period is 15 to 50 days. Sick children must be kept at home until physician advises return. Consult your physician for prophylactic protection of your child.

—Hepatitis B:

Characterized by loss of appetite, abdominal discomfort, nausea, and vomiting. Joint pain and rash may occur as well as jaundice and a mild fever. The incubation period is 6 weeks to 6 months. Sick children must be kept at home during acute illness, and children with chronic disease who bite or cannot contain secretions will be excluded.

—Impetigo:

Starts with multiple skin lesions, usually around the face and mouth and other exposed areas, such as the elbows, legs, and knees. The lesions vary in size and shape and begin as blisters but rapidly change to yellow crusted areas on a reddened base. The incubation period is 1 to 10 days. Children must remain home until they have received at least 48 hours of effective antibiotic therapy.

—Infectious mononucleosis:

An acute syndrome characterized by fever, sore throat, weakness, and enlarged lymph nodes (glands), especially in the neck. The incubation period is 5 to 7 weeks. Child must be kept at home until symptoms disappear and he or she is able to tolerate general activity.

—Influenza:

An acute illness characterized by fever, chills, headache, muscle aches, mild sore throat, and cough. The incubation period is 1 to 3 days. Sick children must be kept at home until general activity is tolerated.

—Lice (pediculosis):

Severe itching and scratching of the scalp. Eggs of head lice (nits attached to hairs) are small round gray lumps. Children with head lice should remain at home until they have been treated and have no visible nits in the hair. Advise examination of household and other close personal contacts, with concurrent treatment as indicated. Clothing, bedding, and other vehicles of transmission should be treated by laundering in hot water, by dry cleaning, or by application of an effective chemical insecticide.

—Measles (rubeola):

Runny nose, sneezing, coughing, watery eyes, and fever, with a red blotchy rash appearing on the third to seventh day. The incubation period is 6 to 21 days; commonly, 10 to 12 days. Sick children are to be kept home for a minimum of 5 days from the appearance of the rash. Consult your physician for prophylactic protection of household contacts who have not had measles or who have not been immunized against measles.

—Meningitis:

- Meningococcal infection is characterized by sudden onset of fever, intense headache, nausea and often vomiting, stiff neck, and frequently a rash. The incubation period varies from 2 to 10 days; commonly, 3 to 4 days. Consult your physician regarding prophylactic treatment of your child.
- *Haemophilus influenzae* infection has a sudden onset of fever, vomiting, lethargy, and stiff neck and back. Progressive stupor and coma are common. The incubation period is 2 to 14 days. Consult your physician regarding prophylactic treatment of your child.

—Mumps (parotitis):

Fever with swelling and tenderness in front of and below the ear or under the jaw. The incubation period is 12 to 25 days. Sick children must be kept home until the swelling of all glands involved and all symptoms have disappeared.

—Nonspecific respiratory infection:

Runny nose, sneezing, lacrimation, irritated nasopharynx, and malaise lasting 2 to 7 days. The incubation period is usually 12 to 72 hours. Child will be allowed to attend, as long as he or she has no fever and is able to function within the normal activities of the class, including outdoor activities.

—Roseola:

Characterized by sudden fever, sometimes as high as 106° F (41° C), which lasts 3 to 5 days. A rash appears on the chest and abdomen with moderate involvement of the face and extremities as the temperature returns to normal. Rash lasts 1 to 2 days. Child may return to school when rash disappears.

—Rotavirus:

Sporadic severe diarrhea and vomiting, often with dehydration. The child will not be allowed to attend until he or she is asymptomatic.

—Scabies:

Begins as itchy raised areas or burrows around finger webs, wrists, elbows, arm pits, and the belt line. Extensive scratching often occurs, especially at night, with secondary sores. The incubation period is 2 to 6 weeks; 1 to 4 days after repeat exposure. Children with scabies should be kept at home until they have been treated.

—Streptococcal infections (sore throat or scarlet fever):

Sudden illness with vomiting, fever, sore throat, and headache. Usually within 24 hours, a bright red rash appears. Some cases may not have a rash, although disease is just as serious. The incubation period is 1 to 3 days. If your child has any of these symptoms, you should contact your physician. Sick children are to be kept at home until 24 hours after initiation of effective antibiotic therapy with clinical improvement.

—Tuberculosis:

Fatigue, fever, and weight loss may occur early, while cough, chest pain, hoarseness, and coughing up blood may occur in more advanced disease. The incubation period is 2 to 10 weeks. Consult your physician regarding prophylactic treatment of your child.

—Whooping cough (pertussis):

A persistent cough that later comes in spells and may have an associated whoop. Coughing may cause vomiting. Many cases have persistent cough but never whoop. The incubation period is 7 to 21 days. Sick children should be kept at home until 5 to 7 days after initiation of effective antibiotic therapy with clinical improvement.

—Worms:

Worms passed in the stool or, occasionally, from the mouth or nose may be accompanied by wheezing, coughing, fever, diarrhea, abdominal pain, or itching around the rectum. The incubation period is about 2 months after ingestion of the worm eggs. Sick children must be kept at home until all symptoms have disappeared.

Section V

Specific Infections

11

Adenovirus

SCOTT A. HALPERIN, M.D.

CLINICAL MANIFESTATIONS

Adenovirus is a common viral infection with diverse clinical manifestations. Occasionally, these manifestations may be so distinct that a clinical diagnosis can be made with assurance. In most cases, however, adenovirus causes an illness indistinguishable from that caused by a variety of other pathogens. Adenovirus most frequently causes infection of the respiratory and gastrointestinal tracts. It is an unusual cause of the common cold but a very common cause of upper respiratory infection with pharyngitis and fever. Adenovirus causes conjunctivitis, exudative tonsillitis, laryngotracheitis (croup), bronchitis, bronchiolitis, and pneumonia. Adenovirus also is the cause of a characteristic syndrome called pharyngoconjunctival fever, which occurs in epidemics most commonly associated with contaminated swimming pool water.

In addition to these infections to the upper respiratory tract, adenovirus is a major cause of childhood diarrhea. The so-called enteric adenoviruses are not cultivatable in routine tissue culture and are usually identifiable on electron microscopy of the stool. Upper respiratory symptoms also may occur in children with enteric adenovirus infection.

ETIOLOGIC AGENT

Adenoviruses are nonenveloped, double-stranded DNA viruses. In humans, 47 distinct serotypes have been identified; additional serotypes have been isolated from other species. Adenoviruses attach to target cells, and the viral DNA enters the nucleus. Viral DNA replication occurs in the nucleus, giving rise to the characteristic inclusions. Adenovirus infection of a cell can result in a lytic infection where there is rapid proliferation of the virus, which results in cell death. Adenovirus can also cause latent infection, usually of lymphoid cells such as those of the tonsils. Finally, adenovirus is capable of oncogenic transformation. The importance of this final adenovirus-cell interaction in human disease is not clear.

EPIDEMIOLOGY

Source of the Organism. Adenovirus can be found in the respiratory secretions, conjunctiva, and the stool of infected individuals.

High-Risk Populations. Adenovirus infection occurs most often and is more severe in young infants and children. Outbreaks occur commonly in situations where close contact is common, including child care centers, schools, and hospitals. Particularly severe epidemics occur in military recruit populations. Infections in immunocompromised patients are not common but are severe when they do occur.

Mode of Spread. Spread of adenovirus infection is by small-droplet aerosols. Infection is initiated when virus-containing particles come in contact with the nose, throat, or conjunctival mucosa of susceptible individuals. Adenovirus also is spread by the fecal-oral route.

Incubation Period. Two to fourteen days.

DIAGNOSIS

In most situations, an etiologic diagnosis of adenovirus infection is not made. Typically, a clinical syndrome such as conjunctivitis, croup, bronchiolitis, pneumonia, or gastroenteritis is made without identifying the specific pathogen. A definitive diagnosis can be made through viral culture, electron microscopic examination, antigen detection in infected secretions, or demonstration of an antibody rise to adenovirus in paired serum specimens. Enteric adenoviruses are noncultivatable in routine tissue culture and are detected through electron microscopy or through antigen detection assays.

THERAPY

No specific therapy is available for the treatment of adenovirus infections. Most infections are not severe and do not require hospitalization; however, in the very young or immunocompromised patients, the infection may be severe and require hospitalization for supportive care.

INFECTIOUS PERIOD

Adenovirus can be isolated in respiratory secretions from 2 days prior to symptoms to 8 days after the onset of symptoms. Enteric adenoviruses are usually found in the stool for 8 days following the onset of diarrhea, although excretion can occur for 2 to 3 months. Adenovirus can be cultured from the conjunctiva for 2 weeks after the onset of symptoms.

INFECTION CONTROL

Vaccine.   A vaccine for certain adenovirus types is available and is used routinely in military recruits. Adenovirus vaccine is not used in children.

Exclusion from Child Care or Preschool Attendance.   No exclusion is required for respiratory infection due to adenovirus. The child's own condition should determine continued participation in child care. Children with enteric adenovirus infection should be excluded from child care until they are no longer having diarrhea. Adenoviral conjunctivitis often occurs in epidemics that are difficult to control; therefore, if an epidemic of keratoconjunctivitis is present, children should be excluded for 2 weeks after the onset of symptoms.

Recommendations for Other Children.   Since exposure has already occurred before onset of symptoms, no specific steps need be taken once adenovirus infection has occurred. The children should be monitored for any symptoms suggestive of more serious disease that may require a visit to the child's physician. The possibility of a more severe disease in immunocompromised children should be remembered.

Recommendations for Personnel.   There is no increased risk for adult caretakers due to adenovirus infection. Particular attention to handwashing and care with infected secretions, particularly stool, will prevent continued spread within the center.

Parental Advice.   Adenovirus infections are usually mild and self-limited. However, parents should be aware that complications such as otitis media, dehydration, and pneumonia may occur, which would require a visit to the family physician.

12

Amebiasis

WILLIAM J. RODRIGUEZ, M.D., PH.D., AND BARBARA A. JANTAUSCH, M.D.

CLINICAL MANIFESTATIONS

Most amebic infections are asymptomatic. Some persons in whom a chronic state of *intestinal amebiasis* develops may experience intermittent diarrhea, constipation, flatulence, vague abdominal complaints, cramps, and tiredness. Those persons in whom diarrhea develops usually have cramps.

Acute amebic dysentery occurs less frequently. The patient may have fever and dysentery (i.e., stools that are liquid and mixed with blood or mucus), abdominal pain, and chills. Headache and tenesmus could also be present. Leukocytosis may be present.

Ulcerative lesions may lead to metastases of the parasite to the liver through the portal vein (1 to 5% of patients), resulting in *hepatic abscess*. In approximately one fourth of instances, enlargement of the liver with pain occurs. Jaundice is rare, but leukocytosis and elevated alkaline phosphatase are common. A radiograph may show elevation of the right hemidiaphragm. Metastases can occur to the lung, brain, and skin. On rare occasion, perforation of the colon, peritonitis, and death can occur.

ETIOLOGIC AGENT

Entamoeba histolytica is a protozoan parasite that has a global distribution. The *E. histolytica* cyst is the infectious particle and is usually found in formed stool. After ingestion, cysts mature into active trophozoites that primarily remain in the liquid portion of the bowel contents.

EPIDEMIOLOGY

Source of the Organism.   Humans are the reservoir of *E. histolytica* and transmit the infection to animals including dogs, cats, and pigs. Food and water contaminated with amebic cysts, such as raw fruits and vegetables washed in contaminated water, are additional sources of infection.

High-Risk Populations.   Travelers to endemic areas and children in day care centers have potential for acquisition of disease.

Mode of Spread.   Fecal-oral, person-to-person transmission, and ingestion of contaminated food and drink result in infection.

Incubation Period.   The incubation period is usually 2 to 4 weeks but may range from just a few days to several months.

DIAGNOSIS

Intestinal Amebiasis.   The diagnosis is made on finding cysts or trophozoites in fresh stool or bowel wall scrapings. Three stool specimens should be submitted 24 hours apart for evaluation, because cyst shedding may be intermittent. Cysts are more likely to be found in formed stool and trophozoites in liquid stool. Trophozoites may lose viability and morphology quickly, hence a *fresh* stool specimen or one properly preserved should be examined.

Acute Dysentery.   Mobile trophozoites with ingested red cells may be seen in dysenteric stools. Amebic ulcers may be seen on sigmoidoscopy. Serologic testing, specifically the indirect hemagglutination test with a titer of 1:128 or greater, is helpful in the diagnosis of acute dysentery or hepatic abscess. Also available are enzyme-linked immunosorbent assay, immunofluorescence, and counterimmunoelectrophoresis.

Hepatic Abscess.   Serology is very helpful (*E. histolytica*–specific IgG and IgA titers). In addition to serology, imaging results provide useful diagnostic information. Elevation of the right hemidiaphragm may be seen in 50% of patients on chest x-ray. Ultrasound of the abdomen and liver scan can confirm the presence of a hepatic lesion.

THERAPY

Asymptomatic excretors should be treated with iodoquinol, 30 mg/kg/day (maximum 2, g/day) orally, divided every 8 hours for 20 days. Two alternative drugs, diloxanide furoate, 20 mg/kg/day divided every 8 hours for 10 days, or paromomycin, 25 to 30 mg/kg/day orally, divided every 8 hours for 7 days. Diloxanide furoate is not currently licensed but may be obtained from the Centers for Disease Control. For intestinal amebiasis, liver abscess, or other invasive forms of disease, a tissue amebicide such as metronidazole, 35 mg/kg/day (maximum, 2250 mg/day) orally, divided every 8 hours for 10 days, should be used in conjunction with iodoquinol or paromomycin in the dose above for 20 days.

INFECTIOUS PERIOD

Individuals are infectious for as long as cysts are being shed in the stool.

INFECTION CONTROL

Vaccine.   None available.

Exclusion from Child Care or Preschool Attendance.   Infected children should be kept out of the child care or preschool setting until they are treated and asymptomatic and their stools are free of oocysts.

Recommendations for Other Children.   Children who develop gastrointestinal symptoms should be removed from the setting, and their stools examined for *E. histolytica*.

Recommendations for Personnel.   Personnel should practice good handwashing, especially after using the toilet and handling diapers. Personnel who become symptomatic with gastrointestinal symptoms should remain at home and have their stool examined for oocysts. New children should not be admitted to the center during an outbreak.

Parental Advice.   Parents should observe their children for gastrointestinal symptoms. Symptomatic children should be kept at home and be seen by their pediatrician, and their stool should be submitted for ova and parasite evaluation.

13

Ancylostoma duodenale
(Hookworm)

ANDREA J. RUFF, M.D.

CLINICAL MANIFESTATIONS

The initial manifestation may consist of pruritus and a papular rash at the site of larval penetration into the skin. While light infections often are asymptomatic, heavy infections may be associated with the development of abdominal pain, anorexia, diarrhea, and weight loss. Gastrointestinal symptoms appear to be more common in *Ancylostoma duodenale* infections than in infections caused by the other human hookworm, *Necator americanus*. The most significant consequence of hookworm infection is the development of iron-deficiency anemia due to gastrointestinal blood loss. The severity of the anemia depends on the parasite burden and dietary iron intake. It may be associated with pallor, listlessness, dyspnea, palpitations, cardiomegaly, and stunted growth. Other findings in hookworm infections may include hypoalbuminemia, peripheral eosinophilia, and occult blood in the stool.

ETIOLOGIC AGENT

Ancylostoma duodenale is one of two species of hookworms that cause widespread human infection. Humans acquire hookworm infection by coming into contact with infective larvae present in contaminated soil. The larvae penetrate the skin, pass into the circulation, and are carried to the lungs. They then penetrate the alveolar walls, ascend the trachea, and are swallowed, ending up in the small intestine where they mature into adult worms. The adult worms produce thousands of eggs that are passed in the stools, completing their development in soil. Under suitable conditions, the larvae will hatch and molt, becoming infective for humans. This process generally requires 5 to 10 days, during which time the eggs and larvae are not infective for humans.

EPIDEMIOLOGY

Source of the Organism.   Hookworms are found predominantly in tropical and subtropical zones, with *A. duodenale* predominating in southern Europe, northern Africa, northern Asia, and parts of South America. These areas provide appropriate environmental conditions for the development of hookworm eggs. The infective larvae are found in soil contaminated with human feces, and most infections result from direct contact with the soil, generally through bare feet. Rarely, food contaminated with *A. duodenale* larvae can serve as the source of the infection. The possibility of transmammary transmission of *A. duodenale* also has been considered, although to date the larvae have not been demonstrated in breast milk.

High-Risk Populations.   Individuals who have direct contact with fecally polluted soil in endemic areas will have a significant risk of acquiring hookworm infections. Children's propensity to play in dirt and to be barefoot increases their risk of infection. However, since effective transmission requires development of the larvae in soil, direct person-to-person spread of hookworm infection does not occur. Therefore, institutional or child care settings should not increase a child's risk of infection.

Mode of Spread.   Transmission occurs through skin contact with soil containing infective larvae. In a few instances, food contaminated with larvae has been implicated in the transmission of *A. duodenale*.

Incubation Period.   The time interval between acquisition of *A. duodenale* and the appearance of eggs in the feces has been reported to range from 43 to 105 days. The longer intervals reflect a period of interrupted development that some larvae undergo after infecting humans. Considerable variability also is observed in the time between infection and the development of symptoms; individuals may develop gastrointestinal symptoms approximately 20 to 38 days following an acute hookworm infection.

DIAGNOSIS

The diagnosis is established by identifying characteristic hookworm eggs in the feces; *A. duodenale* eggs cannot be distinguished from those of *N. americanus.* Although direct microscopic examination of a fecal smear will generally be adequate for the detection of moderate and severe infections, concentration techniques may be required to demonstrate eggs in light infections. Either the zinc sulfate flotation technique or the formalin-ether technique may be used. The larvae or adult worms are rarely seen in stool specimens, and although larvae can be grown from specimens by using Harada-Mori fecal cultures, this technique is rarely used diagnostically.

THERAPY

In countries where hookworms are endemic and reinfection is common, light infections often are not treated. In this country, hookworm infections are generally treated with either mebendazole or pyrantel pamoate. Mebendazole is given in a dose of 100 mg twice a day for 3 days. Pyrantel pamoate is given as a single daily dose of 11 mg/kg (maximum 1 g), repeated for 3 days. Although pyrantel pamoate is an approved drug, the U.S. Food and Drug Administration considers it investigational for this condition. Although both regimens appear to be well tolerated, experience with either in children less than 2 years of age is limited; the decision to treat a child in this age group should be made on an individual basis after determining the potential risks and benefits of therapy. Albendazole, available in a number of other countries, also has been shown to be efficacious in the treatment of hookworm infections. A repeat stool examination should be performed 1 to 2 weeks following therapy, and retreatment should be undertaken if hookworm infection is persistent.

In addition to the use of antihelminthic drugs, iron supplementation should be provided to individuals with significant anemia.

INFECTIOUS PERIOD

Without therapy, hookworm infections may persist for many years, although egg production tends to decrease over time.

INFECTION CONTROL

Vaccine.   None available.

Exclusion from Child Care or Preschool Attendance.   Isolation is not indicated for children infected with hookworms. Since human-to-human transmission does not occur and the eggs passed in feces are not infectious, an infected child does not need to be kept out of any child care or preschool setting.

Recommendations for Other Children.   Other children are not at risk of acquiring hookworm infection unless they are exposed to soil with infective larvae. Unlike the situation with many other enteric pathogens, children should not acquire the infection if they inadvertently ingest fecal material contaminated with hookworm eggs. Therefore, no additional precautions need to be undertaken for children in a center when one child is found to have hookworm infection.

Recommendations for Personnel.   Personnel should be instructed to continue techniques that decrease fecal-oral transmission of pathogens, including good handwashing and appropriate disposal of fecal material. In areas of the country where fecal contamination of the soil may be a problem, children in the child care or preschool setting should not be allowed to wander barefoot or play in the soil.

Parental Advice.   Parents should be told that the risk of person-to-person transmission is minimal. If the attendee appears to have acquired the hookworm infection locally, the need for sanitary disposal of feces and the potential for spread through contaminated soil should be reviewed with all of the parents.

14

Ascaris lumbricoides
(Roundworm)

ANDREA J. RUFF, M.D.

CLINICAL MANIFESTATIONS

During the initial phases of infection with *Ascaris lumbricoides,* larvae migrate through the lungs. Infected individuals may be asymptomatic or have symptoms ranging from a mild transient cough to severe pneumonitis. In heavy infections, fever, eosinophilia, and pulmonary infiltrates may occur transiently with the pneumonitis. Once the larvae have passed into the small intestine and have matured into adult worms, ascariasis is generally asymptomatic. Spontaneous passage of the worms may be the first indication of infection. Some individuals with ascariasis complain of vague abdominal discomfort, and a small number develop intestinal obstruction due to the adult worms. Migration of adult worms may occasionally be associated with intestinal perforation or blockage of the bile duct.

ETIOLOGIC AGENT

A. lumbricoides is the largest intestinal roundworm parasitizing humans. Infection is acquired through the ingestion of eggs containing infective larvae. After ingestion, the larvae hatch, penetrate the intestinal wall, and migrate via venules or lymphatics, passing through the liver and heart to the lungs. They then penetrate the alveolar walls, migrate through the upper respiratory tract, enter the esophagus and pass into the small intestine where they mature into adult worms. Female worms pass thousands of eggs daily in the feces; these eggs under appropriate environmental conditions can develop into infective-stage larvae within a few weeks. Unfertilized eggs or eggs that have not embryonated are not infectious.

EPIDEMIOLOGY

Source of the Organism. Although *A. lumbricoides* has a cosmopolitan distribution, it is most prevalent in areas with poor socioeconomic standards. Inadequate sanitation and the use of human feces as fertilizer contribute to the prevalence of ascariasis by maintaining infective eggs in the soil. Transmission of the infection results from direct ingestion of soil, as in the case of some children, or indirectly through contaminated hands or food.

High-Risk Populations. Children are at risk of acquiring ascariasis primarily because of their extended contact with soil and ingestion of soil either directly or indirectly through unwashed hands and food. This is reflected in the age distribution of ascariasis in endemic areas, where the prevalence increases sharply during the first 2 to 3 years of life.

Mode of Spread. Transmission occurs through ingestion of *A. lumbricoides* eggs containing infective larvae. Since the eggs passed in human feces are not infectious until they have matured for several weeks, person-to-person transmission does not occur.

Incubation Period. The interval between acquisition of infection and the development of adult worms capable of passing eggs is approximately 8 to 12 weeks. Individuals who develop pulmonary symptoms do so approximately 5 to 14 days after infection, during which time the larvae are migrating through lung tissue.

DIAGNOSIS

During early stages of the infection, when the larvae have not matured into adult worms, the diagnosis may occasionally be established by finding larvae in sputum or gastric washings. Once adult worms are present, the diagnosis is readily established by finding *A. lumbricoides* eggs in fecal specimens. Occasionally, the diagnosis is made after the infected individual passes adult worms by mouth or per rectum.

THERAPY

Several relatively nontoxic drugs are now available for the treatment of ascariasis. Pyrantel pamoate offers the advantage of requiring a single oral dose of 11 mg/kg (maximum, 1 g) for effective therapy. Mebendazole also is effective but must be given in a dose of 100 mg twice daily over 3 days. Neither of these drugs has been used extensively in children less than 2 years old; therefore, the decision to treat a child of that age group should be made on an individual basis. In cases of intestinal obstruction due to ascariasis, piperazine citrate may be effective; the drug paralyzes adult worms, which may then be evacuated by the intestinal peristalsis.

INFECTIOUS PERIOD

In untreated individuals, *A. lumbricoides* adults may survive for 12 to 18 months.

INFECTION CONTROL

Vaccine.   None available.

Exclusion from Child Care or Preschool Attendance.   Children with ascariasis are not at risk of directly transmitting the infection to other children, and they therefore do not need to be kept out of the child care setting.

Recommendations for Other Children.   Feces passed by a child with ascariasis will not be directly infectious to other children. Therefore, other children in the center are at risk of acquiring ascariasis only if they ingest soil containing eggs that have developed infective larvae. To prevent potential transmission of a number of intestinal parasites, children should be kept from eating dirt, and good hygiene with handwashing should be emphasized.

Recommendations for Personnel.   Prevention of spread through the maintenance of good hygiene and appropriate disposal of all fecal material should be emphasized. Personnel should specifically be cautioned to avoid inadvertent contamination of hands, food, and utensils with soil potentially containing infective eggs.

Parental Advice.   The means of transmission, including the absence of person-to-person spread, should be discussed with parents. The need to prevent geophagia and to maintain good hygiene among their children also should be emphasized.

15

Campylobacter

MARIAN G. MICHAELS, M.D., M.P.H.

CLINICAL MANIFESTATIONS

Campylobacter jejuni has been found to be a major cause of gastrointestinal infection in both children and adults. The infection it causes presents in a similar fashion to many of the other enteric infections. The majority of patients have acute onset of diarrhea and abdominal discomfort of variable severity. A febrile prodrome is not uncommon, and malaise, headache, and nausea often accompany or just precede the diarrhea. Frank blood in the stool is somewhat more common in *Campylobacter* enteritis than in infections caused by *Shigella* or *Salmonella*, while vomiting appears to be a slightly less frequent finding.

Most often the disease is self-limited, lasting less than a week. However, even when clinical symptoms have disappeared, patients can continue to shed bacteria for up to 7 weeks. This prolonged shedding is the rationale for antibiotic treatment of children in day care or preschool.

Though complications are unusual, a protracted, relapsing course occasionally develops that can be confused with inflammatory bowel disease. Also, bacteremia, postinfectious arthritis, Guillain-Barré syndrome, carditis, megacolon, cholecystitis, and meningitis have been reported, albeit rarely.

ETIOLOGIC AGENT

Campylobacter is a microaerophilic, motile, spiral-shaped Gram-negative rod. There are several different species, but the most common one to cause enteritis is *Campylobacter jejuni. C. fetus* occasionally causes systemic disease in premature infants and other immuno-compromised hosts.

EPIDEMIOLOGY

C. jejuni has worldwide distribution. In recent times, it has been more common than *Shigella* and *Salmonella* as a cause of bacterial diarrhea in children. In the United States infection occurs throughout the year, with peaks in the summer and early fall. The actual prevalence of *C. jejuni* in a community is difficult to ascertain, as most people, even those with diarrhea, do not have stool cultured. In patients with diarrhea in developing countries who have had cultures obtained, the rate of isolation ranges from 4 to 45%. *C. jejuni* is not commonly found in the stool of asymptomatic people in the United States.

Source of the Organism.   Animal and bird species are common reservoirs for *Campylobacter*. Commercial chicken carcasses have often been found to be contaminated, as well as the carcasses of sheep, cattle, and swine. *C. jejuni* can also infect household pets and cause diarrhea in these animals, especially while they are young. Another source associated with outbreaks of *C. jejuni* enteritis is the consumption of unpasteurized milk or untreated water.

High-Risk Populations.   Day care centers with children who are not toilet-trained are predisposed to transmitting *C. jejuni* infections, in similar fashion to the transmission of other infectious diarrheal diseases. Children drinking unpasteurized milk or untreated waters or those eating undercooked foods are at increased risk, as are those who have new puppies or kittens that have diarrheal illnesses.

Mode of Spread.   Ingestion of contaminated foods or water and fecal-oral spread are the primary modes of transmission. Direct contact with infected animal feces is also a method of spread. Maternal transmission of the bacteria to the newborn at the time of delivery has been reported.

Incubation Period.   Incubation is between 1 and 7 days, with most illness occurring 2 to 4 days after exposure, but can be variable, dependent on the size of the inoculum.

DIAGNOSIS

Diagnosis is made either by direct microscopy of fecal material using special stains or by isolation of *C. jejuni* in stool culture. Special isolation techniques are required. These include using either blood-based media containing antibiotics or a filtration system and then incubating the media at 42° C in an atmosphere containing 5% oxygen, 10% carbon dioxide, and 85% nitrogen. Specimens should be inoculated with minimal delay. If more than a 2-hour delay is anticipated, specimens should be stored at 5° C in Cary and Blair transport media.

THERAPY

The enteritis caused by *C. jejuni* is, in general, a self-limited disease often requiring only symptomatic treatment with oral rehydration fluids. The value of antibiotic treatment is controversial, as it does not appear to alter the course of the disease. However, many researchers have demonstrated that despite continued symptoms, the shedding of *C. jejuni* is halted within 72 hours of administering antibiotics. Thus, in the child care setting where children are not toilet-trained, it is prudent to treat with antibiotics.

Erythromycin is the drug of choice. Doses for children are 30 to 50 mg/kg/day given orally in four divided doses for 5 to 7 days. The dose for older children and adults is 250 mg four times a day orally, again for 5 to 7 days.

Systemic infections usually require hospitalization and administration of parenteral antibiotics. In vitro testing shows that *C. jejuni* are usually resistant to the penicillins and cephalosporins but are normally sensitive to many other antimicrobial agents including erythromycin (as mentioned above, this is the drug of choice in patients treated orally), the nitrofurans, the aminoglycosides, chloramphenicol, clindamycin, the quinolones, and the tetracyclines. Typically, the latter two types of drugs are contraindicated in young children. Newer macrolide antibiotics such as clarithromycin and azithromycin have activity against *C. jejuni* and, therefore, are alternate drugs which could be used to halt the shedding of bacteria.

INFECTIOUS PERIOD

Children are contagious 2 to 3 days after appropriate antibiotics are begun. Those who have not been treated can continue to shed organisms in their stool for 5 to 7 weeks. Adults who have not had gastrointestinal symptoms have rarely, if ever, been implicated in the spread of *C. jejuni.*

INFECTION CONTROL

Vaccine.   None available.

Exclusion from Child Care or Preschool Attendance.   Two days after beginning antibiotics or until the child is asymptomatic, whichever is the shorter period of time.

Recommendations for Other Children.   Good hygiene.

Recommendations for Personnel.   Extra-careful attention should be paid to handwashing after changing diapers and before food preparation. Toys and countertops should be cleaned more frequently, especially if used by children with diarrhea.

Parental Advice.   Parents should enforce good personal hygiene in their toilet-trained children. They can be reassured that their child does NOT require a stool culture unless he or she becomes symptomatic.

16

Candida
(Thrush, Diaper Dermatitis)

CHARLES M. GINSBURG, M.D.

CLINICAL MANIFESTATIONS

The skin and the mucous membranes are the most common sites of involvement in infections caused by the various species of *Candida*. In most instances, the infection is superficial and acute; however, in neonates and immunocompromised patients of all ages, the pathogen may be invasive and has the potential to cause disseminated or chronic disease.

Oral candidiasis (thrush), the most common infection caused by *Candida* species, is an acute inflammation of the tongue and oral mucous membranes that is manifested as white or greyish-white focal or diffuse plaques on the mucous membranes. In severe disease the lesions may extend to the angles of the mouth (perlèche) where fissuring and cracking may occur. The plaques are tightly adherent to the mucosa, and attempts to remove them generally produce bleeding and result in a tender erosion in the mucosa.

The diaper area and the intertriginous areas of the axillae, groin, and intergluteal fold are the most common sites for candidal invasion of the skin. Regardless of the area involved, the clinical appearance is similar; the affected skin is fiery red and, depending on the duration of infection, contains lesions that range from slightly raised red papules to discrete eroded lesions with a red raised border.

Often, there also are discrete macular or papular satellite lesions in areas that are separated from the primary site of involvement by normal skin. *Candida* also may infect the skin surrounding the nails of the hands and feet, particularly in infants and children who suck their thumbs or other digits. The paronychial lesions are similar to those that occur on other areas of the skin; however, the lesions are generally more edematous than those that occur on glabrous skin, and often, there is purulent drainage from the lesions as a result of secondary bacterial infection caused by strains of staphylococci.

ETIOLOGIC AGENT

Although there are multiple species of *Candida*, one species, *Candida albicans*, is responsible for the majority of infections in normal hosts.

EPIDEMIOLOGY

Source of the Organism.   *Candida* species are ubiquitous in the environment, largely as the result of human-to-human transmission. The digestive tract, the vagina and, less commonly, the skin are the principal reservoirs for the organism.

High-Risk Populations.   Neonates, immunocompromised patients, and those with chronic endocrine disorders such as diabetes mellitus are predisposed to infection with species of *Candida*. In normal hosts, the organism has a proclivity to invade traumatized skin or mucous membranes or those areas of the skin that become macerated as a result of excess moisture.

Mode of Spread.   The mode of spread of *Candida* is dependent on the age of the patient. Newborns generally acquire the organism from their mother's colonized vagina during the birth process. By contrast, infants and older children acquire the organism from their mother's skin or hands or from unsterilized nipples or bottles. Additionally, in situations where there are breaks in the mucosal or epidermal barrier, children may acquire the organism from infected individuals.

Incubation Period.   The incubation period for *Candida* infections is not known.

DIAGNOSIS

The presumptive diagnosis of most superficial *Candida* infections can be made on clinical grounds. In instances where the diagnosis is unclear, a definitive diagnosis can be made by obtaining scrapings from the surface of the infected lesions for microscopic examination and for culture on Sabouraud agar. The material obtained from scrapings can be stained with Calcuflor or with potassium hydroxide and then examined under the microscope. Although round thin-walled cells may be visualized, they are not indicative of tissue invasion; segmented mycelia are the only forms that are routinely associated with tissue invasion.

THERAPY

Oral or superficial cutaneous *Candida* infections may be treated with nystatin suspension administered three to four times daily for 5 to 7 days. Additional important ancillary measures for treatment of cutaneous disease consist of keeping the affected area dry and, possibly, administering a corticosteroid cream to patients with severe highly inflammatory cutaneous lesions. Caretakers of diapered infants should be reminded to change the diapers frequently, clean the skin with soap and water, and avoid occlusive pants, cornstarch, and baby powders.

INFECTIOUS PERIOD

Patients are infective while active lesions are present.

INFECTION CONTROL

Vaccine.   None available.

Exclusion from Child Care or Preschool Attendance.   Since most children with candidiasis do not have systemic symptoms and their activities of daily living are not compromised, they may attend day care or preschool without limitation.

Recommendations for Other Children.   If careful hygienic procedures are followed by the adult personnel in the center and the infected patient is on effective therapy, there is little risk to the other children in the center.

Recommendations for Personnel.   Normal hosts who work in the center are at little risk for acquisition of the pathogen, provided that careful handwashing techniques are utilized. This latter aspect is particularly important for personnel caring for children with oral or cutaneous candidal infections. Immunosuppressed hosts who work in the center should avoid direct contact with infected children but may work with uninfected children, since the risk for aerosol transmission of the organism is small.

Parental Advice.   Since this agent is ubiquitous and the pathogenicity of the organism for normal hosts is small, it is probably unnecessary to inform parents of normal children that there are cases of *Candida* infection at the center. Parents of children who are immunocompromised should be informed of cases of *Candida* at the center so that they can consult their child's physician to obtain recommendations about management of their child.

17

Chlamydia

MARGARET R. HAMMERSCHLAG, M.D.

CLINICAL MANIFESTATIONS

Chlamydia trachomatis: Major clinical manifestations of *C. trachomatis* infection are conjunctivitis and pneumonia. The conjunctivitis may present unilaterally or bilaterally. The clinical presentation is extremely variable, ranging from mild conjunctival infection and discharge to severe inflammation with chemosis, pseudomembrane formation, and copious mucopurulent discharge. The conjunctivae may be very friable and may bleed when stroked with a swab.

The clinical presentation of pneumonia due to *C. trachomatis* is very characteristic. The onset is gradual with rhinitis and cough. The infants are usually afebrile. Physical examination reveals tachypnea and the presence of rales. Wheezing is distinctly uncommon. Chest radiographs demonstrate hyperexpansion and variable infiltrates. A very suggestive laboratory finding is peripheral eosinophilia (>400 cells/mm^3).

Chlamydia pneumoniae (TWAR): This recently described *Chlamydia* species appears to cause an atypical pneumonia very similar in presentation to *Mycoplasma* pneumonia. Clinical manifestations include coryza, fever, development of cough, sore throat, pleuritic chest pain, and, possibly, pleural effusions. *C. pneumoniae* also has been associated with exacerbations of asthma.

ETIOLOGIC AGENT

C. trachomatis: An obligate intracellular bacterium. All members of the genus have a unique developmental cycle including a 48- to 72-hour life cycle and distinct infectious and reproductive forms (elementary body and reticulate body). The organisms form characteristic intracytoplasmic inclusions that can be detected by staining with Giemsa stain, iodine, or specific fluorescein-conjugated monoclonal antibodies in tissue culture. McCoy cells, a murine-derived fibroblast line, or HeLa 229 cells are the cell lines frequently used in clinical laboratories for *Chlamydia* culture.

C. pneumoniae (TWAR): Shares the same lipopolysaccharide antigen as other members of the genus. It also forms inclusions, and the major difference from *C. trachomatis* is that they do not stain with iodine.

EPIDEMIOLOGY

Source of the Organism.   *C. trachomatis:* Among adults, *C. trachomatis* is primarily a sexually transmitted disease. The adult genital tract is the major reservoir. In many adults, especially women, the infection is frequently asymptomatic and may persist for years if not treated.

C. pneumoniae: Believed to be a primary human respiratory pathogen. The upper respiratory tract may be the primary reservoir. Preliminary clinical data suggest that *C. pneumoniae* may cause prolonged asymptomatic infection of the respiratory tract.

High-Risk Populations.   *C. trachomatis:* Since infection is acquired from an infected mother at delivery, risk factors are those for infection in the mother: young age, early sexual activity, and multiple sexual partners.

C. pneumoniae: Not known.

Mode of Spread.   *C. trachomatis:* Vertical transmission from infected mother to infant during passage through an infected birth canal. If delivery has been by cesarean section without rupture of membranes, transmission is unlikely to occur. There are no data supporting any form of horizontal transmission postnatally.

C. pneumoniae: Believed to be person-to-person by aerosol droplet or respiratory secretions.

Incubation Period.   *C. trachomatis:* Conjunctivitis—5 to 14 days; pneumonia—14 days to 2 months.

C. pneumoniae: Not known. Some preliminary data suggest 3 to 4 days.

DIAGNOSIS

C. trachomatis: Conjunctivitis—determined by isolation of the organism from conjunctival culture or demonstration of chlamydial antigen by either direct fluorescent antibody test or enzyme immunoassay in conjunctival smear or secretions; pneumonia—determined by isolation of the organism from nasopharyngeal secretions obtained by swab or nasopharyngeal aspirate or by antigen detection methods as described above. There are no readily available serologic methods.

C. pneumoniae: As this is a relatively newly described organism, cultures are being performed only in a few laboratories.

THERAPY

C. trachomatis: Conjunctivitis—oral erythromycin suspension, 50 mg/kg/day in four divided doses for 10 to 14 days. Additional topical therapy is not necessary; pneumonia—same dose as for conjunctivitis.

C. pneumoniae: Oral erythromycin at same dose as for *C. trachomatis* infection. Alternatives include clarithromycin, 20 mg/kg/day in two divided doses for 10 days, and azithromycin, 5 to 10 mg/kg/day everyday for 5 days. The optimum dose and duration of therapy are not known.

INFECTIOUS PERIOD

C. trachomatis: Not applicable, as horizontal transmission does not appear to occur.

C. pneumoniae: Not known.

INFECTION CONTROL

Vaccine. *C. trachomatis:* None available.

C. pneumoniae: None available.

Exclusion from Child Care or Preschool Attendance. *C. trachomatis:* It is not necessary to keep the child home, since horizontal transmission (child-to-child) appears to be very unlikely.

C. pneumoniae: Until asymptomatic and on appropriate therapy.

Recommendations for Other Children.   *C. trachomatis:* None.

C. pneumoniae: If infection is symptomatic, children should be taken to their physician.

Recommendations for Personnel.   *C. trachomatis:* None.

C. pneumoniae: If infection is symptomatic, personnel should seek medical attention.

Parental Advice.   *C. trachomatis:* None for parents of other children. Parents of infected children should be advised to seek treatment for themselves.

C. pneumoniae: Inform parents that this infection can progress to pneumonia. Children should be watched closely and brought to medical attention if symptomatic.

18

Coronaviruses
(Common Cold)

RONALD B. TURNER, M.D.

CLINICAL MANIFESTATIONS

The spectrum of clinical illness produced by the coronavirus infection is not clearly defined. The major clinical syndrome caused by these viruses seems to be the common cold. Colds produced by coronaviruses are similar to rhinovirus colds. Some volunteers with coronavirus colds complain of mild gastrointestinal symptoms.

Gastroenteritis has been suggested to be a symptom of coronavirus infection; however, this association has not been clearly established. Necrotizing enterocolitis has been reported in association with coronavirus infection of newborn infants.

ETIOLOGIC AGENT

The coronaviruses are RNA viruses not closely related to other human viral pathogens. Two serologically distinct groups of coronaviruses are recognized, 229E and OC43. The antigenic interrelationships between different strains of virus within these major groups are complex and poorly understood. Experiments in humans inoculated with 229E indicate that solid immunity to reinfection is produced against the infecting strain of virus, but protection does not extend to other 229E strains.

EPIDEMIOLOGY

Source of the Organism.   Infection with the human strains of coronavirus is limited to humans, and no animal or inanimate reservoir of infection has been identified.

High-Risk Populations.   No populations have been identified that are at high risk for acquisition of infection. Newborn infants may be at increased risk of severe disease once infected. The factors that predispose to infection are not known.

Mode of Spread.   The data available suggest that coronaviruses may spread by small-particle aerosols. Further study will be necessary to confirm this observation.

Incubation Period.   The incubation period for coronavirus colds is 48 to 72 hours.

DIAGNOSIS

The coronaviruses grow poorly, if at all, in cell cultures, and no reliable antigen detection methods are available. Diagnosis is rarely attempted; however, serologic techniques have been used in some situations.

THERAPY

There is no specific therapy available for treatment of coronavirus infection.

INFECTIOUS PERIOD

The period of infectivity is not known.

INFECTION CONTROL

Vaccine.   None available.

Exclusion from Child Care or Preschool Attendance.   Exclusion from child care or preschool settings is not necessary for children infected with coronavirus.

Recommendations for Other Children.   No special precautions are indicated.

Recommendations for Personnel.   No special precautions are indicated.

Parental Advice.   Coronavirus colds generally are mild upper respiratory illnesses, and no special precautions are necessary.

19

Coxsackievirus A16
(Hand-Foot-and-Mouth Disease)

ZIAD M. SHEHAB, M.D.

CLINICAL MANIFESTATIONS

Hand-foot-and-mouth disease is an illness characterized by the development of an enanthem consisting of ulcers usually located on the buccal mucosa, tongue, or gums. About 2 days after the onset of the enanthem, an exanthem develops that is characterized by a vesicular eruption over the hands and/or the feet. In addition, the buttocks are sometimes involved, but the rash there tends not to be vesicular.

ETIOLOGIC AGENT

Hand-foot-and-mouth disease is usually caused by coxsackievirus A16. Other types of coxsackieviruses have also been associated with this syndrome, such as coxsackievirus A4, A5, A9, A10, B2, B5, and enterovirus 71.

EPIDEMIOLOGY

Source of the Organism.   Humans are the only natural host for enteroviruses.

High-Risk Populations.   Young children are particularly susceptible to this infection because of their immunologic innocence. Household members are also at increased risk.

Mode of Spread.   The virus is transmitted by the fecal-oral or oral-oral routes.

Incubation Period.   Usually 4 to 6 days.

DIAGNOSIS

The infection is diagnosed based on the typical course and manifestations of the illness. It can be confirmed by viral cultures of the throat and rectal swabs.

THERAPY

No specific therapy is available. Treatment is entirely symptomatic. Hospitalization is not required.

INFECTIOUS PERIOD

The infectivity of patients with hand-foot-and-mouth disease is prolonged, spanning from before the onset of the enanthem to weeks following resolution of the illness. Keep in mind that most infections are entirely asymptomatic.

INFECTION CONTROL

Vaccine.   None available.

Exclusion from Child Care or Preschool Attendance.   Excretion of the virus in hand-foot-and-mouth disease is prolonged, and most infections are asymptomatic. Therefore, removal of the child from day care or preschool is not warranted and would have little to no impact on the spread of the infection.

Recommendations for Other Children.   Emphasize basic hygiene regarding handwashing.

Recommendations for Personnel.   Emphasize basic hygienic measures, i.e., handwashing, with all children and staff in the center.

Parental Advice.   Reassure parents that this is a self-limited, mild, and, in most instances, asymptomatic infection with no serious sequelae.

20

Cryptosporidia

WILLIAM J. RODRIGUEZ, M.D., PH.D., AND BARBARA A. JANTAUSCH, M.D.

CLINICAL MANIFESTATIONS

Cryptosporidium causes severe diarrhea in immunocompromised patients and self-limited disease in immunocompetent hosts. *Cryptosporidium* was first identified as the cause of human enteritis in 1976 and was initially thought to represent an opportunistic pathogen. *Cryptosporidium* is now recognized as a common enteric pathogen throughout the world, being more common in developing countries, and as a cause of diarrheal outbreaks in child care centers and preschools in the United States.

Immunocompromised patients have severe, protracted, watery, foul-smelling diarrhea with large stools, abdominal cramping, malabsorption, and weight loss. A minority of patients may experience mild self-limited disease. Cholecystitis has been recently described in acquired immunodeficiency syndrome patients. Immunocompetent patients experience self-limited disease and have watery stools, abdominal pain, and weight loss for approximately 10 to 14 days. Vomiting has been noted in one third of patients, and fever in the range of 38.5° to 38.9° C has been reported. Rarely, patients may be asymptomatic carriers.

ETIOLOGIC AGENT

Cryptosporidium, meaning "hidden spore" in Greek, is a protozoan parasite belonging to the class Sporozoa and the order Eucoccidiida, which also includes *Toxoplasma gondii, Isospora,* and *Plasmodium*

113

species. The organism has a monoxenous life cycle similar to *Isospora* and passes through sporozoite, trophozoite, merozoite, and gametocyte stages within the same host. The oocyst is the infective particle. Seventeen species of *Cryptosporidium* have been identified; *Cryptosporidium parvum* and *Cryptosporidium muris* have been associated with mammalian infection.

EPIDEMIOLOGY

Source of the Organism.   The organism is found in the gastrointestinal tract of infected humans and animals, specifically reptiles, birds, and mammals, and in contaminated food and water and on fomites. Cryptosporidia exist in nature as a zoonosis of cows and sheep.

High-Risk Populations.   Immunocompromised persons, healthy homosexual men, travelers, especially to developing countries, animal handlers, household contacts of infected persons, hospitalized persons, children in child care centers, preschools, and hospitals, and child care personnel with exposure to infected persons are at greatest risk for acquiring disease.

Mode of Spread.   Spread occurs through fecal-oral transmission, person-to-person transmission, and direct and indirect contact of infected feces, contaminated food, water, and surfaces.

Incubation Period.   The incubation period is estimated to be between 5 and 10 days.

DIAGNOSIS

Diagnosis is made by detection of *Cryptosporidium* oocysts in stool by using special staining techniques including modified Kinyoun acid-fast, fluorescent auramine-rhodamine, and periodic acid-Schiff and carbol-fuchsin-negative stains. The organism also can be identified by light and electron microscopy of intestinal biopsy samples.

THERAPY

As the disease is self-limited in the immunocompetent host, hospitalization is usually not necessary but may be required in severe cases. There is currently no proven effective standard therapy available for eradication of the parasites or palliation of symptoms. There have been isolated reports of success with spiramycin. Therapy with spiramycin, paromomycin, or azithromycin may be beneficial in some cases (doses and duration range from 4 g/24 hr orally, divided four times a day for 3 to 4 weeks, to 100 mg/kg/24 hr divided every 12 hours for 10 days). Clindamycin and quinine have also been used but have not proven to be efficacious. Antiperistaltic agents have not been found to be beneficial and have been noted to worsen abdominal cramping.

INFECTIOUS PERIOD

Oocysts may be shed in the stool of immunocompetent patients for 2 to 5 weeks, although in most cases this stops less than 12 days after resolution of symptoms or until death in immunocompromised patients.

INFECTION CONTROL

Vaccine.   None available.

Exclusion from Child Care or Preschool Attendance.   Children should be kept out of the child care or preschool setting until they are asymptomatic.

Recommendations for Other Children.   Children who develop diarrhea should be removed from the child care or preschool setting and have their stools evaluated for oocysts. Good handwashing, proper disposal of stools, and cohorting of patients should be practiced.

Recommendations for Personnel.   Personnel should practice good handwashing, especially after using the toilet and handling diapers. The organism is resistant to chlorine. Use of an ammonia solution to decontaminate the environment may inactivate cysts. Personnel who become symptomatic should remain at home and have their stools evaluated for oocysts.

Parental Advice.   Parents should monitor their children for symptoms of diarrhea. Symptomatic children should be removed from the child care or preschool setting, be seen by their pediatrician and have their stools evaluated for oocysts.

21

Cytomegalovirus

STUART P. ADLER, M.D.

CLINICAL MANIFESTATIONS

The majority of children with infections due to cytomegalovirus (CMV) acquired after birth have no symptoms. Occasionally, particularly in older children and adults, CMV will cause infectious mononucleosis with sore throat, swollen lymph nodes in the neck, enlarged liver, rash, and atypical white cells in the blood. However, this is very rare, especially in young children in day care or preschool.

ETIOLOGIC AGENT

CMV infects only humans. CMV is the largest and most complex virus that infects humans. Only one major serotype exists.

EPIDEMIOLOGY

Source of the Organism.   The virus is acquired by transmission from human to human, and nearly all humans eventually become infected. Infections occur more frequently when there is crowding and intimate contact.

High-Risk Populations.   Everyone in the population eventually acquires an infection with CMV. In immunocompromised patients, infection can be severe and/or prolonged. Infection in susceptible pregnant women can result in fetal infection.

Mode of Spread.   The exact mode of spread of the virus is unknown, although we assume that intimate contact, i.e., diaper changing, kissing, feeding, bathing, and other activities that result in contact with infected urine or saliva, is important for spread. The virus will remain alive on surfaces and diapers for several hours.

Incubation Period.   The incubation period for this infection is approximately 1 month.

DIAGNOSIS

CMV infection is best diagnosed by obtaining a sample of urine for culture. Seroconversion is also possible but requires a serum obtained before infection and one obtained after infection.

THERAPY

No therapy is available.

INFECTIOUS PERIOD

Most children who acquire CMV infections shed the virus for many months, with a range of 6 months to 2 years. Adults shed for a shorter period, probably less than 6 months.

INFECTION CONTROL

Vaccine.   None available.

Exclusion from Child Care or Preschool Attendance.   Children excreting CMV should not be kept out of day care.

Recommendations for Other Children.   No attempts should be made to prevent children from spreading CMV from child to child in the child care center or preschool, as many children will naturally be infected with this virus.

Recommendations for Personnel.   Pregnant personnel should assume that all children are excreting the virus. Before pregnancy, women should be tested to determine whether they have immunoglobulin G (IgG) antibodies to CMV (immunity) and therefore are very unlikely to give birth to a child damaged by this virus. If a pregnant woman lacks immunity (tests seronegative), she should be advised either to avoid contact with children less than 2 years of age during pregnancy or to avoid intimate contact with young children—particularly contact with a child's urine and saliva. She should avoid unnecessary kissing and handling of young children.

She should either wear gloves or practice frequent handwashing after contact with children. She should not share eating utensils or towels with young children.

Parental Advice.   Pregnant women with a child under age 2 years in group child care or preschool should assume their child is shedding the virus. Routine testing of serum for IgG antibodies for pregnant mothers is not advised. Pregnant mothers should be advised, to the extent possible, to avoid intimate contact with their child under age 2 years during pregnancy.

22

Diphtheria

MOSES GROSSMAN, M.D.

CLINICAL MANIFESTATIONS

Diphtheria may be nasal, tonsillopharyngeal, laryngotracheo-bronchial, or limited to the skin. Diphtheria toxin produces serious damage to the myocardium, the nervous system, and the kidney, resulting in life-threatening complications.

Tonsillopharyngeal diphtheria, the most common form, is manifested by a febrile illness with a severe sore throat, systemic toxicity, and the presence of a yellowish, white exudate over the pharynx, tonsils, or uvula. The exudate becomes organized into a pseudomembrane and may spread to a considerable extent.

In laryngotracheobronchial diphtheria, the exudate involves the larynx and produces life-threatening airway obstruction.

Nasal diphtheria is a mild form of the disease, often devoid of toxic manifestations, and is more likely to affect very young children.

Skin or mucous membrane diphtheria may be found in warm climates presenting as a shallow ulcer, often coated with a pseudomembrane.

ETIOLOGIC AGENT

The causative organism is *Corynebacterium diphtheriae,* a Gram-positive non-spore-forming, slender rod with a tendency to branch, which sometimes gives a palisade-like appearance on Gram stain. *C. diphtheriae* has been divided into gravis, mitis, and intermedius types. All are capable of producing a potent toxin when induced by a lysogenic bacteriophage.

EPIDEMIOLOGY

Source of the Organism.   Infection is limited to humans. Infected persons as well as carriers may spread the organisms. Carriers are usually contacts of infected individuals.

High-Risk Populations.   Crowding, which generally occurs in low socioeconomic settings, facilitates the spread of the organism. Unimmunized or partially immunized individuals are particularly susceptible to the disease, though immunization does not provide 100% protection.

Mode of Spread.   The organism is spread by intimate contact through nasal or oral secretion or contact with infected skin.

Incubation Period.   The incubation period for diphtheria is usually 2 to 6 days.

DIAGNOSIS

The diagnosis is based entirely on isolation of the organism from culture obtained from the infected site. Isolation requires the use of special media both for transport and for growth; thus, the laboratory needs to know that it is *C. diphtheriae* that is suspected. The final link in diagnosis is the demonstration of toxigenicity of the isolated organism.

THERAPY

The cornerstone of therapy is the early administration of diphtheria antitoxin in order to neutralize the circulating diphtheria toxin. The antitoxin is prepared from horse serum; tests for sensitivity must be done before initiating therapy with antitoxin. The administration is intravenous, and the dose is empiric, based on the extent of involvement. Antimicrobial therapy is important because it shortens the duration of communicability. Erythromycin is the preferred antimicrobial; penicillin is also effective.

The child always needs to be hospitalized and may require extensive support measures and monitoring of vital functions, depending on the degree of involvement. Cardiac function and paralysis, particularly cranial nerve involvement, may present serious management problems.

INFECTIOUS PERIOD

Untreated, patients are usually infectious up to 2 weeks but occasionally may harbor organisms for months. Treatment usually eradicates organisms after 4 days.

INFECTION CONTROL

Vaccine.   All children attending day care *must* be fully immunized against diphtheria. All previously immunized individuals who are exposed to a child with diphtheria should receive a booster of toxoid if their last dose of toxoid was 5 or more years before exposure.

Exclusion from Child Care or Preschool Attendance.   The infected child should be kept out of the child care or preschool setting for at least 1 week after initiation of antibiotic therapy. A negative culture should be documented before returning the child to the center.

Recommendations for Other Children.   An outbreak of diphtheria in a child care or preschool setting would be most unusual. It would certainly create a panic among parents and providers and should bring in public health authorities at a very early stage. It would be wise to have a meeting of all concerned to explain the issue and answer questions.

Children, providers, and the family of the index case must be cultured and placed under clinical surveillance for a week.

Those who have been immunized but have not had a booster during the preceding 5 years require a booster dose of diphtheria toxoid. Care must be taken to give only the adult type of toxoid to adults. Immunization should be given to those who have not been previously immunized.

Additionally, all close contacts of the index case should receive antimicrobial prophylaxis—oral erythromycin (40–50 mg/kg/day for 7 days, maximum 2 g/day). Intramuscular benzathine penicillin G (600,000 to 1.2 million units) is an alternative to erythromycin.

Recommendations for Personnel.   Personnel should be cultured and placed under clinical surveillance for 1 week. Those who have not been immunized should be immunized. Those who have been immunized but were immunized more than 5 years before exposure should receive a booster dose of diphtheria toxoid. Culture-positive or very close contacts should receive 1 week of prophylactic antibiotic therapy with either oral erythromycin or injectable penicillin.

Parental Advice.   All parents should be notified in writing of the occurrence of diphtheria in the center. Written recommendations as outlined above should be distributed to all parents, and documented compliance required for return to the child care center or preschool.

23

Enterobius vermicularis
(Pinworm)

ANDREA J. RUFF, M.D.

CLINICAL MANIFESTATIONS

Pruritus ani is the most common symptom associated with enterobiasis. Much less often, pruritus vulvae may be associated with infection. In rare cases, aberrant migration of the adult worm from the perineum has been associated with vaginitis, salpingitis, and peritonitis. Although a number of other manifestations, such as anorexia, weight loss, abdominal pain, enuresis, and teeth grinding, have been attributed to enterobiasis, no controlled studies have indicated a causal relationship between those symptoms and *Enterobius vermicularis* infections.

ETIOLOGIC AGENT

E. vermicularis, the human pinworm, is an intestinal nematode. Humans acquire enterobiasis by ingesting infective eggs. The larvae hatch in the intestines, developing into adult worms that live in the cecum and surrounding colon. Gravid female worms migrate to the anus and deposit their eggs on the perianal and perineal skin. The females die after laying their eggs. Within a few hours the deposited eggs are mature and capable of transmitting infection if they are ingested.

EPIDEMIOLOGY

Source of the Organism.   Enterobiasis, the most common human helminth infection, occurs worldwide. The infective eggs, which are transmitted from person to person or indirectly through contaminated objects, appear to be relatively resistant to disinfectants and under optimal environmental conditions may remain viable for up to 13 days.

High-Risk Populations.   Due to their lack of hygiene, children are more likely to ingest *E. vermicularis* eggs and become infected than are adults. Therefore, enterobiasis tends to be prevalent in almost any setting where groups of children can be found. This includes large families, schools, child care centers, and mental institutions. In these settings the infection is often ubiquitous with continuous transmission and reinfection of the children. Good personal hygiene can diminish the risk of enterobiasis, and if bathing and changes of undergarments are infrequent within a population, infection is even more likely to be a significant problem.

Mode of Spread.   Transmission occurs through ingestion of *E. vermicularis* eggs. Persons with enterobiasis may be reinfected if they scratch themselves and transfer eggs from their anal area to their mouth. Those in close contact with an infected individual may be exposed to contaminated fomites. Transmission of *E. vermicularis* eggs can also occur through contact with soiled clothing or bed linens or through ingestion of eggs in house dust.

Incubation Period.   The time period between acquisition of infection and the deposition of eggs by the female worm has not been well established. Estimates range from 2 weeks to 2 months.

DIAGNOSIS

The diagnosis is established by detecting the eggs deposited in the perianal region. This is best done by applying transparent adhesive tape to the perianal region in the morning before a stool is passed or before a bath. After mounting the tape on a glass slide, it can be examined for the presence of *E. vermicularis* eggs. The test may need to be repeated one or more times to rule out enterobiasis. Less often, the characteristic eggs may be identified in a stool specimen, or the female worm may be observed in the perianal area.

THERAPY

Several effective and reasonably nontoxic drugs are available for the treatment of enterobiasis. Pyrantel pamoate can be given as a single oral dose of 11 mg/kg (maximum, 1 g). Mebendazole can also be given as a single oral dose of 100 mg. It is generally recommended that treatment with these agents be repeated in 2 to 3 weeks to eliminate any remaining adult worms. Some authorities recommend treating all individuals in the household of an infected child, while others recommend treating only those who are symptomatic or known to be infected. Limited data are available regarding use of either pyrantel pamoate or mebendazole in children less than 2 years old; therefore, the risks and benefits of therapy should be carefully considered, and a decision to treat a child in this age group should be made on an individual basis.

INFECTIOUS PERIOD

Individuals will have the potential of transmitting *E. vermicularis* as long as they harbor adult male and female worms; although the female worm dies after laying her eggs, reinfection of the host is common, providing an ongoing source of adult worms.

INFECTION CONTROL

Vaccine.   None available.

Exclusion from Child Care or Preschool Attendance.   Once the diagnosis of enterobiasis has been made, the child should be treated with one of the recommended regimens. After appropriate treatment the child does not need to be kept out of the child care or preschool.

Recommendations for Other Children.   Given the prevalence of enterobiasis, particularly within groups of children, it is highly likely that other children will also be infected. Any children noted by parents or center personnel to have pruritus ani should be checked for *E. vermicularis* and treated appropriately if the infection is present.

Recommendations for Personnel.   Personnel should be made aware of the means of transmission and of the potential for them to be infected by the children. Good hygiene among the children and personnel with washing of hands, bedclothes, and toys should be emphasized. It should, however, also be understood that total prevention within a child care center or preschool is very unlikely, if not impossible.

Parental Advice.   Parents should understand that enterobiasis is ubiquitous and often unavoidable among children in any group setting. They should be educated regarding the mode of transmission, clinical manifestations, means of diagnosis, and therapeutic options. Lastly, they should be reassured that the diagnosis of enterobiasis in their child or in another attendee is not necessarily an indication of poor hygienic conditions.

24

Enteroviruses

ZIAD M. SHEHAB, M.D.

CLINICAL MANIFESTATIONS

Enteroviral infections are relatively widespread and include infections with polioviruses, coxsackieviruses, echoviruses, and enteroviruses. They are divided into polio and nonpolio enteroviruses.

Infection with polioviruses results in an asymptomatic infection in 90 to 95% of cases. In addition, a minor illness may result. Occasionally, an aseptic meningitis can ensue. The most dramatic result of poliovirus infection is paralytic poliomyelitis.

The majority of infections with nonpolio enteroviruses also are asymptomatic. The spectrum of illnesses caused by these viruses span from asymptomatic to life-threatening. Of the symptomatic infections, most are nonspecific febrile illnesses. Some specific enanthems and exanthems have been associated with them, such as herpangina, a febrile illness with papulovesicular enanthem of the palate and tonsillar pillars, or hand-foot-and-mouth disease. Other diseases caused by enteroviruses include exanthems with or without meningitis, aseptic meningitis, epidemic pleurodynia, respiratory diseases, gastroenteritis, hemorrhagic conjunctivitis, and, rarely, myocarditis, pericarditis, or paralytic disease.

ETIOLOGIC AGENT

Enteroviruses are single-stranded RNA viruses that are ubiquitous. They are prevalent during the summer and fall.

Enteroviruses of humans consist of the following antigenic types:

Poliomyelitis
Polioviruses 1, 2, 3

Coxsackie A viruses
A1 to A22 and A24

Coxsackie B viruses
1 to 16

Echoviruses
1 to 9, 11 to 27, 29 to 33

Enteroviruses
68 to 72

EPIDEMIOLOGY

Source of the Organism.   The only known reservoir of human enteroviruses is the human being.

High-Risk Populations.   Young children are especially susceptible to these infections because of lack of prior exposure. In immunocompromised hosts, enteroviruses can establish persistent infections.

Mode of Spread.   The virus is transmitted via a fecal-oral or oral-oral route.

Incubation Period.   The incubation period is usually 7 to 14 days, although incubation periods of 2 to 35 days are not uncommon.

DIAGNOSIS

The diagnosis is established by virus isolation from a throat swab, stool specimen, and, occasionally, cerebrospinal fluid, or occasionally by demonstration of a rise in specific antibody titer. Recently, detection of viral RNA by the polymerase chain reaction has resulted in a more rapid and sensitive diagnostic method for meningitis and infections in the neonate using cerebrospinal fluid, serum, or urine.

THERAPY

No specific therapy is available for enteroviral infection. The treatment is supportive. In the more severe illnesses, such as meningoencephalitis, myocarditis, or poliomyelitis, hospitalization is often required. Bed rest and support for respiratory failure may be required in cases of poliomyelitis.

INFECTIOUS PERIOD

The infectivity of patients with enteroviral infections is prolonged, spanning from before the onset of the clinical illness to weeks following its resolution. Note that most infections are entirely asymptomatic.

INFECTION CONTROL

Vaccine.   No vaccines are available for nonpolio enteroviruses. Two poliovirus vaccines are presently available. The live attenuated oral poliovirus vaccine is recommended for routine immunization at 2, 4, and 18 months of age and again at 4 to 6 years. The inactivated polio vaccine should be used in individuals who are immunocompromised and in household contacts of immunocompromised persons.

Exclusion from Child Care or Preschool Attendance.   Excretion of the virus in nonpolio enteroviral infections is prolonged, and most infections are asymptomatic. Therefore, removal of the child from day care is not warranted and would have little to no impact on the spread of the infection. Children with nonvaccine poliovirus infections should be kept out of child care or preschool until shedding of poliovirus has resolved.

Recommendations for Other Children.   Emphasize basic hygiene regarding handwashing. In the care of poliomyelitis, children whose immunizations are incomplete should receive polio vaccine.

Recommendations for Personnel.   Emphasize basic hygiene measures (i.e., handwashing) with all children and staff in the day care center. A booster dose of inactivated polio vaccine should be considered.

Parental Advice.   Emphasize basic hygiene regarding handwashing. In the case of poliomyelitis, children whose immunizations are incomplete should receive polio vaccine, and inactivated polio vaccine should be given to all household contacts.

25

Escherichia coli
(Diarrhea)

WILLIAM J. RODRIGUEZ, M.D., PH.D., AND BARBARA A. JANTAUSCH, M.D.

CLINICAL MANIFESTATIONS

Disease caused by the various types of *Escherichia coli* is not very prevalent in the United States. Five major mechanisms of disease are postulated: enterotoxigenic strains (ETEC), enteropathogenic strains (EPEC), enteroinvasive strains (EIEC), enterohemorrhagic strains (EHEC), and enteroadherent strains (EAEC).

ETEC: These produce either heat-labile, heat-stable, or both kinds of enterotoxins, causing disease by affecting the small bowel absorptive mechanism. This results in loss of electrolytes and water. Cramps, diarrhea, some vomiting, and very little if no fever are the hallmarks. Disease usually lasts 5 days. Enterotoxigenic strains are a common cause of traveler's diarrhea and diarrhea in infants in underdeveloped countries.

EPEC: These *E. coli* strains are serotypeable but not enterotoxigenic or invasive. Those strains that destroy the villi in the small intestine cause lowering of disaccharidases and may cause malabsorption. Although they usually cause self-limiting diseases in older children and adults, younger children and infants may have prolonged diarrhea lasting 2 weeks or longer. These latter patients may experience voluminous diarrhea without blood or mucus. These strains produce outbreaks of diarrhea in infants in the United States.

EIEC: These strains belong to restricted serotypes and cause disease with a clinical picture comparable to that seen with *Shigella*. These strains affect the colon and distal small bowel. Affected patients usually have fever, headache, and stool with mucus and blood.

EHEC: These strains, common in Argentina and South Africa, are represented in the United States in *E. coli* O157H7. They produce a syndrome associated with severe abdominal cramps with a predominantly afebrile state accompanied by grossly bloody diarrhea and occasional chills. Hemolytic uremic syndrome has been found to be associated with these strains. Symptoms are usually self-limited and last about 5 days.

EAEC: These strains have been postulated to be a cause of traveler's diarrhea in adults and in some cases of protracted infant diarrhea.

ETIOLOGIC AGENT

ETEC traditionally have not been classified under the classical serotypes; a plasmid encodes for enterotoxin production, and some associated serotypes are O6, O27, O78, O148, and O159. EPEC have multiple classical serotypes: O26:B6, O55, O111, and O128. These organisms lack the ability to produce heat-labile or heat-stable enterotoxin and are noninvasive. EIEC also have classic serotypes such as O124, O136, O144, and O152, which are not prevalent in the United States. Enterohemorrhagic strains such as O157H7 produce enterohemorrhagic toxin, occur in multiple strains, and have a worldwide distribution. In addition to these strains, some noninvasive EPEC produce a *Shigella*-like toxin or verotoxin, so named because of its activity against vero cells in tissue culture. The majority of EAEC do not belong to classic EPEC serogroups and adhere to Hep-2 cells.

EPIDEMIOLOGY

Source of the Organism.   Infected persons and food or water contaminated with feces are sources of the organism.

High-Risk Populations.   *ETEC:* Newborn, travelers.

EPEC: Newborn (uncommon).

EIEC: Contaminated food.

EHEC: Person-to-person in some outbreaks, fecal-oral, contaminated food, water.

EAEC: Travelers (primarily adults); infants.

Mode of Spread.   The organism is spread via fecal-oral transmission and person to person: caregiver to infant, patient to patient.

Incubation Period.   The incubation period is 2 to 6 days and usually shorter in cases of foodborne acquisition.

DIAGNOSIS

ETEC: The diagnosis is made by detecting heat-labile or heat-stable enterotoxin in an animal system, by cell culture, or through immunoassay. Tissue culture (Chinese hamster ovarian or y-1 mouse adrenal Ca line) or immunoassay will detect heat-labile toxin. While the suckling mouse assay and immunoassays may detect heat-stable enterotoxin, these tests are not generally available.

EPEC: There is no generally reliable commercially available system. Specialized immunologic methods are available in a limited number of laboratories.

EIEC: The organism is identified by demonstrating invasiveness in tissue culture or the conjunctival sac of animals or by identification of specific serotypes.

EHEC: Strains are first identified by demonstrating the presence of a sorbitol nonfermenter on sorbitol McConkey agar (SMAC). The strain is next tested for agglutination with 0:157 antiserum and its identity as an *E. coli* is then verified. Cultures for these microbes should be requested early in the illness (first 7 days).

EAEC: Strains of *E. coli* negative for heat-labile and heat-stable enterotoxin are tested for the presence of adherence to Hep-2 cells. A rise in titer of the O antigen of the specific strain is then sought.

THERAPY

ETEC: This is the only *E. coli* that is treatable early because diagnosis of the others is usually difficult. Trimethoprim-sulfamethoxazole (TMP-SMZ) is given empirically. Doxycycline represents a reasonable alternative for those older than 8 years of age.

EPEC: Neomycin, colistin, or TMP-SMZ.

EIEC: TMP-SMZ, amoxicillin, absorbable antibiotic.

EHEC: No antibiotic.

EAEC: No general treatment is available; for those infants with protracted diarrhea, limited experience with parenteral gentamicin suggests efficacy.

Fluid and electrolyte supplementation is of paramount importance in treating any of these infections.

INFECTIOUS PERIOD

The infectious period is generally considered to be while the person is symptomatic. The degree and extent of shedding may vary beyond that period.

INFECTION CONTROL

Vaccine.   None available.

Exclusion from Child Care or Preschool Attendance.   The child should be kept out of the child care or preschool setting until he or she is asymptomatic and has negative stool cultures. In the case of enterohemorrhagic *E. coli* the child should remain out of the child care setting until at least two serial stool cultures are negative or until 10 days after cessation of symptoms. (See under EHEC for screening assays.)

Recommendations for Other Children.   Close contacts of a symptomatic child with an enteroinvasive strain may need to be cultured and, if their stool is positive, should be considered for treatment even if asymptomatic. Public Health authorities should be notified immediately of an outbreak of EHEC.

Recommendations for Personnel.   Personnel should be cohorted, practice good handwashing, and stay at home and be cultured if symptomatic. If initial contact measures are not successful, it may be necessary to close the center temporarily.

Parental Advice.   Parents should report even mild gastroenteritis symptoms in their child. Symptomatic children should be removed from day care, seen by their pediatrician, and have their stool examined.

Giardia lamblia

THERESA A. SCHLAGER, M.D.

CLINICAL MANIFESTATIONS

Infants and children infected with *Giardia lamblia* can be asymptomatic or can be symptomatic with either a brief episode of diarrhea or a chronic illness with multiple symptoms. Asymptomatic infection may be seen in as many as 50% of the infected children. Surveys of the prevalence of *G. lamblia* in stool reveal rates ranging from 1% to 26%. An increased rate of asymptomatic infection has been seen in day care settings during outbreaks of diarrhea due to *G. lamblia*. Symptomatic infants and children with a brief illness will usually have diarrhea that is profuse and watery but unassociated with significant fever, toxicity, or dehydration and that usually resolves without specific dietary alteration or drug therapy. Symptomatic patients who develop a chronic illness ordinarily have protracted, intermittent symptoms including watery diarrhea, abdominal cramps, a protuberant abdomen, wasted extremities, edema, significant weight loss, retarded growth, and anemia. Their stools contain an increased amount of fat but do not usually contain visible blood, pus, or mucus.

ETIOLOGIC AGENT

G. lamblia is a flagellated protozoan type of parasite. Only two species appear to infect humans. The protozoan exists in two forms: a trophozoite form that inhabits the lumen of the upper small intestine where it can cause symptoms, and a cyst form that inhabits the lower small intestine and the large intestine and that when excreted in stool is infectious. When cysts are ingested by a susceptible host, trophozoites are released following the exposure of the cysts to the acidity of the stomach. The trophozoites can then inhabit the intestine, sometimes in very large numbers.

EPIDEMIOLOGY

Source of the Organism.   *G. lamblia* is distributed throughout the world. Humans are the principal reservoir of infection, but dogs and beavers are other sources of infection. Feces or objects (toys, diaper-changing tables, eating utensils) soiled with feces, water, or food contaminated with cysts are infectious by the oral route even if small numbers of cysts are ingested. Most epidemics result from contaminated water supplies. Prevention of waterborne outbreaks requires adequate filtration of municipal water obtained from surface water sources, because concentrations of chlorine used to disinfect drinking water are not effective against the cysts.

High-Risk Populations.   High-risk populations include:

- Infants and children in day care centers or preschools. In some areas, *G. lamblia* is the most common cause of diarrhea in child care centers and preschools—both in outbreaks and in sporadic cases. The children most frequently infected are non-toilet-trained toddlers. Following child care center or preschool outbreaks, 12 to 25% of family members of children (especially non–toilet-trained children) attending the center have become infected. There is increasing evidence that children in day care centers are a common source for spread of *G. lamblia* to the surrounding community.

- Infants and children exposed to unprocessed water sources.

- Patients with acquired immunodeficiency syndrome.

- Patients with hypogammaglobulinemia.

- Malnourished children.

- Children who have had previous stomach surgery with removal of part of the stomach wall.

- Children with reduced gastric acidity.

Mode of Spread.   Infection is spread via the fecal-oral route after the ingestion of cysts contained in feces, water, or food or on shared objects (toys, diaper-changing tables, eating utensils) contaminated with infested feces.

Incubation Period.   The incubation period is 1 to 4 weeks.

DIAGNOSIS

The parasite can be detected by new antigen detection assays, microscopic examination of a stool specimen, duodenal contents, or jejunal biopsy material. Because *Giardia* are excreted intermittently in stool, multiple specimens obtained on different days need to be examined for cysts and trophozoites. Take-home stool collection kits containing a vial of 10% formalin and a vial of polyvinyl alcohol fixative in childproof containers are convenient for collecting multiple specimens. To enhance detection, stool should be mixed, placed in fixative, concentrated, and examined by both wet mount and permanent stain. The examination of a single stool specimen will detect 50 to 75% of infections; the examination of specimens from three separate stools will detect about 95% of infections. The presence of trophozoites or cysts in a stool specimen is seen with infection but may not correlate with symptomatic disease. Duodenal contents can be obtained by direct aspiration with a tube inserted through the mouth or nose past the stomach into the upper small intestine or by using a commercially available string test (Enterotest) that requires swallowing a string that passes into the duodenum. The aspirate obtained through the tube or the absorbed duodenal contents on the removed string are examined microscopically. Examination of duodenal contents is more likely to detect infection with *G. lamblia* than is examination of a stool specimen, and the presence of the parasite in duodenal contents is more likely to be associated with symptomatic disease. Rarely, biopsy of the small intestine with a special instrument (Crosby capsule) that is swallowed is used to obtain a mucosal specimen for microscopic examination. Antigen assays detect *G. lamblia* by immunofluorescence (IFA) or enzyme-linked immunosorbent assay (ELISA) or enzyme immunoassay (EIA). They are most helpful when *G. lamblia* is the only parasite under consideration or when used as a screening tool during an outbreak. They are comparable in cost to ova and parasite exam and are 85 to 98% sensitive and 90 to 100% specific. With use of the antigen detection assays or careful search for parasites on a stool ova and parasite exam, sampling of duodenal contents will usually not be needed.

THERAPY

At present, only symptomatic infections are treated; the benefits and risks of treating asymptomatic patients have not been characterized. Three drugs are available for treatment of giardiasis: quinacrine (Atabrine), metronidazole (Flagyl), and furazolidone (Furoxone). However, none of these therapies is ideal. Quinacrine hydrochloride and metronidazole have cure rates of 90% or more, while the efficacy of furazolidone is only about 80%. Quinacrine is less expensive than the other agents but is poorly tolerated in children because of associated nausea, vomiting, yellow discoloration of skin, and, rarely, psychosis during therapy. Metronidazole is better tolerated than quinacrine but is not currently licensed for treatment of giardiasis. Furazolidone has the advantage of a liquid formulation, which makes it easier to administer to infants but may cause nausea, vomiting, brown discoloration of the urine, and occasional hemolysis in children with glucose-6-phosphate dehydrogenase deficiency. While animal data have suggested that both metronidazole and furazolidone may be carcinogenic, no evidence has been produced that short-term therapy results in such an effect in humans.

Patients are treated for 7 to 10 days, and if treatment fails, a repeat course is indicated. Relapse is common in immunocompromised patients and may require continuous therapy for prolonged periods of time. Hospitalization may be required for patients with severe malnutrition, dehydration, and weight loss.

INFECTIOUS PERIOD

Patients are infectious as long as they excrete cysts, and they may excrete cysts in their stools for prolonged periods (12 to 14 months). Excreted cysts may remain infectious for months if they remain in a moist environment.

INFECTION CONTROL

Vaccine.   A vaccine is not presently available.

Exclusion from Child Care or Preschool Attendance.   Children with symptomatic giardiasis who have completed a course of therapy should be allowed to return to the child care or preschool setting when diarrhea is no longer present. The local health department should be notified.

Recommendations for Other Children.   Symptomatic infected children should be treated. Routine testing is not recommended for children exposed to a child with *G. lamblia*. Washing of children's hands on arrival at the center, after a diaper change or use of the toilet, and before meals and snacks should be consistently practiced. Use of liquid soap in a dispenser along with disposable paper towels is recommended. Shared surfaces and toys may be disinfected on a daily basis with a freshly prepared solution of commercially available cleanser (detergents, disinfectant detergents, or chemical germicides).

Recommendations for Personnel.   Symptomatic infected staff members should be treated. Without failure, staff members should practice careful handwashing (10 seconds with soap and warm running water) upon arrival at the center, after changing a child's diaper, after using or providing assistance to a child using the toilet, and before food handling. Disinfecting diaper-changing surfaces along with proper disposal of diapers is recommended.

Parental Advice.   A child care center or preschool should notify parents of children who have been in direct contact with a child who has diarrhea and from whom *G. lamblia* has been identified. Parents should contact their physician for advice if their child develops diarrhea or signs of chronic illness as described.

27

Gonococcus

THOMAS A. BELL, M.D., M.P.H.

CLINICAL MANIFESTATIONS

In adults, the most common manifestations of gonorrhea are purulent discharge from the urethra or endocervix. In men, the organism may spread to the epididymis. In women, it may spread to the endometrium, fallopian tubes, or liver capsule. In either sex, it may spread to the joints, skin, leptomeninges, or cardiac valves. Pharyngitis may occur from direct inoculation. Many cases are asymptomatic. In newborns, the most common manifestation is purulent conjunctivitis. Less commonly infected sites are joints and the nasopharynx. Older children may develop vaginitis, proctitis, or urethritis.

ETIOLOGIC AGENT

Neisseria gonorrhoeae is a Gram-negative coccus with tropism for mucous membranes, endometrium, and the epithelium of the fallopian tubes. It may infect other epithelial surfaces, too, especially synovial membranes, cardiac valves, and leptomeninges. Approximately 200 auxotype/serovar phenotypes have been described. Strains also vary by susceptibility to antimicrobials, and plasmids may be useful in differentiating between strains. Determination of the phenotype may be useful for epidemiologic and forensic purposes.

EPIDEMIOLOGY

Source of the Organism.   In adults, coitus is the only plausible means of transmission other than accidental inoculation by laboratory workers or medical practitioners. Newborns may acquire the organism from their mothers, either during delivery or, more rarely, while still *in utero*. Transmission by kissing is so rare that its occurrence is reportable.

In older children, acquisition is almost exclusively sexual. Older literature that claimed transmission by rectal thermometers is of dubious validity, as are claims of transmission by bedding in tropical environments. The age beyond which the presence of the organism indicates sexual transmission instead of persistent perinatal infection is unknown.

High-Risk Populations.   Gonorrhea in pregnant women is usually associated with youth, poverty, and psychosocial problems. Older children with gonorrhea tend to come from similar backgrounds because they promulgate sexual abuse by infected persons.

Mode of Spread.   The vector of practical importance is infected genital secretions. In theory, purulent conjunctival discharge could be infectious, but such transmission is extremely rare. Urine from an infected person may be a vector when used as a folk remedy for conjunctivitis. Laboratory workers have accidentally infected themselves.

Incubation Period.   The incubation period is usually 2 or 3 days, but several months' incubation of perinatally acquired infection has been reported.

DIAGNOSIS

In adults with genital infections, the organism may be presumptively diagnosed by a Gram-stained smear. Isolation on digested sheep-blood ("chocolate") agar with antimicrobials to inhibit commensal flora and incubated in an atmosphere enriched with carbon dioxide is preferable for women. Isolation from anatomic sites with scant or no commensal flora is better done on chocolate agar without inhibitory antimicrobials. Isolation is mandatory in any case with legal ramifications, as would be the case for diagnosis of almost any child except a newborn.

N. gonorrhoeae may be confused with other *Neisseriaceae*. The identity of isolates from children should be confirmed by at least two tests that detect different properties of the organism, such as its pattern of fermenting sugars and its antigens.

THERAPY

Adults are easily treated with cefixime in a dose of 400 mg given orally once. Alternative regimens include intramuscular spectinomycin, certain orally and parenterally administered cephalosporins, and trimethoprim-sulfamethoxazole. Exposed or infected newborns should receive ceftriaxone, 25 mg/kg intramuscularly, once; hospitalization is required only for management of complications such as severe conjunctivitis or for management of the social situation in sexually abused children. Older children with genitourinary or rectal infections may be treated as adults, with adjustments for weight.

INFECTIOUS PERIOD

The infected person is no longer contagious within hours of receiving effective treatment such as cefixime. Without therapy, the period of contagiousness may last for months.

INFECTION CONTROL

Vaccine.   None available.

Exclusion from Child Care or Preschool Attendance.   The child may return to day care the day after treatment with an effective treatment such as cefixime.

Recommendations for Other Children.   The risk of nonsexual transmission to other children is inconsequential. If the child was infected elsewhere, no further measures for control of infection are necessary, but the child may be subject to emotional and behavioral problems.

Recommendations for Personnel.   The risk of transmission to personnel is inconsequential.

Parental Advice.   If the infection was not acquired at the child care center or preschool, other parents should not be informed because the infection is stigmatizing and the risk of transmission is negligible. Detection of the infection may have forensic implications for the child care center or preschool.

28

Haemophilus influenzae
(Meningitis, Cellulitis, Epiglottitis, Pneumonia, Arthritis)

TRUDY V. MURPHY, M.D.

CLINICAL MANIFESTATIONS

Before the introduction of universal vaccination, strains of *Haemophilus influenzae* that elaborate the serotype b polysaccharide capsule were responsible for 97% of the serious invasive infections in children caused by *H. influenzae*. These infections require public health intervention when the patient has been attending a child care or preschool facility.

Systemic or invasive infection begins when *H. influenzae* type b reaches the bloodstream, providing access to many body sites. Invasion is accompanied by a worsening in the child's condition and rapid development of fever. The most common infections are meningitis, cellulitis, epiglottitis, pneumonia, and arthritis. All sites of invasive infection have the same importance for public health purposes. Although *H. influenzae* type b is isolated from the middle ear in a small percentage of cases, otitis media is not considered a systemic or invasive infection.

H. influenzae that elaborate a polysaccharide capsule other than serotype b (a, c–f) or that do not elaborate a capsule (nontypeable strains) are a rare cause of invasive infection in children. Nontypeable strains are isolated from the middle ear in about 20% of children with acute otitis media. They also cause sinusitis. Infections caused by nontypeable strains of *H. influenzae* and strains with capsular types other than type b do not require public health intervention and will not be covered further.

ETIOLOGIC AGENT

The bacterium *H. influenzae* is a small, pleomorphic, Gram-negative rod. Strains are divided based on the presence of a serologically distinct polysaccharide capsule (capsular types a–f) or on the absence of capsule (nontypeable strains).

EPIDEMIOLOGY

Source of the Organism.   Infection with *H. influenzae*, in the absence of disease, is called colonization or carrier state. Prior to universal use of the conjugated *H. influenzae* vaccine in infants, up to 5% of healthy preschool children were colonized in the nose and throat with type b *H. influenzae*. Older children and adults had rates of asymptomatic colonization of about 0.1%. Colonization persisted for a few weeks or for several months and contributed to the natural acquisition of antibody that protects against systemic infection. Prior to universal vaccination, at least a third of all children became carriers at some time before 5 years of age; 1 in 200 to 250 children developed invasive infection. Since 1993, invasive infections have been uncommon in the United States.

High-Risk Populations.   Serious, invasive infections with *H. influenzae* type b occur primarily in young children and in the elderly. In the United States, 75 to 90% of systemic infections in children occur before 2 years of age. Children who are immunodeficient, are immunocompromised, who have abnormal or no splenic function (e.g., sickle cell disease), and young children attending child care centers or preschools may have increased rates of infection caused by *H. influenzae* type b.

Children who are younger than 4 years of age and who are siblings or household contacts exposed to a case of invasive *H. influenzae* type b infection are at increased risk of (secondary) invasive infection. Children who are younger than 24 months of age and who are exposed to a case in a classmate at day care also may be at slightly increased risk of invasive infection.

Mode of Spread.   *H. influenzae* type b bacteria are found in high concentrations in nasal secretions (and occasionally in low concentrations in saliva) of healthy children who are carriers. In nasal secretions, some bacteria remain viable for several hours on nonabsorbent surfaces, e.g., plastic. Spread probably occurs after infected secretions reach the mucous membranes of the nose, eye, or mouth either after coughing or sneezing. Spread also occurs when contaminated face cloths or nose wipes, food, toys, or hands, etc. come in contact with the mucous membranes. Spread is usually "slow," compared with that of other infections, e.g., chickenpox.

Incubation Period.   No incubation period for invasive infection with *H. influenzae* type b has been determined. Clusters of cases occur rarely, and usually within 60 days. The long and variable interval between "primary" and "subsequent" cases in both households and day care suggests they arise after common exposure to children who are carriers, rather than from direct exposure to the primary case patient.

DIAGNOSIS

The only certain method of diagnosing invasive *H. influenzae* type b infection is by isolation of the bacterium from a normally sterile body fluid or tissue, e.g., blood, cerebrospinal, pleural, or joint fluid, or the aspirate of an area of cellulitis. Positive cultures obtained from the throat, ear, or eye (conjunctiva) indicate local, not invasive, infection and can miss *H. influenzae* type b, if present, unless special culture medium is used.

Urine or cerebrospinal fluid can be tested for the presence of type b capsular antigen by latex or other antigen detection tests. A positive result suggests invasive infection but must be interpreted within the context of the clinical findings. The value of these tests is limited by significant rates of false-negative results. False-positive results arise from vaccine capsular antigen eliminated in urine during the first few days following vaccination. False-negative results occur early in infection, when capsular antigen is in small concentration, or when the sample is dilute (e.g., urine).

THERAPY

Treatment of invasive *H. influenzae* type b infections is usually started in the hospital in order to monitor for complications of the infection. Antibiotic treatment for 10 days is recommended; it is started by using intravenous antibiotics, e.g., a third-generation cephalosporin such as cefotaxime or ceftriaxone, or ampicillin and chloramphenicol. Children who have meningitis should have their hearing tested after recovering.

INFECTIOUS PERIOD

Parenteral antibiotic therapy of invasive *H. influenzae* type b infection usually suppresses or eradicates colonization in less than 24 hours, rendering the child noncontagious during therapy. After treatment, *H. influenzae* type b has been recovered again from the nasopharynx of some patients. Children and patients who are carriers of *H. influenzae* type b are potentially contagious.

INFECTION CONTROL

Vaccine.   *Routine Use.* To prevent invasive *H. influenzae* type b infections, three or four doses of a conjugate vaccine are strongly recommended for all children starting at 2 months of age, including children attending day care. Children 15 months to 5 years of age require one dose of conjugate vaccine.

Exclusion from Child Care or Preschool Attendance.   Children who have invasive *H. influenzae* type b infection may return to the child care or preschool setting as soon as they are well enough to participate in the program. Because a few patients will be carriers even after treatment of the invasive infection, prophylactic treatment with oral rifampin should be given before the patient returns. Most children receiving prophylaxis will not be contagious after taking the second dose of rifampin. Children less than 2 years of age should also be vaccinated starting 1 month after recovery from the invasive infection.

Recommendations for Other Children.   When a primary (first) case of invasive *H. influenzae* type b infection occurs in a child attending a child care center or preschool, the patient could have acquired the infection from siblings, playmates, or other contacts and may not have transmitted the bacteria to classmates in the child care center or preschool. The patient also could have acquired the infection at the child care center or preschool from classmates who are healthy carriers. Before universal vaccination, the risk of a second case in the same group of children was estimated to be 0 to 1.3% during 1 to 60 days after the primary case among children younger than 24 months of age. Since the risk of a second case is variable, children should be carefully monitored for the occurrence of another case. In addition, general measures as outlined above are warranted to reduce the spread of infected secretions from child to child. Recommendations that apply to children and adult care providers in the same classroom or care group as the child with invasive *H. influenzae* type b infection are:

1. Confirm that the child's infection is invasive, such as meningitis, epiglottitis, pneumonia, cellulitis, or bacteremia (but not ear, sinus, or conjunctival infection), and that the infection is caused by *H. influenzae* type b.

2. Report confirmed cases to appropriate health department officials (required by law in many states).

3. Consult with local health officials, the facility medical advisor, or the patient's physician to develop a recommendation for managing contacts at the facility.

4. If all classmates of the case patient are 24 months of age or older, notifying parents of the illness is sufficient intervention. The risk of another case among contacts is not significantly increased. Parents should assure that their child is vaccinated.

5. If classmates of the case patient are younger than 24 months of age and unvaccinated, parents should be notified of the illness and they should check their child's vaccination status. Rifampin prophylaxis can be considered.

   Rifampin prophylaxis of classmates and adult caretakers in child care or preschool is advocated by some authorities after a single (first) case. The decision to give rifampin prophylaxis should take into account the following: (a) the availability of resources to prescribe, to purchase, and to administer rifampin in an effective manner, (b) the potential side effects, (c) the risk of subsequent infection, (d) that rifampin prophylaxis is not uniformly effective in preventing subsequent cases, and (e) that children less than 1 year of age may be protected against invasive infection after receiving two doses of conjugate vaccine, and most older children are protected after a single dose of vaccine.

A second case in a classroom group is more likely than a single case to indicate the presence of *H. influenzae* type b colonization among children in the classroom group. If a second case occurs within 1 to 60 days and incompletely vaccinated children remain in the group, carefully supervised administration of rifampin prophylaxis is recommended by most authorities.

6. Rifampin prophylaxis. The common oral antibiotics used to treat pharyngitis or ear infections have low rates of success in eradicating colonization. Rifampin is the only antibiotic that is 90 to 95% effective in temporarily eradicating *H. influenzae* type b from the nasopharynx. *H. influenzae* type b bacteria resistant to rifampin are uncommon. The efficacy of rifampin prophylaxis in preventing subsequent cases in day care is unknown. Failures are reported.

Prophylaxis should be given as soon as possible after diagnosis of the case. Prophylaxis is most likely to be effective if given to all children at the same time. This prevents reacquisition from untreated children. All members of the classroom or group are candidates for prophylaxis, including vaccinated children, those older than 24 months, those unexposed or enrolled after the case-patient's illness, and adult care providers.

Rifampin is a prescription antibiotic that should be given only with sufficient knowledge of the child's or the adult's health, to exclude allergy and conditions that might preclude its use. Consider possible contraindications (e.g., pregnancy, liver disease) and drug interactions (e.g., lowered efficacy of birth control pills, displacing protein-bound drugs, increased hepatic metabolism). Rifampin turns urine, saliva, and tears an orange color, which can stain clothing and soft contact lenses. Some individuals experience nausea or vomiting or rash while taking rifampin.

Rifampin is taken orally at a dosage of 20 mg/kg/day (maximum dose, 600 mg/day), once a day for 4 days. Infants less than 2 months of age are not given rifampin, or they are given a reduced dosage of 10 mg/kg/day. Rifampin is available in

150-mg and 300-mg capsules, which can be cut to provide a dose to the nearest 75 mg. The powder is removed from the capsule and dispensed in a teaspoon of ice cream or applesauce. Rifampin also can be mixed by the pharmacist in suspension of 85% flavored sucrose solution, but this must be shaken well before measuring and still shows wide fluctuations in the dispensed dose. For adequate absorption, rifampin should be given when the stomach is empty.

7. There are no specific recommendations regarding enrollment of new children at a facility after a case of invasive *H. influenzae* type b infection. Children who are eligible for vaccine (2 months of age or older) should have had at least one dose of *H. influenzae* type b conjugate vaccine before starting to attend the facility. If rifampin prophylaxis is to be given, new children who will be assigned to a case classroom should wait to attend the facility until prophylactic treatment is completed.

Recommendations for Personnel. Care providers of children in classroom groups with a case of invasive *H. influenzae* type b infection are at extremely low risk of infection. However, up to 7% are carriers when two or more cases occur in a day care center or preschool classroom. Thus, when rifampin prophylaxis is given to children, it should also be given to care providers.

Parental Advice. The parents of children who are in the classroom or group with any case child with invasive *H. influenzae* type b infection should be notified in writing. The notification letter should inform of (a) the date of the infection, (b) the classroom or group assignment of the case child, (c) the correct name of the germ, and (d) the recommendations for all children at the facility. Parents should also be informed of the signs of infection, and the importance of prompt medical attention and notification of the child care provider in the event their child becomes ill. Parents should be encouraged to make sure their child is fully immunized with conjugate vaccine.

29

Hepatitis A

TIMOTHY R. TOWNSEND, M.D.

CLINICAL MANIFESTATIONS

Only about one quarter of children infected with the hepatitis A virus (HAV) have any symptoms, as opposed to infections among adults where three quarters are symptomatic. Often, the initial clue that HAV transmission is occurring in a group child care setting is the occurrence of clinical illness among the adults, either caretakers or family members of the children, who are in contact with the children. Typical signs and symptoms found among symptomatic children are jaundice, dark urine, malaise, and light-colored stools. Diarrhea is a common finding among children but is rare among adults. There is no evidence that HAV causes a persistent infection and progressive liver damage.

ETIOLOGIC AGENT

The HAV is a small, nonenveloped RNA virus in the same family, Picornaviridae, as the rhinoviruses and the enteroviruses. There is a single antigenic strain found worldwide.

EPIDEMIOLOGY

Source of the Organism. Humans are the only source of the HAV. There is no evidence for an animal or inanimate reservoir of the virus.

High-Risk Populations. There are no markers such as age, race, or gender that place a person at higher susceptibility to infection. Exposure, primarily through oral ingestion, to fecally contaminated objects defines the risk of infection. Child care centers and preschools that have children who are not toilet-trained are at higher risk of having HAV transmission than those where only toilet-trained children are clients. Among centers with non–toilet-trained children, those that have poor infection control practices that permit greater fecal contamination associated with diaper changing are at greater risk for having HAV transmission than those with good infection control practices.

Mode of Spread.   Hepatitis A is transmitted primarily by the fecal-oral route, although there have been a few transfusion-associated cases reported.

Incubation Period.   The incubation period is 15 to 50 days.

DIAGNOSIS

Since most infections among children are asymptomatic, serologic testing is the most reliable means of diagnosing HAV infection. A single serum specimen tested for immunoglobulin M (IgM) anti-HAV and immunoglobulin G (IgG) anti-HAV can indicate that an IgM-negative, IgG-negative person is susceptible and not currently infected; an IgM-positive, IgG-negative person is currently infected or was infected within the past few months; an IgM-positive, IgG-positive person was infected approximately 2 to 6 months ago; and an IgM-negative, IgG-positive person was infected more than 6 months ago.

THERAPY

There is no known effective therapy for HAV infection. Supportive therapy to maintain fluid and caloric intake is usually sufficient, and hospitalization is rarely required.

INFECTIOUS PERIOD

Among symptomatic persons, 10 days after the onset of dark urine, viral particles are no longer detectable in stool, and epidemiologic evidence supports the concept that by the time a person is ill enough to seek treatment, infectivity has waned.

INFECTION CONTROL

Vaccine.   An inactivated hepatitis A virus vaccine was licensed in 1995. A three-dose regimen with the first and second dose given

1 month apart and the booster dose following the first dose by 6 to 12 months is used in children and adolescents age 2 to 18. Adults are given a single initial dose of a more potent formulation of the vaccine with a booster dose 6 to 12 months later. The duration of protection is unknown but the vaccine efficacy in the first year or two following vaccination has ranged from 85 to 95%. The vaccine's indications list several populations in which the vaccine should be used and one of these is all employees in child day care centers.

Exclusion from Child Care or Preschool Attendance. Symptomatic children could return to a child care or preschool setting 10 days after onset of symptoms. Asymptomatic children will be identified in the context of an outbreak, and the epidemiologic circumstances will determine when it is safe for them to return. (The outbreak investigators, usually health authorities, are in the best position to make this decision.)

Recommendations for Other Children and Personnel/Parental Advice. Since hepatitis A is a reportable disease and the occurrence of a single symptomatically infected child, family member of a child in child care, or adult caretaker often means an outbreak is occurring at the child care center or preschool, it is important to notify the local health authority. The health authorities are the only ones with the expertise to investigate the situation and make recommendations concerning other children, personnel, and parents of children at the center. Issues such as serotesting, use of immune serum globulin, and vaccine and/or closure of the center involve considerable expense and should be approached judiciously. Until the proper authorities can investigate and recommend control measures, parents of children can be taught simple infection control measures to minimize fecal-oral transmission so as to protect family members from further spread; personnel can examine diaper changing and handwashing practices so as to prevent further spread; and other children can be carefully observed for onset of illness. Finally, the child care center or preschool must communicate with each family it serves, both to transmit information from the health authorities and to assist the authorities with their investigation. Closing the center as the initial response to an outbreak will force infected children to other child care centers and preschools, thereby worsening the situation.

30

Hepatitis B

TIMOTHY R. TOWNSEND, M.D.

CLINICAL MANIFESTATIONS

Hepatitis B virus (HBV) infection in children is symptomatic in less than 10% of cases. When it is symptomatic, the typical signs and symptoms of fatigue, anorexia, jaundice, dark urine, light stools, nausea, vomiting, and abdominal pain are indistinguishable from other causes of hepatitis. The younger a person is at the time of infection, the greater the risk of becoming a chronic HBV carrier, which is associated with a greater risk of developing chronic active hepatitis and cirrhosis later in life.

ETIOLOGIC AGENT

HBV is an incompletely double-stranded DNA virus that is coated with a surface protein (hepatitis B surface antigen [HBsAg]) and has a central core (hepatitis B core antigen [HBcAg]) containing the DNA and a protein, the hepatitis e antigen. A group-specific genetic determinant 'a' and two pairs of genetic subdeterminants, 'd' 'y' and 'w' 'r', make for different strains, but in a given geographic location a single strain predominates. Immunity is group-specific, so infection with one subtype usually confers immunity to other subtypes.

EPIDEMIOLOGY

Source of the Organism.   The source of infection is a person either acutely infected or a chronic carrier of HBV. The virus is found in highest concentrations in blood or bloody body fluids and in much lower concentration in other body fluids such as saliva, urine, or stool.

High-Risk Populations.   In the United States, infection among preadolescents is very uncommon, since HBV is a behaviorally associated infection (sexual activity, parenteral drug abuse). Those preadolescents that are infected are those born to acutely infected or chronic carrier women. Now that universal screening for HBsAg of pregnant women is recommended and widely practiced, identification of at-risk and infected infants should be facilitated. For those infants or children whose mothers were not screened during pregnancy, reliance on maternal risk history (immigrant from Asia, Africa, or the Middle East, parenteral drug use, sexual activity with multiple partners) is relatively poor in accurately identifying infected women.

Mode of Spread.   HBV is transmitted via percutaneous or permucosal exposure to infective blood or other infectious body fluids from a person who is HBsAg-positive. Transmission can occur in household settings or in institutions for persons with mental retardation, but the risk of transmission in these settings only becomes significant over time with repeated exposures. These exposures usually consist of sharing toothbrushes or razors or aggressive behavior such as biting. When institutionalized children with mental retardation have been placed in normal school classrooms, the risk of transmission has been less than 1% per year even with the children with disabilities showing aggressive or self-mutilative behavior and sharing food, eating utensils, and toys they put in their mouth. There has been only one reported instance where transmission occurred in a child care setting. In this report, the infected child was engaging in unusually aggressive behavior. In another reported instance a known chronic carrier with severe eczema who had been documented to have transmitted HBV to a household member did not transmit the infection to others in a child care setting despite being in that setting a number of months.

Incubation Period.   The incubation period ranges from 6 weeks to 6 months.

DIAGNOSIS

Since most infections are asymptomatic, serologic testing is the most accurate means to diagnose HBV infection. A person with a positive HBsAg and positive IgM anti-HBc is acutely infected. A person with a positive HBsAg and a positive IgG anti-HBc is a chronic carrier (must be positive for HBsAg 6 months later to confirm this). A person who is anti-HBs-positive has been infected in the past or has been vaccinated and is now immune. A person who is negative for HBsAg, anti-HBc, and anti-HBs is not and has not been infected but is susceptible to infection.

THERAPY

There is no therapy available for HBV infection.

INFECTIOUS PERIOD

Persons are considered infectious if their HBsAg test is positive. There have been rare reports of persons who have a negative HBsAg test but a positive anti-HBc test that have transmitted HBV, but most persons with this serologic profile are noninfectious.

INFECTION CONTROL

Vaccine.   A very effective vaccine is available and is recommended for children attending child care centers and preschools. It should be mandatory for a child care center or preschool that has one or more chronic carriers that cannot be excluded and that exhibit aggressive behavior. Now that universal immunization of infants for hepatitis B is taking place, hepatitis B should be less of an issue in the future.

Exclusion from Child Care or Preschool Attendance.   HBV-infected children need not be excluded from the child care or preschool setting. Other than the single instance of transmission described earlier, there have been no reported outbreaks of HBV in child care settings. As noted above, in transmission studies of deinstitutionalized children with mental retardation whose behaviors are more likely to transmit HBV than children in the noninstitutional child care setting the risk was extremely low. Exclusion should only be considered after education of parents, personnel, and children on ways to prevent transmission has failed and universal vaccination has not yet occurred. If a child is excluded, then exclusion should last only as long as the child tests positive for HBsAg.

Recommendations for Other Children.   Children should be taught how to minimize the risk of transmission: Don't bite, put a bandage on cuts and scrapes, and don't share toothbrushes.

Recommendations for Personnel.   It is suggested that all personnel receive the hepatitis B vaccine. Personnel are at very low risk of becoming infected by a child. Personnel should be instructed to observe the children for biting or other aggressive behavior, uncovered cuts or scrapes, and toothbrush sharing. If universal vaccination has not occurred and the behavior continues to be a problem, then the use of vaccine or exclusion of the infected child should be reconsidered by the management of the center.

Parental Advice.   Parents should be informed of the very low risk and the steps being taken to minimize the risk. They should be told of the recommended option of vaccination and exclusion of the infected child and what events or situations will cause the child care center or preschool to choose either of those options. Finally, they should be told that exclusion would be the option of last resort and that in the case of deinstitutionalized retarded children in school classrooms, exclusion was legally indefensible when transmission could not be demonstrated.

31

Hepatitis C

TIMOTHY R. TOWNSEND, M.D.

CLINICAL MANIFESTATIONS

Hepatitis C virus (HCV) is clinically indistinguishable from hepatitis due to hepatitis A virus or hepatitis B virus, although in most cases the signs, symptoms, and biochemical abnormalities are not as severe. Posttransfusion HCV infection is symptomatic in about 25% of cases. Chronic asymptomatic liver disease develops in approximately 50% of patients with HCV infection, and chronic active hepatitis or cirrhosis develops in 20 to 40% of those patients.

ETIOLOGIC AGENT

The hepatitis C virus is a single-stranded RNA virus classified as a separate genus in the Flaviviridae genus.

EPIDEMIOLOGY

Source of the Organism.   The reservoir for HCV is the chronic HCV carrier.

High-Risk Populations.   With the exception of transfusion-related HCV infection in children, few data exist concerning HCV in children. Children receiving blood or blood products probably are at the same risk (3 per 10,000 units) as adults. Perinatal transmission has been documented but the significance has not been defined.

Mode of Spread.   The mode of spread has been described epidemiologically: 5 to 10% of cases have a history of transfusion; 40%, a history of parenteral drug abuse; 10%, a history of heterosexual activity with multiple partners or household contact with or sexual exposure to a person with hepatitis; less than 5%, a history of occupational blood exposure; and 40%, no known exposure history. There have been no reports of transmission of HCV in child care settings.

Incubation Period.   The incubation period of HCV averages 7 to 9 weeks (range, 2 to 24 weeks).

DIAGNOSIS

A diagnostic serologic test for anti-HCV has been available since 1990. This test is usually positive in patients with HCV infection but does not necessarily indicate ongoing infection.

THERAPY

Recombinant alpha-interferon has been licensed for treatment of chronically infected patients but is not uniformly effective.

INFECTIOUS PERIOD

The period of infectivity is estimated to last from about 1 week following infection to as long as 6 years in a chronically infected individual (including during periods of normal liver function tests).

INFECTION CONTROL

Vaccine.   None available.

Exclusion from Child Care or Preschool Attendance/Recommendations for Other Children and Personnel/Parental Advice. Until there are data demonstrating that transmission of HCV occurs in a child care or preschool setting, firm recommendations concerning exclusion of the infected child or management of other children, personnel, or parents are not possible. To date, no outbreaks of HCV have been reported in these settings, nor have there been case reports suggesting possible disease transmission in a child care or preschool setting. Adherence to scrupulous universal precautions in this setting should prevent transmission of HCV.

32

Hepatitis Delta

TIMOTHY R. TOWNSEND, M.D.

CLINICAL MANIFESTATIONS

Infection with hepatitis delta virus (HDV) can occur only in a person with an active (acute or chronic carrier) hepatitis B (HBV) infection. Infection can occur simultaneously with infection with HBV (coinfection), in which case the clinical manifestations of both infections are the same as those of HBV alone except that the risk of fulminant hepatitis is greater with coinfection. Infection can occur in a person who is a chronic HBV carrier (superinfection). This superinfection can be asymptomatic or symptomatic and indistinguishable from a symptomatic HBV infection. Both coinfection and superinfection can lead to a chronic HDV carrier state associated with chronic active hepatitis and cirrhosis.

ETIOLOGIC AGENT

HDV is considered a defective virus in that its ability to infect and cause hepatitis is dependent on the presence of active HBV infection. The virus consists of an outer coat of hepatitis B surface antigen and an internal protein antigen, the delta antigen, containing a very-low-molecular-weight single strand of RNA.

EPIDEMIOLOGY

Source of the Organism.   The reservoir for HDV is the chronic HDV-HBV carrier.

High-Risk Populations.   In the United States, approximately 6%

of chronic HBV carriers have antibody to HDV, suggesting HDV is much less of a problem than in endemic areas such as southern Italy. Higher prevalences have been found in some intravenous drug abuser populations and hemophiliacs.

Mode of Spread.   HDV is spread the same way HBV is spread.

Incubation Period.   The incubation period for coinfection is the same as that for HBV, 6 weeks to 6 months. For superinfection the incubation period may be shorter.

DIAGNOSIS

The diagnosis should be suspected in any fulminant HBV infection. Serologic testing using immunoglobulins G and M, anti-HDV, and delta antigen will confirm the diagnosis and permit an estimate of the recency of infection.

THERAPY

There is no known therapy for HDV.

INFECTIOUS PERIOD

In an acutely coinfected person when there is evidence that active HBV infection is over (disappearance of the hepatitis B surface antigen), HDV should no longer be able to be transmitted. A superinfected person that is a chronic carrier of both HBV and HDV is infectious for as long as the HBV carrier state lasts.

INFECTION CONTROL

Vaccine.   There is no vaccine available against HDV. Vaccination against HBV would be protective, indirectly, against HDV; therefore, all recommendations for HBV should be followed.

Exclusion from Child Care or Preschool Attendance/Recommendations for Other Children and Personnel/Parental Advice.   Recommendations concerning HDV infection in a child care setting should be no different from those for HBV infection.

33

Hepatitis E

TIMOTHY R. TOWNSEND, M.D.

CLINICAL MANIFESTATIONS

Hepatitis E virus (HEV) is the enterically transmitted non-A, non-B hepatitis virus. Clinical disease is similar to that of the other viral hepatitides and includes jaundice, fever, anorexia, malaise, and arthralgia. Chronic infection does not occur with HEV infection.

ETIOLOGIC AGENT

The hepatitis E virus is a single-stranded RNA virus.

EPIDEMIOLOGY

Source of the Organism.   The reservoir of HEV is infected humans and fecally contaminated food and water.

High-Risk Populations.   Adults are more commonly infected than children. Endemic and epidemic disease is present in Mexico, Asia, and Africa. Infection of travelers to endemic areas has been reported.

Mode of Spread.   The most common modes of transmission are fecal-oral, associated with person-to-person spread, and ingestion of contaminated water.

Incubation Period.   The incubation period is approximately 6 weeks (range, 2 to 9 weeks).

DIAGNOSIS

The diagnosis of HEV infection is by excluding the other acute viral hepatitides (A, B, C, D) and hepatitis associated with cytomegalovirus and Epstein-Barr virus infection. No test is commercially available.

THERAPY

There is no proven therapy for HEV infection.

INFECTIOUS PERIOD

The infectious period for HEV infection is not known. There is not, however, a chronic carrier state associated with HEV infection.

INFECTION CONTROL

Vaccine.   None available.

Exclusion from Child Care or Preschool Attendance.   The child should not attend day care or preschool until symptoms have resolved.

Recommendations for Other Children.   Adherence to careful sanitation and handwashing.

Recommendations for Personnel.   Strict adherence to sanitation practices and handwashing.

Parental Advice.   Until there are data demonstrating that transmission of HEV occurs in a child care or preschool setting, firm recommendations concerning exclusion of the infected child or management of children, personnel, or parents are not possible. However, given the epidemiology of this pathogen, children should be monitored for signs and symptoms of hepatitis and brought to their primary care provider, if symptomatic.

34

Herpes Simplex Virus
(Gingivostomatitis)

RICHARD J. WHITLEY, M.D.

CLINICAL MANIFESTATIONS

Herpes simplex virus infections cause a wide spectrum of diseases ranging from asymptomatic and benign infections such as fever blisters to life-threatening diseases such as neonatal herpes and herpes simplex encephalitis. Infections caused by herpes simplex virus in individuals who are immunocompromised can be severe. The most common childhood manifestation of herpes simplex infections are herpes simplex gingivostomatitis, a disease of the oropharynx characterized by vesicular ulcerative lesions in association with fever and a painful mouth. The oral pain can lead to hospitalization because of inadequate oral fluid intake.

Other childhood manifestations of herpes simplex infections include herpes simplex keratoconjunctivitis, neonatal herpes simplex virus infection presenting within the first 4 weeks of life, and herpes simplex encephalitis. Children who are immunocompromised can reactivate a latent infection that results in severe and progressive orofacial disease.

Patients with herpes simplex infections are only contagious to other individuals when skin vesicles are present.

ETIOLOGIC AGENT

Herpes simplex virus consists of two serotypes: herpes simplex type 1, which generally causes infections above the belt, and herpes simplex type 2, which generally causes infections below the belt. Herpes simplex types 1 and 2 are members of the herpesvirus family. Other members of this family include: cytomegalovirus, Epstein-Barr virus, varicella-zoster virus, and human herpesvirus 6. All members of the herpesvirus family are large DNA viruses containing double-stranded DNA that resides in the core of the virus.

EPIDEMIOLOGY

Source of the Organism.   The virus is only found in infectious secretions of individuals actively replicating herpes simplex virus. Sites from which herpes simplex virus can be retrieved are vesicular lesions, the oropharynx during gingivostomatitis, tissue obtained at biopsy of individuals with severely progressive disease, and lesions of the genital tract with episodes of recurrent genital herpes.

High-Risk Populations.   High-risk populations include individuals who are immunocompromised or babies born to women who have genital herpetic infection at delivery.

Mode of Spread.   Transmission of herpes simplex virus is by direct and intimate personal contact. Virus has not been known to be transmitted from inanimate objects to human beings. Intimate personal human contact is the only mechanism known today for transmission of this infection.

Incubation Period.   The incubation period is from 3 to 5 days.

DIAGNOSIS

Infections caused by herpes simplex virus are usually diagnosed by clinical manifestations. In most individuals the vesicular rash is diagnostic; however, virus can be isolated in cell culture systems. Under unusual circumstances, the diagnosis of neonatal herpes simplex infection and herpes simplex encephalitis is often more difficult. Excretion of virus from peripheral sites in such individuals is often rare, and therefore, obtaining tissue for isolation of virus is essential.

THERAPY

The only forms of herpes simplex virus infections that require therapy are those involving the newborn, children with herpes simplex encephalitis, and the immunocompromised child with recurrent herpes simplex infections. Acyclovir is the treatment of choice, and the only formulation currently licensed for use in children is that for intravenous administration (5 to 10 mg/kg given every 8 hours).

INFECTIOUS PERIOD

The duration of infectivity is approximately 4 to 5 days once intravenous acyclovir has been initiated. In the absence of therapy, however, infectivity can persist for as long as 3 weeks.

INFECTION CONTROL

Vaccine.   None available.

Exclusion from Child Care or Preschool Attendance.   The child should not attend the child care center or preschool until cutaneous lesions are scabbed.

Recommendations for Other Children.   Once a child is infected, avoid person-to-person contact and contact with vesicles. To accomplish such a goal, existing vesicles can be covered.

Recommendations for Personnel.   Strict handwashing and the use of gloves when changing or manipulating skin that has a vesicular rash will prevent transmission of this virus.

Parental Advice.   There is little likelihood that this infection will be transmitted from one child to another. Since many individuals are infected symptomatically, acquisition of this infection early in life may be to the child's benefit.

35

Human Immunodeficiency Virus Infections and Acquired Immunodeficiency Syndrome

GWENDOLYN B. SCOTT, M.D.

CLINICAL MANIFESTATIONS

Infection with human immunodeficiency virus type-1 (HIV-1) results in a progressive deterioration of the immune system, ultimately leading to opportunistic infections, malignancies, and other conditions representative of the acquired immunodeficiency syndrome (AIDS). At the end of 1995, more than 6600 children with AIDS had been reported to the Centers for Disease Control and Prevention (CDC). In recent years, the majority of children have acquired HIV infection through perinatal transmission. It is estimated that approximately 7000 women with HIV infection deliver an infant in the United States yearly. Of these infants, between 20 and 30% will be infected unless zidovudine was taken for reduction of perinatal transmission, in which case the transmission rate is reduced to 8%. During infancy and early childhood, many of these children will attend child care or preschool.

HIV infection in children is a chronic multisystem disease characterized by a wide range of complications and conditions. Between 10 and 20% of children develop progressive disease with significant immune suppression during the first 2 years of life, with survival less than 4 years. The remainder of children will have a variable clinical course with a median survival of 8 years. In Miami, 28% of the 350 living children followed in our clinic with perinatally acquired HIV infection range in age from 8 to 16 years of age.

The clinical course of HIV infection is variable but generally progressive. Particularly for older children, acute complicating infections may be interspersed with periods during which the child functions relatively normally. As the disease progresses, involvement of multiple organ systems and the occurrence of multiple infections or conditions simultaneously are common.

Common early clinical manifestations of HIV infection in children with perinatal infection include failure to thrive or wasting; chronic or recurrent diarrhea without specific cause; generalized lymphadenopathy, hepatosplenomegaly and parotitis; persistent or recurrent oral candidiasis; and a variety of recurrent infections including otitis media, pneumonia, and meningitis, usually of bacterial origin but also including viral, fungal, and parasitic pathogens.

Central nervous system involvement with HIV may present in the infant or young child as developmental delay or loss of milestones. Progressive encephalopathy occurs in about 10% of infected children and is usually associated with significant immune deficiency, failure to thrive, spasticity, poor head growth, and evidence of brain atrophy and/or basal ganglia calcifications on computed tomography scanning of the brain. This condition is associated with a poor prognosis. Older children may manifest learning disabilities or attention deficit disorders. Thus, developmental testing is an important part of routine care so these conditions can be detected early and interventions prescribed. Cardiomyopathy, hepatitis, and nephropathy also occur in some children. Malignancies, particularly non-Hodgkin's lymphomas, occur in about 2% of HIV-infected children.

AIDS is the "late stage" of infection with HIV. The definition, which has been revised several times, includes the presence of opportunistic infection, certain malignancies, recurrent serious bacterial infections, lymphoid interstitial pneumonia in children under 13 years of age, and low levels of CD4-positive lymphocytes in adults and adolescents. Separate disease classification systems have been developed for both children and adults which relate clinical and immunological status and describe the spectrum of disease.

Lymphoid interstitial pneumonitis occurs in approximately one third of infected children and is usually associated with a good prognosis, although chronic lung disease may occur as a complication in some children. Pneumonia caused by *Pneumocystis carinii* is the most frequently described opportunistic infection in AIDS. Other common opportunistic infections include Candida esophagitis, disseminated cytomegalovirus infection, and disseminated mycobacterial infection, most often caused by *Mycobacterium avium* complex. Both pulmonary and nonpulmonary tuberculosis are an increasingly common problem, particularly among adults in selected populations. In some areas, tuberculosis and tuberculosis resistant to multiple drugs in people with AIDS has become a significant public health problem.

ETIOLOGIC AGENT

Human immunodeficiency virus (HIV) is an RNA cytopathic retrovirus not known to infect other animals naturally: nonhuman primates such as chimpanzees can be infected in the laboratory but do not develop disease. Humans are the only known reservoir of HIV. Two major types of HIV have been identified: HIV-1 and HIV-2. Although both subtypes have been associated with AIDS and related clinical syndromes, HIV-1 has been the predominant cause of disease in the world. HIV-2 infection is endemic in western African countries and is extremely rare in the United States. Considerable genetic variation exists among different isolates of HIV-1 from different individuals. Selected regions of the envelope genes of HIV-1 mutate relatively rapidly, giving rise to numerous strains.

HIV attaches to the cell through the interaction between the viral envelope glycoprotein and its receptor, the CD4 molecule, located on the cell surface. Thus, the cells most commonly infected are CD4+ lymphocytes and cells of the monocyte-macrophage series. Once a cell has been infected with HIV, the proviral genome is integrated into the host cell DNA and establishes a persistent chronic infection. HIV has a complex gene structure with a number of regulatory genes that appear to control the rate of viral replication, although the interaction of this regulatory mechanism with the infected cell is not yet fully understood.

EPIDEMIOLOGY

Source of the Organism.   Humans are the only known reservoir of HIV.

High-Risk Populations.   In the United States, HIV infection and AIDS primarily occur in young adults. Adults (and adolescents) currently at highest risk of acquiring HIV infection include men who have sex with men (homosexual or bisexual males), people who inject drugs or use crack cocaine (the latter because of its association with multiple sex partners), and men and women who have multiple sex partners (some of whom may be at high risk). Approximately 2% of all cases of AIDS reported in the United States have occurred in children or adolescents. Children at highest risk for HIV infection are those born to women who are infected; the highest risk for women is injection of drugs, using crack cocaine, having multiple sex partners, or being the sex partner of a man at high risk. Children or adults who have clotting factor disorders (including classic hemophilia) and who received clotting factor therapy before the mid-1980s also are at high risk of HIV infection and AIDS. Major improvements have been made in the safety of clotting factor concentrates since the mid-1980s, and people with hemophilia not infected before 1986 are no longer at high risk of HIV infection through that route. The majority of cases of HIV infection associated with transfusion of infected blood or blood products occurred before 1985. Since 1985, all donated blood has been screened for HIV antibody and the estimated risk of transmission of HIV by screened blood in the United States is 1 in every 440,000 to 660,000 donated units. This risk usually occurs when the donor has been recently infected and detectable HIV antibodies have not developed.

Mode of Spread.   HIV infection is acquired through: (a) sexual contact with an infected person, whether homosexual or heterosexual; (b) direct inoculation of infectious blood or tissue through use of contaminated needles during intravenous drug injection, a mucous membrane exposure, penetrating injury with a needle or sharp object containing infected blood, tissue or organ transplantation or, rarely, through receipt of a blood transfusion; and (c) perinatal transmission from an infected woman to her fetus or at delivery to her infant, or postnatally during breast feeding. For children with HIV in the United States, perinatal transmission accounts for over 95% of cases. In the United States, the risk of perinatal infection to the infant of an infected mother who has not received zidovudine during pregnancy and delivery is between 13 and 39%. The risk of perinatal transmission has been reduced to approximately 8% through the maternal use of zidovudine during pregnancy and delivery and in the infant for the first 6 weeks of life.

Transmission by other means such as through food or water, fomites, or casual contact in a household, workplace, or school setting has not been documented to have occurred. Several studies of individuals living in households with HIV-infected adults or children have shown no transmission and include 300 children of differing ages followed for more than 1700 person years. Independent of these studies, there are six case reports of household transmission of HIV involving children. In most of these cases the means of transmission is unknown but percutaneous or intravenous exposure to blood from the infected household contact is possible.

Biting is a common behavior in young children. Although HIV has been isolated from saliva of some infected persons, transmission to another person from saliva is not known to have occurred. The actual risk of transmission of HIV through biting is thought to be negligible. Fluids implicated in the transmission of HIV infection include blood, cervical secretions, semen, and breast milk.

Incubation Period.   In adults, acute self-limited illness caused by HIV may occur within a few weeks after infection. Onset of chronic illness usually occurs years after infection, with approximately half of infected adults diagnosed with AIDS 10 years after infection. In children with perinatal infection, clinical illness often is apparent during the first or second year of life, although it may occur years later. With other types of infection (e.g., transfusion), clinical illness and a diagnosis of AIDS may not occur for years.

DIAGNOSIS

The diagnosis of symptomatic HIV infection and AIDS is based on the clinical, serologic, and immunologic findings and exclusion of other causes of immunodeficiency. The presence of certain clinical conditions or opportunistic infections may suggest a diagnosis of HIV infection. Serologic tests for HIV infection are highly sensitive and specific if performed by a reliable laboratory. Confirmation is essential. In a child 2 years of age or older, HIV infection is diagnosed by an HIV antibody test that is repeatedly reactive and confirmed by a Western blot assay or an immunofluorescence test. Before 24 months of age, diagnosis is more complex because a positive HIV antibody test may only reflect in utero passive transfer of maternal antibody. Standard tests for diagnosis of HIV infection in infants and children under 24 months of age include the polymerase chain reaction (PCR) for detection of HIV DNA sequences, an HIV culture, or a p24 antigen test. The sensitivity of both culture or PCR for diagnosis of HIV is greater than 95% by 3 months of age. The p24 antigen assay is specific, but less sensitive than the other two tests. Thus, the majority of infected infants should be identified by 6 months of age. Special problems in young children (e,g., immunologic tolerance or hypogammaglobulinemia) that may impair test accuracy should be kept in mind. Consent for testing the infant or child for HIV should be obtained from the parent or legal guardian prior to testing.

THERAPY

Children with HIV infection need close medical supervision with monitoring of their clinical, neurologic, and immunologic, status. Most infants and children with HIV infection are seen at 3- to 6-month intervals depending on their clinical status. The child with HIV infection should receive routine childhood care including vaccinations and should be evaluated promptly if infection or fever occurs. Therapy for HIV infection includes prophylaxis against *Pneumocystis carinii* and other infections, antiretroviral therapy and, in certain instances, intravenous gamma globulin.

The American Academy of Pediatrics and the Centers for Disease Control and Prevention have published recommendations for immunization of children with HIV infection against other diseases, and current recommendations should be consulted. Briefly, both symptomatic and asymptomatic children with HIV infection should receive diphtheria-pertussis-tetanus (DPT) vaccine, measles-mumps-rubella (MMR) vaccine, inactivated polio vaccine (IPV), *Haemophilus influenzae* type b conjugate and hepatitis B vaccine following the routine immunization schedule. In general, live viral (e.g., oral polio [OPV] and varicella vaccine) and bacterial (e.g., bacillus Calmette-Guerin [BCG]) vaccines should not be given but MMR is recommended, since measles can cause severe or fatal illness in HIV-infected children. Pneumococcal vaccine is suggested for infected children over the age of 2 years, and annual influenza vaccine should be considered for children 6 months or older. Since children with symptomatic HIV infection often have a poor immunologic response to vaccines, these children should be considered candidates for postexposure prophylaxis (e.g., immunoglobulin, varicella-zoster immune globulin) if exposed to diseases for which this is available.

Zidovudine (azidothymidine [AZT]), didanosine (ddI), and lamivudine (3TC) have been approved with some restrictions for treatment of symptomatic HIV infection in children. Several other drugs have been approved for use in adults and adolescents used alone or in combination with other available antiretroviral agents, including stavudine (d4T), zalcitabine (ddC), and saquinavir, a protease inhibitor. Combination therapy using different antivirals is being studied in children. Data from recent trials in both children and adults show that initiation of therapy with didanosine alone or in combination with zidovudine provides greater long-term benefit than zidovudine monotherapy. Therapy for HIV infection and its complications continues to evolve rapidly, and current recommendations should be sought. The benefit of therapy in asymptomatic infants with normal immune parameters has not been determined. Optimal therapy for treatment of advanced HIV disease associated with significant immune impairment is being studied through clinical trials. New antiretroviral agents, vaccines, and immunomodulators, alone and in various combinations also are being evaluated in clinical trials. These agents all have side effects and close clinical and laboratory monitoring of the child is essential.

Monthly administration of intravenous immunoglobulin (IVIG) to HIV-infected children is indicated for children with HIV infection who have hypogammaglobulinemia (immunoglobulin G levels below 250 mg%). In the past, it was widely used in children with recurrent serious bacterial infections. However, a recent double-blind, placebo controlled study showed that although IVIG therapy did reduce the number of serious bacterial infections in children, this benefit was limited to children who were not receiving trimethoprim-sulfamethoxazole prophylaxis and it did not improve overall survival.

Intravenous gamma globulin has also been recommended as therapy for children with chronic bronchiectasis, for those children with no antibody response to measles immunization living in areas where measles is prevalent, and for treatment of severe HIV-associated thrombocytopenia.

Prompt diagnosis and aggressive treatment of opportunistic infections, maintenance of nutritional status, developmental assessment, and good supportive care are important elements of ongoing medical followup. Prophylaxis against *P. carinii* pneumonia (PCP) with trimethoprim-sulfamethoxazole is recommended for all children at risk for HIV until their HIV status is determined and for all infected children during the first year of life. Continuation of PCP prophylaxis after 1 year of age in the infected child is determined by the child's clinical and immune status. Prophylaxis against atypical mycobacterial infection (*Mycobacterium avium complex* [MAC]), *candida* species, herpes simplex, and cytomegalovirus infections are used depending on the clinical situation.

INFECTIOUS PERIOD

Since HIV establishes a chronic infection, an infected person is presumably infectious throughout life. Degree of transmissibility of HIV may vary with the state of infection.

INFECTION CONTROL

Vaccine.   No effective vaccine for prevention of HIV is currently available.

Exclusion from Child Care or Preschool Attendance.   HIV-infected children should be allowed to attend day care centers and schools and allowed to participate in all activities to the extent that their health permits. Attendance at a day care center should be decided on an individual basis by qualified persons. including the child's physician. Factors to be considered include the type of care the child will receive and whether the infected child would be at significant risk of being exposed to serious infectious diseases. Although the risk of transmission of HIV from one infant or child to another in a child care setting is unmeasurable and highly improbable based on known means of transmission, it has been a major consideration in all discussions about including HIV-infected children in these settings. In general, young children who have open skin lesions should not be in a child care setting with other small children. Because of neurologic impairment and developmental delays with HIV infection, decisions about appropriate care settings should be based on developmental stage rather than chronologic age. Periodic reassessment of the child is urged. The American Academy of Pediatrics publishes current recommendations to provide a guide for evaluation of children in this setting. In addition, other infectious conditions in an HIV-infected child should be evaluated to determine whether they pose a risk to other children or adults in the care setting. Preschool care programs should develop policies to inform all parents when a highly infectious illness, such as measles or chickenpox, occurs in a child, so families can take appropriate measures to protect their immunodeficient children.

Recommendations for Other Children.   Based on studies of HIV-Infected children and adults that have shown no transmission of HIV in a family setting, HIV is highly unlikely to be transmitted from one child to another in a child care center or preschool. No special precautions are warranted; therefore, admission or continued attendance of an HIV-infected child should be based on a careful case-by-case review as recommended above. Screening of children for HIV in a child care setting for HIV infection before admission or after an infected child has been found is not justified.

Recommendations for Personnel.   Since a child may not be known to be infected with HIV (or other bloodborne infectious agents such as hepatitis B virus), all child care centers and preschools should adopt reasonable policies and procedures for managing accidents such as a nosebleed, for all students, and for cleaning and disinfecting surfaces contaminated with blood. Gloves should be used if readily available, but direct contact with blood can also be avoided by using several thicknesses of paper towels or folded cloths. Blood-contaminated surfaces should be cleaned and disinfected with freshly prepared chlorine bleach solution (1:10 to 1:100 dilution). Gloves do not need to be used for feeding a child or wiping secretions that do not contain visible blood; they should be used, however (in addition to careful handwashing), for changing diapers that contain bloody stools. Good handwashing is fundamental in prevention of

HIV and other infectious diseases. All personnel should have knowledge of appropriate infection control procedures and have access to necessary supplies.

Personnel who are directly involved with the care of an HIV-infected child in a child care setting and who have a need to know should be informed of that fact and should be instructed about the need to respect and maintain the rights of the child and family to privacy and confidentiality of the information; the minimum number of persons necessary should be informed. If medical records are maintained, confidentiality must be assured.

HIV-Infected Personnel.   The American Academy of Pediatrics has stated that HIV-infected adults do not pose a risk of infection to children in child care settings if they do not have open or exudative skin lesions or other medical conditions that would allow contact with potentially infectious (i.e., bloody) fluids. HIV-infected personnel who have other infectious conditions (e.g., active tuberculosis) that may be transmitted to others in the care setting should be evaluated to determine appropriate management and whether temporary or permanent exclusion from the care setting is warranted. Immunocompromised adults may be highly susceptible to the infectious agents that young children attending child care centers or preschools are likely to have, and they should seek advice from their physician about the advisability of such work and what precautions are recommended.

Parental Advice.   Since the risk of transmission of HIV infection among children in a child care setting is only hypothetical, there is no urgent need to inform parents about the attendance of an infected child at a center. In lieu of special notice, it may be preferable to provide parents with general information about management of infectious diseases, including HIV, before a specific instance arises.

36

Infectious
Mononucleosis

CIRO V. SUMAYA, M.D.

CLINICAL MANIFESTATIONS

Most infections by this virus occur mainly in young children and produce no problems (i.e., they are asymptomatic). In some instances, at a frequency that is not very clear, an infection can produce infectious mononucleosis. This illness consists of a typical clinical picture with fever, tiredness, enlarged neck lymph nodes, inflamed throat and tonsils, and enlargement of abdominal organs (liver and/or spleen). The clinical illness may last 1 to 2 or more weeks.

Sometimes, significant complications can occur during the infectious mononucleosis episode and involve the respiratory tract (pneumonia, severe airway obstruction), nervous system (seizures, meningoencephalitis, nerve palsies) and blood system (decline in platelets and anemia), among others. However, virtually all cases have a transient course with complete resolution and no aftereffects. It also is believed that this virus can cause illnesses characterized by isolated manifestations such as inflamed throats or pneumonia instead of an infectious mononucleosis episode.

ETIOLOGIC AGENT

Epstein-Barr virus (EBV), the cause of infectious mononucleosis, belongs to the herpesvirus group of viruses that produces chickenpox (varicella-zoster virus) and fever blisters or genital herpes (herpes simplex virus).

EPIDEMIOLOGY

Source of the Organism.   It is believed that this virus is present in salival secretions and therefore can be transmitted through body contact that permits salival exchange.

High-Risk Populations.   The virus spreads mainly among children, presumably more rapidly in closed or overcrowded conditions. Why an infection with this virus usually produces no ill effects in young children, while in young adults it is quite likely to produce the infectious mononucleosis syndrome, is unclear. It also seems that if one child in a family develops infectious mononucleosis, there is a greater chance for another child in the family to develop that illness even after a long lapse in time following the initial case. Children with special problems with their immune system or those who have recently received organ or bone marrow transplants are at greater risk for experiencing a serious disease with an infectious mononucleosis episode or other manifestations from their EBV infection.

Mode of Spread.   It is believed that the virus is transmitted through salival exchange. The spread of this virus, however, is not as efficient as that of other herpesviruses, such as herpes simplex or varicella-zoster virus. The transmission of EBV via blood products with the subsequent development of an infectious mononucleosis-like illness is quite uncommon.

Incubation Period.   The incubation period of infectious mononucleosis is usually quite long, 5 to 7 weeks after exposure. The incubation period seems to be a few weeks shorter if the exposure to EBV was through a blood transfusion.

DIAGNOSIS

The diagnosis is made by the presence of the following triad of findings: (a) typical signs and symptoms as mentioned above, (b) a blood count showing a relative lymphocytosis and atypical lymphocyte formation, and (c) a serologic assay indicating the presence of heterophil antibodies or specific EBV antibodies reflecting an acute infection.

THERAPY

Simple measures to reduce or alleviate the signs and symptoms, such as antipyretics to decrease the fever, reduction of activity and bed rest for the malaise, are commonly recommended for the patient with infectious mononucleosis. Contact sports should be avoided during the time the spleen is felt to be enlarged. Corticosteroids are sometimes administered when the patient has significant complications or an otherwise severe clinical course. The efficacy of the corticosteroids in this condition, however, is still quite obscure. The few patients that may develop pronounced respiratory obstruction because of immense tonsillar inflammation may receive an emergency tonsillectomy or intubation. An antiviral medication, acyclovir, does reduce the amount of EBV in salival excretions of patients with infectious mononucleosis, but does not significantly alter the signs, symptoms, or course of the disease.

INFECTIOUS PERIOD

The length of infectivity is quite unclear, because patients with infectious mononucleosis or other forms of acute EBV infections may excrete the virus intermittently in their saliva for many months, if not years, following their infection. It is presumed, though, that the amount of virus in the saliva during the acute episode of infectious mononucleosis or other form of EBV infection is at its peak and, therefore, more likely to be transmittable to close contacts, in comparison with later in convalescence or after resolution of the illness, when there are progressively decreasing titers of virus present.

INFECTION CONTROL

Vaccine.   An experimental vaccine is being tested but is not available for general use.

Exclusion from Child Care or Preschool Attendance.   The child should probably be removed from the child care setting during the period of time that he or she feels ill and unable to tolerate much general activity. In most cases, this is about 1 to 2 weeks.

Recommendations for Other Children.   There are no specific recommendations for other children in the center other than the adherence to common hygienic practices such as the washing of hands when potentially contaminated with human secretions and the avoidance of mouthing of toys or mouth-to-mouth kissing.

Recommendations for Personnel.   There are no specific recommendations other than the adherence to common hygienic practices as noted. The risk of significant problems to a pregnant woman (and her unborn child) from exposure to a child with infectious mononucleosis is considered extremely low.

Parental Advice.   The parent (or physician) should notify the center supervisor about the diagnosis. An assurance can be provided that this illness is not easily spread (i.e., the development of a second case or more cases of infectious mononucleosis in the center that are related to contact with the initial case should be a rare event).

37

Influenza (Flu)

SCOTT A. HALPERIN, M.D.

CLINICAL MANIFESTATIONS

Influenza virus causes a spectrum of clinical symptoms that make up the "flu syndrome." In the first several days of infection, fever, headache, myalgias, and chills are prominent. Burning and tearing of the eyes also occur during this period. Respiratory symptoms, including cough and rhinorrhea, are present at the onset but predominate after the third day when the fever and systemic manifestations subside. Respiratory symptoms persist for 3 or 4 days, although the cough may persist for 1 to 2 weeks.

Influenza infections occur in epidemics during the winter months. The spread is rapid through a community, with widespread absenteeism from work and school. Young children typically have milder disease, although the fever may be higher. Myalgias, arthralgias, and headache are typically seen in older children and adults. Secondary complications occur frequently during influenza epidemics, although these are less common in children. Primary viral pneumonia due to influenza virus can occur, as well as secondary bacterial pneumonia due to *Streptococcus pneumoniae, Haemophilus influenzae,* or *Staphylococcus aureus.* In young children, croup and bronchitis may occur due to infection with influenza virus. A rare but serious complication of an influenza virus infection in children is Reye's syndrome.

ETIOLOGIC AGENT

Influenza virus is an orthomyxovirus. Three virus types are known: influenza A, influenza B, and influenza C. Influenza virus is an enveloped RNA virus. The unique characteristic of influenza virus is the frequency with which it changes its antigenicity. Antigenic variation involves primarily the two external glycoproteins of the virus, neuraminidase and hemagglutinin. With influenza A, antigenic variation occurs on an almost annual basis. Variation also occurs with influenza B but has not been shown with influenza C virus. This antigenic variation enables the virus to evade the immune system and results in repeated epidemics of influenza virus on a yearly basis.

EPIDEMIOLOGY

Source of the Organism.   Influenza virus is found in respiratory secretions of infected individuals.

High-Risk Populations.   Because of continual change of the antigenic composition of the virus, individuals may continue to be susceptible to influenza virus infection from year to year. Particularly severe infections occur when major antigenic shifts occur in the influenza virus. Children at high risk include those with chronic lung disease, such as moderate to severe asthma, cystic fibrosis, and bronchopulmonary dysplasia. Severe disease also occurs in children with significant cardiac anomalies, immunosuppressed children, and children with hemoglobinopathies (including sickle cell disease), diabetes, chronic renal failure, and metabolic diseases.

Mode of Spread.   Influenza is spread from person to person by direct contact with infected secretions or via large- or small-droplet aerosols.

Incubation Period.   1 to 3 days.

DIAGNOSIS

Influenza virus infection may be diagnosed by culture of the virus in egg or tissue culture. The virus also can be detected directly in nasopharyngeal secretions by using direct or indirect immunofluorescent techniques. However, during an epidemic, the diagnosis is usually made clinically.

THERAPY

Most children with influenza virus infection do not require specific therapy. In children at risk for severe or complicated disease due to underlying conditions, amantadine and rimantadine therapy have been shown to be effective in reducing the symptoms caused by influenza A virus only, particularly if started very early in the course of the illness. Therapy is usually continued for 3 to 5 days, depending on symptomatic improvement. Aspirin and aspirin-containing products should be avoided due to their association with the subsequent development of Reye's syndrome in influenza patients. Hospitalization is only required for those with severe illness.

INFECTIOUS PERIOD

The virus may be found in respiratory secretions for 24 hours prior to the onset of symptoms until 5 to 10 days after the symptoms began.

INFECTION CONTROL

Vaccine.   Influenza vaccine is recommended in children considered to be at high risk. These include children with chronic lung disease, including moderate to severe asthma, bronchopulmonary dysplasia, and cystic fibrosis. It is also recommended for children with significant cardiac disease, children receiving immunosuppressive therapy, children with hemoglobinopathies, diabetes, or human immunodeficiency virus infection, and individuals with rheumatoid arthritis or Kawasaki's disease on long-term aspirin therapy.

Exclusion from Child Care or Preschool Attendance.   Once influenza is introduced into a child care facility, most children will have been exposed before the onset of symptoms. Therefore, exclusion of a child with influenza infection is not necessary, and attendance should be based on the condition of the child. However, it is not uncommon for child care facilities to close during an influenza epidemic because of high absenteeism among staff and high absenteeism among children who are too sick to attend.

Recommendations for Other Children.   Children with symptoms of influenza should be monitored for any complications that would require examination by the family physician.

Recommendations for Personnel.   Influenza virus infection is typically spread from children to their caregivers. The infection spreads rapidly through the facility, and most susceptible individuals will become infected. It is recommended that all day care and preschool providers receive yearly influenza vaccine. Careful hand-washing and attention to respiratory secretions may diminish the spread of infection.

Parental Advice.   Parents should be advised that an influenza outbreak is occurring and should be instructed to monitor for any complications or severe infection. Aspirin or aspirin-containing products should be avoided during influenza infections because of the association with Reye's syndrome.

38

Meningococcus
(Bacteremia, Meningitis, Arthritis)

EUGENE D. SHAPIRO, M.D.

CLINICAL MANIFESTATIONS

The most common manifestations of illness caused by *Neisseria meningitidis* in children are meningitis, septicemia (with or without septic shock), arthritis, and pneumonia, any of which may occur alone or in combination with one or more of the others. In children with meningitis, fever usually develops, and they may have a stiff neck and often become irritable or lethargic. This condition may progress to obtundation and coma. Children with meningococcal sepsis (with or without meningitis) may develop a characteristic rash that consists of small, flat red spots (petechiae) on the extremities and/or on the trunk. Occasionally, patients develop a fulminant illness with rapidly progressive septic shock, often associated with a hemorrhagic rash (purpura fulminans).

ETIOLOGIC AGENT

Meningococcal infections are caused by a type of bacteria, *N. meningitidis*. These bacteria are divided into nine different serogroups (A, B [which is responsible for about half of the infections in the United States], C, D, 29E, W-135, X, Y, and Z), based on different characteristics of the outer coating of their cell walls.

EPIDEMIOLOGY

Source of the Organism. The organism is part of the normal bacterial flora of the human mouth. It is usually carried in the nasopharynx (the throat). At any given time, 5 to 10% of asymptomatic people will harbor the bacteria in their throat. However, in a day care center in which a case of an invasive meningococcal infection has occurred, up to 50% or more of the children and adults in the group may be colonized with the organism.

High-Risk Populations.   Children with deficiencies of antibody or complement or who have anatomical or functional asplenia are at increased risk of infection. Although both children and adults who are exposed may be at risk, younger children are at the greatest risk.

Mode of Spread.   The organism is spread by respiratory droplets or by direct oral contact with someone who is colonized with the bacteria. Although many people worry about the organism spreading from an infected child to others, in most instances other children in the group are already colonized before the index child becomes ill. Indeed, the ill child usually acquires the bacteria from other asymptomatic children.

Incubation Period.   The incubation period is from 2 days to several weeks. Most people who acquire the organism become temporarily colonized (for weeks to months) with the bacteria and never develop an invasive, symptomatic infection. The majority of the people who do develop an invasive infection do so within 1 week of exposure. However, because the exposure may be to an asymptomatic carrier rather than to an ill person, it is often impossible to identify accurately the time of exposure.

DIAGNOSIS

The diagnosis is usually made by recovering the bacteria from the cerebrospinal fluid or from the bloodstream. This is accomplished by culturing specimens obtained by performing a lumbar puncture (spinal tap) and by drawing a sample of the blood. Throat cultures are *not* useful for establishing a diagnosis.

THERAPY

Children with meningococcal infections are usually hospitalized and treated with an antibiotic (penicillin) that is administered intravenously. Most patients with uncomplicated illnesses are hospitalized for 7 to 10 days.

INFECTIOUS PERIOD

The occurrence of a meningococcal infection is a marker for a high rate of colonization in the entire child care group or preschool class. Consequently, even though the ill child's infectivity diminishes dramatically within 24 hours of the initiation of antimicrobial treatment, the organism may spread within the day care center from other, asymptomatically colonized children.

INFECTION CONTROL

Vaccine.   A vaccine against serogroups A, C, Y, and W-135 is available, although it may not be effective in children less than 2 years of age. It takes 1 to 2 weeks for antibodies to develop after immunization. Since the period of greatest risk is in the first 2 weeks after exposure, vaccination is generally not recommended routinely in response to sporadic cases of the illness. However, if there seems to be an ongoing epidemic caused by a serogroup contained in the vaccine, it may be appropriate to institute an immunization program.

Exclusion from Child Care or Preschool Attendance.   The child may return as soon as he or she recovers after treatment.

Recommendations for Other Children.   Chemoprophylaxis with rifampin (an antibiotic) is effective for eliminating colonization with the meningococcus. Rifampin (10 mg/kg/dose [maximum, 600 mg/dose], twice a day for 2 days) should be administered to all other children who are regularly cared for in the same room. Rifampin may impart an orangish-red color to urine, tears, and other bodily fluids. Children who develop fever or other symptoms that are consistent with a meningococcal infection should be promptly evaluated by a physician.

Recommendations for Personnel.   Rifampin (600-mg dose), twice a day for 2 days, should be administered to all personnel who are regularly in the same room (with the exception of pregnant women). Personnel in whom fever or other symptoms develop that are consistent with a meningococcal infection should be promptly evaluated by a physician.

Parental Advice.   Rifampin should be administered promptly to all children and adults in the group. It is usually prudent to try to identify one knowledgeable physician to direct this effort. If each parent goes to his or her own physician, there may be several, conflicting recommendations. Since the goal of chemoprophylaxis with rifampin is to eliminate colonization in the *entire* group, its effectiveness is directly related to the completeness and timeliness with which chemoprophylaxis is implemented.

Parents should realize that most children who are exposed do not become ill. However, at the first sign of an illness that is compatible with a meningococcal infection (fever and/or a petechial rash), the child should be evaluated promptly by a physician.

39

Mumps

GREGORY F. HAYDEN, M.D.

CLINICAL MANIFESTATIONS

The clinical spectrum of mumps is broad, ranging from subclinical infection to severe illness with involvement of many organ systems. Clinical diagnosis generally depends upon swelling of the salivary glands with prominent parotid enlargement. Other manifestations of mumps may include meningoencephalitis, deafness (usually unilateral), pancreatitis, arthritis, myocarditis, thyroiditis, nephritis, and hepatitis. Orchitis develops in approximately 20 to 30% of affected postpubertal males, but only about 25% of such cases are bilateral, and only a small fraction of these develop progressive testicular atrophy.

ETIOLOGIC AGENT

Mumps is caused by a paramyxovirus that contains single-stranded RNA in a helical nucleocapsid. Only one serologic type is recognized.

EPIDEMIOLOGY

Source of the Organism.   Humans are the only natural host.

High-Risk Populations.   Mumps infections are uncommon in the first several months of life, but after this age, unvaccinated children remain at high risk of developing mumps, if exposed. The risk of complications, such as orchitis, meningoencephalitis, and arthritis, is higher in older patients.

Mode of Spread.   The virus is spread by droplets and by direct contact with respiratory secretions of an infected patient.

Incubation Period.   The incubation period is usually 16 to 18 days, but it can range from 12 to 25 days.

DIAGNOSIS

The clinical diagnosis of mumps can be confirmed by using virologic or serologic methods. Mumps virus can be cultured from the throat, urine, and spinal fluid, but viral culture is relatively expensive and not universally available. Several serologic techniques are available, including complement fixation (CF), neutralization (NT), hemagglutination inhibition (HI) or enzyme-linked immunosorbent assay (ELISA). A significant rise in titer between acute and convalescent serum specimens is diagnostic of mumps infection. (For CF, NT, and HI tests, this is usually a fourfold or greater rise in titer; for ELISA methods, see the manufacturer's instructions for interpretation of a significant change.) A suspected or confirmed diagnosis of mumps should be reported immediately to the local health department.

THERAPY

No specific therapy is currently available. The selection of treatment, therefore, depends solely on the presence and severity of associated symptoms. Warm or cold compresses and analgesic therapy with acetaminophen, for example, may be used to relieve parotid discomfort. A soft, bland diet may be preferred. Hospitalization is recommended only for those occasional children with very severe or complicated cases requiring intensive supportive care. Children with severe central nervous system involvement, for example, may require hospitalization for bed rest, analgesic/antipyretic therapy, and carefully monitored parenteral fluid therapy.

INFECTIOUS PERIOD

Patients may be contagious up to 7 days before the onset of parotid swelling and may remain contagious for as long as 9 days after onset.

INFECTION CONTROL

Vaccine.   Live, attenuated mumps virus vaccine should be given routinely to children after the first birthday and is usually administered at 12 to 15 months of age as a part of the combined measles-mumps-rubella (MMR) vaccine. The cornerstone of mumps prevention in day care centers and preschools should be the vigilant insistence that all children 15 months or older have received mumps vaccine as a prerequisite for attending the center. There is no evidence for any difference in efficacy when mumps vaccine is administered at 12 versus 15 months of age. A single dose confers long-lasting immunity in over 95% of vaccinees, but a second dose of MMR vaccine is recommended at 4 to 12 years of age.

Contraindications to live mumps vaccination include immunodeficiency, anaphylactic allergy to neomycin, severe febrile illness, pregnancy, and recent receipt of an immune globulin preparation or blood products. Persons with anaphylactic allergy to eggs should receive mumps vaccine only with caution. MMR vaccine is recommended for children infected with the human immunodeficiency virus, even those whose infections have become symptomatic.

Exclusion from Child Care or Preschool Attendance. Since the period of communicability can extend as long as 9 days after the onset of parotid swelling, infected children should be excluded for this interval. By this time, the parotid swelling should have subsided, and any other manifestations of mumps should have resolved. Since patients are often contagious before the onset of parotid swelling, however, and since inapparent infections can be communicable, attempts to control spread by means of isolation are commonly ineffective.

Recommendations for Other Children. The first step is to verify that other children attending the center have already been immunized against mumps in accordance with established center policy. Children with documented previous immunization against mumps are highly unlikely to develop illness and may continue to attend the center. The management of unvaccinated children is somewhat more complex. It is not known whether the administration of mumps vaccine after exposure can prevent or modify illness. Adverse reactions to this vaccine are uncommon, however, and vaccination after exposure is not known to increase the severity of incubating mumps. If an exposed child is not already incubating infection, mumps vaccination should protect the child against subsequent exposures to mumps. Vaccination can, therefore, be recommended for unimmunized children at least 12 months of age, especially if they have been exposed for no more than a few days. Parents must understand, however, that the vaccine may not block the progression of incubating mumps, so that they will not wrongly blame the vaccine for mumps illness that develops after vaccination.

For children under 1 year of age, vaccination is a less attractive option because the rate of seroconversion is lower and protection is less likely. Standard immunoglobulin is ineffective in protecting against mumps infection. These infants could be excluded from the center during the period when they might be expected to become ill and contagious themselves. Since patients may be contagious up to 7 days before the onset of parotid swelling and since the incubation period may vary from 12 to 25 days, this policy would require exclusion of infants from the child care center or preschool for 3 weeks or longer. Since mumps is usually not severe in young infants, simple observation seems reasonable if coupled with careful documentation of immunization among those 12 to 15 months of age or older. If additional cases of mumps were to occur among younger infants, however, a strict exclusionary policy could be enforced.

Recommendations for Personnel.   Ideally, all staff members should provide a documented history of mumps immunization, a physician-documented diagnosis of infection, or serologic evidence of immunity at the time of employment. Strict adherence to such a policy will reduce or eliminate the disruption that can arise among personnel when mumps is diagnosed in a child attending the center. If appropriate preparations have not been made before such a case occurs, the first step is to determine whether any center personnel are likely to be susceptible to mumps. The mumps skin test was unreliable in predicting clinical immunity to mumps and is no longer readily available. A positive mumps neutralization titer or ELISA index strongly suggests mumps immunity, but these tests are not always readily available. The determination of probable immunity usually rests, therefore, upon simple historical information. A definite history of previous mumps illness or immunization is highly predictive of mumps immunity. In contrast, a negative history of mumps illness is poorly predictive of mumps susceptibility. Most adults with such negative histories are immune to mumps on the basis of previous, unrecognized infection. Most persons born before 1957 generally may be considered immune. Younger adults with a negative history of mumps immunization or illness are not at high risk of infection but can consider immunization after the exposure.

Parental Advice.   Parents should be advised that a suspected (or confirmed) case of mumps has occurred in a child at the center. They should be advised that the risk to their child is minimal so long as the child has already received mumps vaccine. Parents of unimmunized children should be advised to seek medical advice immediately concerning the prompt vaccination of children over 1 year of age. Parents should also be urged to verify their own immunity status as well as the immunization status of any older children in the family, especially adolescents, who do not attend the center, and to seek vaccination as appropriate.

40

Mycoplasma pneumoniae
(Pneumonia)

RONALD B. TURNER, M.D.

CLINICAL MANIFESTATIONS

Mycoplasma pneumoniae infection may result in symptoms at any level of the respiratory tract. Pneumonia is the most common clinical manifestation of infection and is characterized by prominent cough and fever. Infection with *Mycoplasma* is usually not associated with rhinorrhea, a characteristic that may help in the clinical differentiation of this infection from other causes of pneumonia. Less important respiratory syndromes associated with mycoplasma infection are otitis media, pharyngitis, croup, and bronchiolitis. Most preschool children infected with *Mycoplasma* are asymptomatic.

M. pneumoniae has rarely been associated with a variety of nonrespiratory illnesses. Arthritis, carditis, and a variety of neurologic syndromes have been reported in patients infected with *M. pneumoniae.* These manifestations of infection have generally been reported in patients older than those who would be seen in a day care setting.

ETIOLOGIC AGENT

M. pneumoniae is a free-living organism that can be cultured on agar or in broth medium. There are ten different *Mycoplasma* organisms that can infect humans; however, only three of these organisms are associated with clinical illness. *M. pneumoniae* causes respiratory illness. *M. hominis* and *Ureaplasma urealyticum* are associated with genitourinary infections.

EPIDEMIOLOGY

Source of the Organism.   *M. pneumoniae* is acquired by person-to-person spread.

High-Risk Populations.   No populations have been identified that are at high risk for acquisition of infection. Infection of children with sickle cell diseases has been associated with severe lower respiratory disease.

Mode of Spread.   The mechanism of transmission is not known with certainty but is thought to be by large-particle aerosols. Small-particle aerosols may rarely play a role in transmission of infection.

Incubation Period.   The incubation period for *Mycoplasma* infection is 2 to 3 weeks.

DIAGNOSIS

Culture of *M. pneumoniae* is relatively easily accomplished by experienced personnel. The organism grows slowly, however, so cultures are not generally useful in the clinical setting. Antigen detection methods are available for diagnosis but are not widely used. Serology is the cornerstone of the etiologic diagnosis of *M. pneumoniae* infection. Complement fixation is the test most frequently used. With this technique, a fourfold rise in titer or a titer greater than 1:128 obtained during a typical illness is usually considered indicative of acute infection.

THERAPY

Erythromycin, 50 mg/kg/day given orally on an every-6-hour dosing schedule for 10 to 14 days, is the usual treatment for *Mycoplasma* infections in children. Hospitalization is usually not necessary. The newer erythromycin-like antibiotics azithromycin and clarithromycin are expected to show similar efficacy against *Mycoplasma* although there has been no formal evaluation in this age group.

INFECTIOUS PERIOD

The period of infectivity is not known; however, infected individuals should be considered capable of transmitting infection for the duration of the cough.

INFECTION CONTROL

Vaccine.   None available.

Exclusion from Child Care or Preschool Attendance.   Exclusion from child care or preschool settings is not necessary for children infected with *Mycoplasma*.

Recommendations for Other Children.   No special precautions are indicated.

Recommendations for Personnel.   No special precautions are indicated.

Parental Advice.   *Mycoplasma* infections spread very slowly and have not been associated with outbreaks in the day care or preschool setting. No special precautions are indicated.

41

Necator americanus
(Hookworm)

ANDREA J. RUFF, M.D.

CLINICAL MANIFESTATIONS

The initial manifestation of an infection with *Necator americanus* may consist of itching and burning, followed by the development of a papular rash at the site of larval penetration into the skin. Although many infected individuals remain asymptomatic, heavy infections can be associated with the development of gastrointestinal symptoms including abdominal pain, anorexia, diarrhea, and weight loss. The most debilitating effect of hookworm infections is due to chronic intestinal blood loss resulting in the development of iron-deficiency anemia. The severity of the anemia is variable, depending on the worm burden and dietary iron intake. It may be associated with pallor, lassitude, dyspnea, palpitations, cardiomegaly, and impaired growth. Infected individuals may also have hypoalbuminemia, hypoproteinemia, and eosinophilia. The hematologic, cardiac, and nutritional effects of hookworm infections contribute significantly to the morbidity of pediatric and adult populations worldwide.

ETIOLOGIC AGENT

Necator americanus is one of the two most common hookworms found in humans. Humans acquire the infection percutaneously, by coming into contact with infective larvae present in contaminated soil. The larvae penetrate the skin, migrate through the circulation to the lungs, pass through the alveolar walls, and ascend the trachea.

They are then swallowed and move to the small intestine where they mature into adults. After mating, the female worms lay eggs, discharging thousands per day in the feces. Under favorable environmental conditions, the eggs will hatch and larvae will develop into infective forms. This process generally requires 5 to 10 days in the soil, during which time the eggs and larvae are not infective for humans.

EPIDEMIOLOGY

Source of the Organism.   Hookworms continue to be endemic in a number of tropical and subtropical areas. *N. americanus* is the prevailing species in parts of the southern United States, Central and South America, the Caribbean, central and southern Africa, and southern Asia. Hookworm has remained endemic in areas where fecal pollution and environmental conditions favoring the development of hookworm eggs are present. The infective larvae are found in soil contaminated with human feces, and transmission is generally the result of direct contact with the soil, often through bare feet. Although transmission of *Ancylostoma duodenale*–infective larvae through food and possibly breast milk has been suggested, this does not appear to occur with *N. americanus.*

High-Risk Populations.   Individuals who have direct contact with fecally contaminated soil in hookworm endemic areas will be at risk of acquiring the infection. Because children are more likely to go barefoot and to play in dirt, they are also likely to acquire hookworm infections. However, since the larvae are not infective unless they undergo development in soil, direct person-to-person spread of hookworm does not appear to occur. Therefore, institutional or child care settings should not increase a child's risk of infection.

Mode of Spread.   Transmission occurs percutaneously through contact with soil containing infective hookworm larvae.

Incubation Period.   The time interval between the acquisition of *N. americanus* and the passage of eggs in the feces ranges from approximately 40 to 60 days. Considerable variability has also been observed in the time between exposure and development of symptoms; some individuals develop gastrointestinal symptoms 20 to 45 days following an acute infection.

DIAGNOSIS

The diagnosis is established by identifying the characteristic hook-worm eggs in feces; *N. americanus* eggs cannot be distinguished from those of *A. duodenale*. Most moderate to severe hookworm infections will be detected by direct microscopic examination of a fecal smear. However, the detection of light infections may require the use of concentration methods such as the zinc sulfate flotation or formalin-ether techniques. Although larvae or adult worms are rarely seen in stool specimens, the larvae can be grown from specimens by using Harada-Mori fecal cultures. This technique is rarely used diagnostically.

THERAPY

In countries where hookworm infections are endemic and reinfection is common, light infections are often not treated. In this country, hookworm infections are generally treated with either mebendazole or pyrantel pamoate. Mebendazole is given in a dose of 100 mg twice a day for 3 days. Pyrantel pamoate is given as a single daily dose of 11 mg/kg (maximum, 1 g), repeated for 3 days. Although pyrantel pamoate is an approved drug, the U.S. Food and Drug Administration considers it investigational for this condition. Both regimens are effective against *N. americanus* and are associated with few significant adverse reactions. However, since neither regimen has been used widely in children less than 2 years old, the drugs should be used with caution, determining the potential risks and benefits of therapy on an individual basis in this age group. Albendazole, an antihelminthic available in a number of other countries, is also efficacious in the treatment of hookworm infections. One to two weeks following treatment with any of the regimens, a repeat stool examination should be performed, and if the infection is still present, retreatment undertaken.

In addition to the use of antihelminthic agents, iron supplementation should be provided to individuals with significant anemia.

INFECTIOUS PERIOD

If untreated, hookworm infections, in particular those caused by *N. americanus*, may persist for many years. Since egg production tends to decrease over time, individuals may become somewhat less infectious.

INFECTION CONTROL

Vaccine.   None available.

Exclusion from Child Care or Preschool Attendance.   Children with hookworm infections do not need to be isolated. Since human-to-human transmission does not occur and the eggs passed in feces are not infectious, an infected child does not need to be kept out of any child care setting.

Recommendations for Other Children.   Other children will acquire hookworm only if they come into contact with soil containing infective larvae. Unlike the situation with many other enteric pathogens, they should not become infected if they inadvertently ingest fecal material contaminated with hookworm eggs. Therefore, no additional precautions need to be undertaken for children in a center when one child is found to have hookworm infection.

Recommendations for Personnel.   Personnel should be instructed to maintain techniques that decrease fecal-oral transmission of pathogens, including good handwashing and appropriate disposal of fecal material. Obviously, no child should be allowed to defecate in the playground areas where fecal contamination of the soil may be a problem, and children should not be allowed to go barefoot or play in the soil.

Parental Advice.   Parents should be told that the risk of person-to-person transmission is minimal. If the attendee appears to have acquired the infection locally, the need for sanitary disposal of feces and the potential for spread through contaminated soil should be reviewed with all of the parents.

42

Papillomaviruses
(Warts)

DAVID A. WHITING, M.D.

CLINICAL MANIFESTATIONS

Warts are unusual in infancy and early childhood and have a peak incidence at 12 to 16 years of age. Warts are intraepidermal tumors that affect skin and mucous membranes and are caused by a DNA virus known as the human papillomavirus.

Common warts (verruca vulgaris): These occur as firm papules with a rough, horny surface that range in size from 1 to 12 mm in diameter and that are usually discrete but may be confluent. They often contain black specks from thrombosed capillaries. They can occur anywhere on the body but are seen most commonly on the backs of the hands and fingers and on the knees. Sixty-five percent disappear spontaneously within 2 years.

Plane warts (verruca plana): These are multiple, small, tan or flesh-colored, flattened, round, or polygonal lesions 1 to 5 mm in diameter and are found mostly on the face, backs of the hands, and shins.

Plantar warts (verruca plantaris): These are inverted, flattened, circumscribed horny papules of the soles often containing black specks from thrombosed capillaries. A wart interrupts the natural skin lines and is separated from the surrounding skin by a plane of cleavage. Plantar warts may be single, multiple, or mosaic. They are rare in the preschool-aged child.

Venereal warts (condylomata acuminata): These manifest as multiple pointed papules, single or confluent, on or around the genitalia and the anus. In children, the possibility of child abuse should always be considered in cases of venereal warts.

ETIOLOGIC AGENT

Human papillomaviruses (HPV), a subgroup of the Papovaviridae family, are small, double-stranded DNA viruses that are host-specific. More than 70 types of HPV have now been characterized by Southern blot testing of the viral genome. The most common viral types are associated with different warts.

Common warts (verruca vulgaris): HPV 2 and 4.

Plane warts (verruca plana): HPV 3.

Plantar warts (verruca plantaris): HPV 1, 2, and 4.

Venereal warts (condylomata acuminata): HPV 6 and 11. (HPV 16 and 18 cause venereal warts less commonly but are oncogenic, and can cause dysplasia in adolescents and adults.)

EPIDEMIOLOGY

Source of the Organism.   Other humans.

High-Risk Populations.   School children of 12 to 16 years of age or immunosuppressed individuals. Abused children may have genital warts.

Mode of Spread.   Warts are spread by direct contact with the infected individual, by indirect contact through contamination of objects and immediate environment, and by autoinoculation.

Incubation Period.   1 to 20 months, with an average of 4 months.

DIAGNOSIS

The clinical appearance is usually diagnostic, and the presence of warts may be confirmed by demonstrating black dots in them after paring down the horny surfaces. A biopsy is sometimes diagnostic.

THERAPY

Therapy is local and is done on an outpatient basis. Hospital admission is not required unless it is for very extensive condylomata acuminata.

There is no specific antiviral therapy, although intralesional alpha-2b interferon has been used successfully in some cases.

Common warts: Light electrodesiccation and curettage, cryosurgery, keratolytics, monochloroacetic acid or bichloracetic acid, laser surgery.

Plane warts: Cryosurgery, monochloroacetic acid or bichloracetic acid, light electrodesiccation and curettage, topical tretinoin.

Plantar warts: Keratolytics, light electrodesiccation and curettage, formalin soaks, laser surgery.

Venereal warts: Podophyllin 25% in compound tincture of benzoin or podophyllotoxin, monochloroacetic acid or bichloracetic acid, cryosurgery, light electrodesiccation and curettage, laser surgery.

Note that a wait-and-see attitude is advisable in children, since many warts disappear spontaneously and wart treatment is often destructive and painful and liable to cause scars. The least destructive therapy possible is always advisable.

INFECTIOUS PERIOD

How long the infectious period will last is uncertain, but it may last as long as the lesion is actually present, which can be months or years.

INFECTION CONTROL

Vaccine.   None available.

Exclusion from Child Care or Preschool Attendance.   Isolation is unnecessary, although it is advisable to cover the warts, if practical.

Recommendations for Other Children.   Wait and see if warts develop, and treat if necessary.

Recommendations for Personnel.   Wait and see if warts develop, and treat if necessary.

Parental Advice.   Wait and see if warts develop, and treat if necessary.

43

Parainfluenza Virus

SCOTT A. HALPERIN, M.D.

CLINICAL MANIFESTATIONS

Parainfluenza virus causes both upper and lower respiratory tract disease in children. Upper respiratory infection with fever is the most common manifestation of parainfluenza virus infection and is indistinguishable from the common cold caused by other viruses. The disease is characterized by coryza, bronchitis, and pharyngitis and may be associated with a low-grade fever.

Parainfluenza virus is the most common etiologic agent of croup, which is characterized by hoarseness, a barking cough, and inspiratory stridor. Parainfluenza viruses also are important causes of bronchiolitis, bronchitis, and pneumonia. Outbreaks of croup caused by parainfluenza virus often occur each fall, although sporadic infection occurs throughout the year. Reinfections with parainfluenza virus occur but are usually mild.

ETIOLOGIC AGENT

Parainfluenza virus is a member of the paramyxoviruses. Parainfluenza viruses are enveloped RNA viruses that, although similar to influenza virus, have remained antigenically stable. There are four antigenic types that cause disease in humans. Parainfluenza virus types 1 and 2 are the most common causes of croup, while parainfluenza virus type 3 is an important etiologic agent of pneumonia and bronchiolitis. Types 1, 2, and 3 also are associated with symptoms of the common cold. Parainfluenza virus type 4 causes very mild disease of the upper respiratory tract.

EPIDEMIOLOGY

Source of the Organism.   Parainfluenza virus is spread from person to person or found in infected respiratory secretions. Although parainfluenza-like viruses exist in animals, these do not cause infection or disease in humans.

High-Risk Populations.   Infants and young children are susceptible to parainfluenza viruses, and almost all children will have been infected with all four types by the age of 6 years. The severity of the illness depends on the parainfluenza virus type, the age of the child and whether it is a primary infection or a reinfection. Severe prolonged infection can occur in the immunocompromised host.

Mode of Spread.   Parainfluenza viruses are spread from person to person by direct contact or by large droplets and contaminated nasopharyngeal secretions.

Incubation Period.   3 to 6 days.

DIAGNOSIS

Diagnosis of parainfluenza virus infection can be established through isolation of the virus in tissue culture. The diagnosis can also be made (a) by detection of the virus in infected secretions by using direct or indirect immunofluorescent techniques or (b) by antigen detection methods. Because of the epidemic nature of certain parainfluenza virus infections, a diagnosis can occasionally be deduced by using knowledge of the predominant viral infection in a community at that time.

THERAPY

No specific antiviral therapy is yet available for parainfluenza virus infection. Most infections due to parainfluenza virus are self-limited; however, parainfluenza virus infections of the lower respiratory tract may be severe and require hospitalization for supportive care. Humidified air, oxygen, and racemic epinephrine are effective in the management of the hospitalized patient with croup; steroid therapy remains controversial.

INFECTIOUS PERIOD

Parainfluenza viruses may be shed for 3 to 16 days, depending on the type.

INFECTION CONTROL

Vaccine.   None available.

Exclusion from Child Care or Preschool Attendance.   Exclusion from child care is not required because of infection with parainfluenza virus. Attendance should be based on the clinical condition of the individual child.

Recommendations for Other Children.   No specific recommendations are required for other children exposed to parainfluenza virus infection. Children with significant lower respiratory tract symptoms may require examination by their family physician.

Recommendations for Personnel.   Since parainfluenza virus is primarily spread by direct contact with infected secretions and by large droplets, handwashing is important in interrupting the spread. In addition, secretion-contaminated toys should be carefully washed prior to use by other children.

Parental Advice.   Children should be monitored for more severe illness that would require a visit to the family physician.

44

Parvovirus B19
(Fifth Disease, Erythema Infectiosum)

WILLIAM C. KOCH, M.D.

CLINICAL MANIFESTATIONS

The most common manifestation of infection with the human parvovirus B19 is a benign rash illness of childhood called erythema infectiosum or "fifth disease." This illness occurs most often in school-aged children with a peak season from late winter to early spring. The illness begins with a prodromal phase of mild fever and nonspecific symptoms of headache, malaise, and myalgia. This lasts for only a few days and is followed by the eruption of the characteristic rash. This begins as an intensely red facial rash, giving the child a "slapped-cheek" appearance. It then spreads to the trunk and the extremities as an erythematous, maculopapular eruption. As the rash progresses, there is central clearing that gives it a reticular or lacy character, especially on the extremities. The palms and soles are spared. When the rash appears, the child has usually begun to feel better and the fever, if present, resolves. The rash may persist for over a week and may recur in response to various stimuli such as sunlight or a warm bath.

B19 also causes more serious illnesses in other groups of individuals. These include a syndrome of acute, self-limited arthritis in adults; aplastic crisis in individuals with chronic hemolytic anemia such as sickle cell anemia or hereditary spherocytosis; fetal hydrops and stillbirth in pregnant women; and chronic anemia in adults and children with impaired immunity. Asymptomatic infections occur commonly and atypical rashes (rubella-like, purpuric, etc.) have been reported. There is no evidence that B19 causes congenital anomalies.

ETIOLOGIC AGENT

B19 is a small, single-stranded DNA virus; it is the smallest DNA-containing virus known to infect mammalian cells. It has no envelope and is heat-stable. B19 is a member of the family Parvoviridae, which includes a number of animal pathogens, but it is infectious only among humans. There is only one serotype of B19.

EPIDEMIOLOGY

Source of the Organism.   The virus is contracted from infected individuals during their period of viremia. Virus can be detected in respiratory secretions at this time, suggesting that these secretions are involved in transmission. For patients with erythema infectiosum, this occurs during the prodromal phase, prior to the onset of the rash. In patients with aplastic crisis, viremia occurs at presentation and is of much greater intensity.

High-Risk Populations.   There are no conditions that predispose to acquisition of B19 infection. Although the infection occurs most commonly in school-aged children, it can be spread to their younger siblings through household contact and subsequently introduced into the child care or preschool setting. There are certain groups who are at risk for more serious consequences if they acquire a B19 infection, and these include children with conditions of chronic hemolysis, immunocompromised patients, and pregnant women.

Mode of Spread.   The virus is spread by close contact, presumably through respiratory secretions. The secondary attack rate for susceptible household contacts is about 50%. In school outbreaks, the secondary attack rate has varied from 10 to 60%. Potential mechanisms of transmission include direct personal contact, large-particle and small-particle droplets, and fomites (shared objects and surfaces such as toys, doorknobs, etc.). Transmission by blood or blood products is also possible.

Incubation Period.   The incubation period for erythema infectiosum is reported to range from 4 to 14 days on average with the longest reported incubation time being 28 days. However, results of experimental B19 infection in adults suggest an incubation period of 17 to 18 days based on time to onset of the rash. This correlates well with the reported case-to-case interval of 6 to 14 days observed in most studies. The incubation period for the B19-related aplastic crisis is generally shorter as it coincides with the onset of viremia, usually 6 to 8 days after exposure.

DIAGNOSIS

Erythema infectiosum is usually diagnosed on clinical grounds. It can be confirmed by serologic tests for B19 antibodies. The most sensitive test for acute infection is detection of anti-B19 immunoglobulin M (IgM). This is detectable by the third day after onset and persists for 60 to 90 days. Infection can also be diagnosed by seroconversion from negative to positive on a test for anti-B19 immunoglobulin G (IgG). IgG is detectable a few days after IgM and persists for life. Unfortunately, there is a limitation on antigen available for these tests, and, therefore, they are performed at only a few reference laboratories around the country. In immunocompromised patients, specific antibody production may be impaired, so diagnosis is usually made by detection of viral DNA.

THERAPY

Children with erythema infectiosum require no therapy, as the great majority will recover without incident. Children with aplastic crisis will usually require hospitalization for supportive care with oxygen and transfusions until their hematocrit and hemoglobin return to baseline. There is no antiviral agent available. Although the use of commercial preparations of immune globulin have been reported to ameliorate B19 infections in immunocompromised children, their use as either treatment or postexposure prophylaxis in pregnant caretakers cannot be recommended until controlled studies are performed.

INFECTIOUS PERIOD

Children with erythema infectiosum are infectious during the prodromal phase of their illness when the virus is detectable in their respiratory secretions, a period of 1 to 6 days. This phase may go unnoticed but usually occurs about 1 week prior to the onset of the rash. The appearance of the rash coincides with production of virus-specific antibodies; once the rash develops the child is no longer infectious.

INFECTION CONTROL

Vaccine.   None available.

Exclusion from Child Care or Preschool Attendance.   Children with erythema infectiosum do not need to be excluded from day care, as they are unlikely to be infectious after the rash appears and the clinical diagnosis is made. Children with aplastic crisis are infectious when they present, and they remain infectious for a longer period of time. Such children will most likely be hospitalized until their hematologic status is stable. They should be isolated for at least 1 week after presentation and should not return to the child care or preschool setting until after this time.

Recommendations for Other Children.   Once an outbreak of erythema infectiosum has been identified in a child care center or preschool, parents of children at risk for more serious complications as a result of B19 infection (chronic hemolytic conditions, immunocompromised, etc.) should be notified. They may wish to consult their pediatricians for individual advice. A general policy of exclusion is not recommended.

Recommendations for Personnel.   There are no studies documenting the efficacy of handwashing or decontamination of toys and environmental surfaces in preventing the transmission of B19; however, handwashing and control of respiratory secretions (disposal of facial tissues, etc.) are recommended.

When an outbreak of erythema infectiosum is identified in a center, there is some risk that the adult personnel will become infected. This is only of particular concern for those who are pregnant. The magnitude of this risk is not known for certain, nor is the time of greatest risk during gestation. Approximately 50% of adults will already be seropositive and, therefore, immune. Personnel who are pregnant should be aware of ways to minimize exposure by proper handwashing, avoidance of shared utensils, etc. If available, serologic testing for the presence of anti-B19 IgG could be of benefit by identifying those women who are already immune. Individuals who desire more information on the risks and management of B19 exposure should contact their health care provider. Again, a routine policy of exclusion of pregnant caretakers is not recommended.

Parental Advice.   Once an outbreak of erythema infectiosum has been identified in a center, parents of children in attendance should be informed of the risk for transmission of the virus both in the center and from susceptible contacts at home. They should be made aware of the generally benign nature of the illness and those underlying conditions that are considered higher risk. Those families who desire more information about B19 infections should be referred to their health care provider or local health officials.

45

Pediculosis (Lice)

DAVID A. WHITING, M.D.

CLINICAL MANIFESTATIONS

The characteristic feature of all types of pediculosis is pruritus. Intense itching, usually worse at night, leads to excoriations, lichenification, pigmentation, secondary infection, and lymphadenopathy. The actual louse bites are relatively painless and cause small, red macules. These may develop into papules over hours or days or, in a sensitized individual, may cause immediate whealing. The nit or egg case of the developing louse is attached firmly to human hair or threads of clothing and is usually somewhat translucent in appearance. It is often easier to find the nit than the actual louse.

Head lice: Pruritus is most severe around the back and sides of the scalp. Nits can be found attached to scalp hair in those areas. Excoriation with secondary infection and lymphadenopathy is common, and foul matted hair can result. Common bacterial invaders causing secondary infection include coagulase-positive *Staphylococcus aureus* and group A *Streptococcus pyogenes.*

Body lice: Body lice can only survive in conditions of poor hygiene and are therefore found in homeless or displaced persons who are unable to maintain any reasonable standard of personal cleanliness. The lice live in clothing and lay eggs on the inner seams of clothes and occasionally on body hairs. Pinpoint red macules, papules, wheals, excoriations, secondary infection, and, perhaps, pigmentation can occur all over the body. Note that body lice are vectors of epidemic or louse-borne typhus (caused by *Rickettsia prowazekii*), trench fever (caused by *Rochalimaea* [*Rickettsia quintana*]) and European or louseborne relapsing fever (caused by *Borrelia recurrentis*). Body lice are human-to-human vectors of murine typhus or are vectors of endemic or fleaborne typhus caused by *Rickettsia typhi* (*mooseri*).

Pubic lice: Pubic lice affect not only the pubic hair but also the adjacent hair on the thighs, abdomen, chest, breasts, and axillae and sometimes the hair on the eyebrows, eyelashes, or scalp. Intense irritation with excoriation and eczematization occurs. Occasionally, blue-grey macules, the so-called maculae ceruleae, are found on the lower abdomen and upper thighs.

ETIOLOGIC AGENT

Sucking lice of the order *Anoplura* are dorsoventrally flattened, wingless insects, and two species of these are obligate parasites of humans. The first is *Pediculus humanus,* a louse 3 to 4 mm long that exists in humans in two distinct populations, namely, *Pediculus humanus capitis,* affecting the scalp, and *Pediculus humanus corporis,* affecting the body. The other species is *Phthirus pubis* or the crab louse, which is 2 to 3 mm in length and is adapted for clinging onto body hairs.

EPIDEMIOLOGY

Source of the Organism.   Human body.

High-Risk Populations.   *Head lice:* Age and sex: Highest prevalence of head lice is usually between the ages of 3 and 10 with equal sex incidence. More females are affected in the teens and in adult life. Socioeconomic and ethnic factors: Head lice can affect all levels of society and all ethnic groups except for low levels of infestation in North American blacks. Lack of grooming: Inadequate washing and grooming as seen in individuals with mental disabilities or in those with elaborate hairstyles can lead to higher populations of head lice.

Body lice: Socioeconomic factors: Body lice are confined to economically deprived persons of no fixed abode and no means of achieving personal cleanliness. The term "vagabond's disease" is self-explanatory here. Lack of personal hygiene: Chronically ill individuals or persons with mental disabilities who are unable to look after themselves also may be infested by body lice, and children living in that environment may become infested.

Pubic lice: Children are not usually affected by this sexually transmitted disease, but the presence of lice or nits in eyelashes or scalp hair in children does indicate the possibility of sexual abuse.

Mode of Spread.   Direct spread is frequent, but lice can survive for at least a week off the human body, so indirect spread can occur.

Head lice: The commonest method of spread is head-to-head contact, especially in crowded sleeping quarters. Head lice also can be spread by infested headgear, towels, hairbrushes, combs, pillows, bedding, and cassette recorder earphones.

Body lice: Body lice are spread by person-to-person contact or contact with infested clothing or bedding.

Crab lice: Crab lice are spread by person-to-person contact and sometimes by infested towels and bedding.

Incubation Period.   The incubation period from egg laying to emerging adult is 17 to 25 days for *Pediculus humanus capitis* and *corporis* and 22 to 27 days for *Phthirus pubis.*

DIAGNOSIS

The diagnosis is established by the identification of nits on hairs or clothing, which show pale blue fluorescence on Wood's light, or the identification of actual lice on skin, hair, or clothing. Supporting the diagnosis is a clinical picture of intense pruritus, excoriations, secondary infection, and lymphadenopathy.

THERAPY

Outpatient therapy is adequate.

Head lice: The treatment of choice, after shampooing and rinsing the hair, is to work 1% permethrin creme rinse (Nix) into the hair and scalp, leave for 10 minutes, and then rinse it out with clear water. An alternative but less effective therapy is to apply 1 to 2 ounces of 1% lindane shampoo to the dry hair and work it in thoroughly. Then add small quantities of water until a lather forms, and leave it in place for 4 minutes. Rinse thoroughly and dry briskly. A new, effective ovicidal treatment available in some countries is 0.5% malathion (Ovide) lotion, applied to the scalp once, for 8 to 12 hours. A recently described method of nit removal is a cream rinse containing 8% formic acid, followed by a metal nit comb (Nit Removal System Step II). These treatments can be repeated weekly if necessary.

Body lice: Current treatment is to sterilize clothing and bedding and to apply 1% lindane lotion from head to toe for 8 to 10 hours or for 6 to 8 hours in small children. A better alternative is to apply 5% permethrin topical cream (Elimite).

Pubic lice: One method of treatment is 1% lindane lotion from neck to toes for 8 to 12 hours. Alternatively, 5% lindane shampoo can be used on the affected hair-bearing areas in the same manner as it is on the scalp, or, preferably, 1% permethrin cream rinse (Nix) can be applied.

Floors, play areas, and furniture should be vacuumed thoroughly for affected hairs. Mattresses and furniture can be sprayed with synergized pyrethrins or synthetic pyrethroids (Li-Ban, R&C Spray). All clothing, bedding, and headgear should be disinfected by machine washing and machine drying or dry cleaning. Clothing can also be bagged and sealed in tight plastic bags for 2 weeks. Combs and brushes should be soaked in 2% Lysol for 1 to 2 hours or boiled in water for 10 minutes. Combs, brushes, grooming aids, towels, sponges, and facecloths should not be shared. Any secondary infection should be treated with appropriate compresses and antibiotics.

INFECTIOUS PERIOD

The child is infectious as long as live lice or viable ova (nits) are present on the child.

INFECTION CONTROL

Vaccine.   None available.

Exclusion from Child Care or Preschool Attendance.   Until live lice and viable ova are eradicated. This usually means isolating the child for 24 hours after effective treatment. Retreatment is advisable after 1 week to eradicate new lice hatching out of any surviving viable ova.

Recommendations for Other Children.   Examine unaffected children for results of pruritus, such as excoriations, infections, and lymphadenopathy, examine with Wood's lamp for nits, and examine for lice. If any symptoms or signs of pediculosis are found or develop, treatment is indicated.

Recommendations for Personnel.   Check personnel for pruritus, excoriations, infections, lymphadenopathy, nits, and lice. If any symptoms or signs develop, treatment is indicated.

Parental Advice.   All domestic contacts should be checked for symptoms or signs and treated as necessary.

46

Pertussis
(Whooping Cough)

JAMES W. BASS, M.D.

CLINICAL MANIFESTATIONS

Pertussis evolves in three clinical stages: catarrhal, paroxysmal, and convalescent. The catarrhal stage is manifested by mucoid rhinorrhea, nasal congestion, sneezing, and cough. This stage lasts 1 day to several days and is indistinguishable from the common cold. The paroxysmal stage follows and is manifested by violent, protracted bouts of coughing in severe paroxysms lasting up to several minutes. Gasping musical inspirations, "the whoop," often occur during these paroxysms in older infants and preschool children, but they may be absent in infants less than 6 months of age and in older children and adults. This stage lasts from only a few days to 3 to 4 weeks but averages about 2 weeks in duration. The convalescent stage begins when cough paroxysms cease while chronic cough continues. It usually lasts 3 to 4 weeks with decrease in frequency and severity of cough. Rarely, this stage may persist for months.

ETIOLOGIC AGENT

Pertussis, or the "whooping cough syndrome," is caused by *Bordetella pertussis* (90 to 95% of cases) or *B. parapertussis* (5%). The clinical illness caused by the two organisms is the same except that *B. parapertussis* infections are said to be less severe. Since immunization against pertussis does not protect against *B. parapertussis* infection, the relative incidence of *B. parapertussis* infection in areas with high pertussis immunization rates has been reported to be as high as 20%. Small outbreaks of whooping cough–like illness due to *B. bronchiseptica* have been reported in families or laboratory workers in contact with small animals. All three organisms are small Gram-negative coccobacilli that are morphologically similar.

EPIDEMIOLOGY

Pertussis is one of the most highly communicable diseases of humans. Attack rates approach 100% of close susceptible contacts. The distribution of the disease is worldwide. It is a leading cause of sickness and death in children in developing countries where immunization against pertussis is not practiced. It is also prevalent in highly industrialized nations where no vaccine or ineffective vaccines are used.

Source of the Organism.   The only natural reservoir of *B. pertussis* and *B. parapertussis* organisms is the human being, and a healthy carrier state in humans has not been demonstrated. Only a few experimental animals have been infected.

High-Risk Populations.   Children younger than 1 year of age are at greatest risk for contracting the disease and are more likely to have severe life-threatening illness. Lack of placentally transferred passive immunity to pertussis and delayed acquisition of active immunity until these infants have received the basic pertussis immunization series leave them vulnerable to pertussis throughout most of the first year of life.

Other populations at risk who may become infected and promote spread of the disease are older children who may not have received pertussis vaccine. In addition, some older children who have received pertussis vaccine may be susceptible, since vaccine-induced immunity is only partial (80 to 90%) and transient (3 years, decreasing thereafter to 12 years when no protection is evident). Most young adults born since 1950 received pertussis vaccine as children, but since pertussis vaccine is not recommended for persons older than 7 years of age and vaccine protection totally dissipates after 12 years, these individuals are fully susceptible to pertussis. They usually have mild or "atypical" disease manifested only by chronic cough. The diagnosis of pertussis is seldom suspected in these individuals, yet they appear to serve as a significant source of infection. Older adults born before 1950 had pertussis as children, and most remain immune, but there is evidence that some may become infected and possibly serve as a source of infection.

Mode of Spread.   Mode of spread is by the airborne route directly by droplets and droplet nuclei from aerosols generated by the intense cough of infected individuals. Less often, infection may be acquired indirectly by handling objects freshly contaminated with nasopharyngeal or oropharyngeal secretions.

Incubation Period.   The incubation period is usually 7 to 10 days but may range from 5 to 20 days.

DIAGNOSIS

Culture of *B. pertussis* from secretions obtained from the posterior nasopharynx (NP) by a through-the-nose swab remains the "gold standard" for laboratory diagnosis of pertussis. Oropharyngeal swab culture and cough plates are less efficient and are no longer used. Calcium alginate NP swabs (cotton inhibits growth) should be immediately plated onto Bordet-Gengou (BG) media with and without added penicillin or Regan-Lowe (RL) media with and without added cephalexin. Recent reports have shown RL media superior to BG media when they are compared on the same study population, so RL media should be selected if only one medium is used. However, recovery of organisms occurs in some cases on BG media where culture is negative on RL media and in some cases on RL media where it is negative on BG media. Also, using either medium with and without added antibiotic yields similar varying results, so for optimal results culture should be performed on both BG and RL media with and without added antibiotic.

Unfortunately, culture requires a minimum of 3 to 5 days for adequate growth for identification, and positive cultures are obtained in only 35 to 80% of patients with obvious clinical pertussis, varying significantly with the experience and skill of the laboratory personnel and with timing of the culture. Organisms are most likely to be recovered from patients in the catarrhal stage of illness when almost pure cultures may be obtained, particularly in very young infants. The diagnosis, however, is seldom suspected until the onset of the paroxysmal stage when the incidence of positive culture remains almost equally high throughout the first week. It decreases thereafter, and it is seldom possible to recover the organism from patients beyond 3 weeks after onset of the paroxysmal stage of illness.

Early presumptive diagnosis may be made by direct examination of NP smears on glass slides stained with fluorescein-conjugated *B. pertussis* and *B. parapertussis* antiserum with examination under fluorescent microscopy. Both false-positive and false-negative results occur. Well-prepared slides stained with high-quality reagents and examined by experienced technologists using positive and negative controls yield results that are as sensitive and specific as other tests that are now generally available. This test can be done at most medical centers or state health laboratories, and results can be reported within minutes. It is probably the best test currently used for immediate presumptive diagnosis of pertussis that will permit early management decisions regarding isolation, pertussis vaccine administration, and antimicrobial prophylaxis.

Serologic tests such as agglutination and complement fixation are not helpful in early diagnosis, and they are not specific. Some individuals who have culture-proven pertussis and are immune fail to develop agglutinins, whereas some who have not had the disease or prior immunization and are susceptible can be shown to have agglutinins.

Other methods of identification of the organism or its components are DNA hybridization by DNA gene probe, enzyme-linked immunosorbent assay, or the assay for adenylate cyclase. These along with newer tests for antibodies against the organism or its components are promising but are still in the developmental stages.

The characteristic lymphocytosis seen with pertussis may be a helpful diagnostic aid, but it is nonspecific. Lymphocyte counts ranging from 20,000 to over 100,000 mm^3 are seen in the late catarrhal stage and throughout most of the paroxysmal stage. Lymphocytosis may not be present in children less than 6 months of age and in adults or in partially immunized individuals.

THERAPY

General Medical Management. Experienced and efficient nursing care is probably the most important factor in survival of infants with severe pertussis. Seventy percent of children who die of pertussis are less than 1 year of age; they are most commonly 2, 3, or 4 months of age. For this reason it is wise to hospitalize children in this age group until it can be determined that the child does not have life-threatening paroxysms, apnea, cyanosis, or severe feeding problems, and safe management at home can be assured. Children with these problems may require frequent suctioning of secretions and oxygen administration during severe paroxysms. Parenteral fluid and electrolyte supplementation and, in protracted cases, parenteral alimentation may be required.

Mist therapy is not helpful. Continuous supplemental well-humidified oxygen may be needed for some patients who have sustained hypoxemia. These patients usually have pulmonary complications such as atelectasis or pneumonia. Cough suppressants, expectorants, and sedatives have not been shown to be of benefit in the treatment of pertussis.

Antimicrobial Agents.   Pertussis organisms are eradicated from patients with the disease if they are treated with antimicrobial agents active against *B. pertussis* organisms, provided that the drug diffuses in significant concentrations into respiratory tract secretions. No antimicrobial drug has been shown to alter the subsequent clinical course of the illness when given in the paroxysmal stage of the disease. However, drugs that meet these criteria attenuate the illness when given in the catarrhal or preparoxysmal stage of the disease and abort or prevent the disease in individuals during incubation (asymptomatic susceptibles who are culture or fluorescent antibody–positive for *B. pertussis*). Their administration to patients at any stage of pertussis regularly produces bacteriologic cure and may render them noninfectious. These reasons constitute the rationale for the use of antimicrobials in pertussis, and for these purposes erythromycin is the most effective and least toxic drug of all studied to date. The optimal dose is 40 to 50 mg/kg/day (maximum, 1 g/day) in four divided doses for 14 days. Treatment for less than 14 days results in a 10% incidence of bacteriologic relapse, and these children may again become contagious. Clarithromycin is currently being evaluated and may present a superior alternative with the advantages of shorter duration of treatment and fewer side effects.

Children who develop fever or an elevated erythrocyte sedimentation rate usually have secondary suppurative infections, most often acute otitis media, sinusitis, or pneumonia. The bacterial pathogens implicated are those that usually cause these infections in infants and children, so that more specific additional antibiotic treatment may be indicated.

Corticosteroids.   Betamethasone given orally at a dosage of 0.075 mg/kg/day and hydrocortisone succinate (Solu-Cortef) given intramuscularly at a dose of 30 mg/kg/day for 2 days, with the dose gradually reduced and discontinued after 1 week, have both been shown to be effective in reducing the incidence and severity of cough paroxysms in controlled studies of children with pertussis. Additional studies are needed, but it appears that corticosteroids may be beneficial in the treatment of pertussis even after onset of paroxysms and that treatment may be indicated in young infants with life-threatening paroxysms. Other corticosteroid preparations at comparable dosages should work equally well.

Albuterol.   Several controlled studies evaluating the use of albuterol in the treatment of pertussis have been reported, and most have shown a beneficial effect. Its use may be indicated for treatment of pertussis in small infants with severe life-threatening paroxysms. A dosage of 0.3 to 0.5 mg/kg/day in three divided doses has been shown to be effective and well tolerated.

INFECTIOUS PERIOD

Individuals with pertussis should be considered infectious from just before the onset of the catarrhal stage of the disease until 3 weeks after the development of the paroxysmal stage.

INFECTION CONTROL

Vaccine.   Pertussis vaccine should only be given to individuals less than 7 years of age. Close contacts in this age group should receive a dose of diphtheria-pertussis-tetanus (DPT) vaccine if they have not completed the four-dose primary series or if they have not received a dose within the previous 3 years. Those who are unimmunized or who have received fewer than four doses of DPT should be immunized in accordance with current recommended schedules.

Exclusion from Child Care or Preschool Attendance.   Children with clinical pertussis should be considered contagious from the earliest signs and symptoms of the catarrhal stage of illness to 3 weeks after onset of the paroxysmal stage. Nearly all children with pertussis who are treated with erythromycin are culture-negative for *B. pertussis* organisms after 5 days, so that if compliance can be assured, these children also may be considered noncontagious at this time and return to the child care setting. However, treatment should be continued for at least 14 days.

Recommendations for Other Children.   All children in a child care center or preschool where pertussis has been confirmed in one or more children should be considered infected, and they should be isolated from other children until it can be determined if they are contagious. After NP swabs for culture and fluorescent antibody studies are obtained, it is recommended that these children be treated with erythromycin as outlined under Therapy.

Recommendations for Personnel.   Most personnel younger than 40 years of age have lost previous immunity conferred by vaccination and are fully susceptible to pertussis. Even those older than 40 years of age who probably had pertussis as a child and are immune to pertussis may have subclinical disease and serve as a source of infection to their contacts. For these reasons when the diagnosis of pertussis has been confirmed, it is recommended that all day care center personnel receive erythromycin as outlined above under Therapy.

Parental Advice.   Parents should be told that pertussis or "whooping cough" has been diagnosed in children in the center and that measures have been taken to control the infection. These include isolation of infected or possibly infected individuals, "booster" pertussis vaccine administration to certain children, and antibiotic treatment or prophylaxis to all children in the center to stop spread of the infection.

47

Pneumococcus
(Otitis Media, Sinusitis, Bacteremia, Pneumonia, Meningitis)

KEITH R. POWELL, M.D.

CLINICAL MANIFESTATIONS

The most common diseases caused by *Streptococcus pneumoniae* are otitis media, sinusitis, bacteremia, pneumonia, and meningitis. *S. pneumoniae* is isolated from 30 to 40% of cases of acute otitis media and acute maxillary sinusitis in which a bacterial pathogen is identified. Pneumococcal otitis media frequently accompanies a viral respiratory infection. There are no clinical features that distinguish acute pneumococcal otitis media or sinusitis from infections with other pathogens. *S. pneumoniae* also can cause purulent conjunctivitis in young infants.

S. pneumoniae pneumonia is characterized by fever, tachypnea, localized findings on chest examination, and consolidative pneumonia of one or more lobes seen on chest roentgenogram. Symptoms usually improve dramatically after 1 or 2 days of an appropriate antibiotic.

Three percent to five percent of children between 3 and 36 months of age with temperatures above 39° C for which no source can be identified will be bacteremic. *S. pneumoniae* can be isolated from the blood in 65 to 75% of such infants. Occult bacteremia is most often associated with upper respiratory infections, pharyngitis, or fever alone.

S. pneumoniae causes about 7 cases of meningitis per 100,000 children younger than 5 years of age per year. Pneumococcal meningitis cannot be distinguished clinically from other types of bacterial meningitis.

ETIOLOGIC AGENT

S. pneumoniae are lancet-shaped Gram-positive cocci that occur in pairs. When grown on blood agar plates there is a greenish discoloration around colonies because of partial (alpha) hemolysis. Pneumococci are serotyped based on chemically distinct capsular polysaccharides. There are currently 84 recognized serotypes.

EPIDEMIOLOGY

Source of the Organism.   *S. pneumoniae* are ubiquitous. Asymptomatic carriage of this organism is extremely common. Seventy-nine of 82 infants studied from birth through 2 years of age carried one or more types of *S. pneumoniae* for varying lengths of time. Between 1970 and 1980, more than 40% of the children in a day care center were found to be *S. pneumoniae* carriers in 95% of the months of observation. During this time, there were no children with systemic disease.

High-Risk Populations.   About 70% of pneumococcal infections in children occur in infants younger than 2 years old, and as many as 25% of children with systemic pneumococcal infections have underlying conditions such as sickle cell disease, malignancy, congenital malformations, and renal disease or have had a splenectomy. There are experimental data that support the hypothesis that viral respiratory tract infections that result in a negative pressure in the middle ear can predispose to pneumococcal otitis media.

Mode of Spread.   The mode of spread of *S. pneumoniae* is from person to person via respiratory droplets. Spread can occur in association with viral upper respiratory tract infections.

Incubation Period.   There is no distinct incubation period for pneumococcal diseases. However, infection most often occurs within 1 month after an individual acquires a new serotype.

DIAGNOSIS

The diagnosis of infection caused by *S. pneumoniae* is usually made by isolation of the organism from body sites that are normally sterile (e.g., blood, spinal fluid). A diagnosis of pneumococcal pneumonia can be made by typical clinical and roentgenographic findings and the presence of Gram-positive lancet-shaped diplococci in an adequate Gram-stained sputum specimen. Since sputum is difficult to obtain in young children, an alternative is to assay concentrated urine for the presence of pneumococcal capsular polysaccharides by countercurrent immunoelectrophoresis or latex particle agglutination.

THERAPY

Penicillin G is the antibiotic of choice for most infections with *S. pneumoniae.* Otitis media, sinusitis, and pneumonia are usually treated empirically with amoxicillin or an antibiotic that will also cover beta-lactamase-producing *H. influenzae* and *Moraxella catarrhalis* (amoxicillin-clavulanate, erythromycin-sulfisoxazole, trimethoprim-sulfamethoxazole). Pneumococci with reduced susceptibility to penicillin, cephalosporins, and trimethoprim-sulfamethoxazole are being isolated with increasing frequency from children in day care settings. Conjunctivitis can be treated with ophthalmic preparations of polymyxin B-bacitracin, sulfacetamide, or erythromycin. Children with bacterial meningitis require hospitalization for 10 days of parenteral antibiotic therapy, and children with more severe pneumococcal pneumonia require hospitalization until they are ready for oral therapy. Children found to have occult pneumococcal bacteremia are usually treated for 10 days. The route of administration and whether the child is hospitalized will depend on the clinical setting.

INFECTIOUS PERIOD

There is no evidence that children with *S. pneumoniae* infections are more likely to transmit the organism than are asymptomatic carriers.

INFECTION CONTROL

Vaccine. A 23-valent pneumococcal vaccine is commercially available but is not effective in children less than 2 years of age. At present, vaccination is recommended for children aged 2 years or older with (a) sickle cell disease, (b) asplenia, or (c) nephrotic syndrome, and (d) prior to cytoreduction therapy for Hodgkin's disease. The effectiveness of more widespread use of the pneumococcal conjugate vaccines in young children is currently under study.

Exclusion from Child Care or Preschool Attendance.   Children should only be kept out of child care or preschool if they are too ill to participate in usual activities.

Recommendations for Other Children.   There are no recommendations for other children in the day care center or preschool once one child is known to be infected with *S. pneumoniae.*

Recommendations for Personnel.   There are no recommendations for personnel in the day care center once one child is known to be infected.

Parental Advice.   Nearly all children have *S. pneumoniae* in their upper respiratory tract at one time or another, and such "colonization" is seldom associated with disease. The fact that one child in the day care center has an illness caused by *S. pneumoniae* probably does not increase the risk of another child having an illness with this bacteria. Children recently treated with antibiotics are more likely to have infections with resistant pneumococci than children who did not receive antibiotics. Antibiotics should be used only when there are clear indications of bacterial infection.

48

Respiratory Syncytial Virus

CAROLINE BREESE HALL, M.D.

CLINICAL MANIFESTATIONS

Respiratory syncytial virus (RSV) is the major cause of lower respiratory tract infection in infants and young children. It is the most frequent cause of bronchiolitis and also the most frequent cause of pneumonia during the first 2 years of life. The lower respiratory tract disease caused by RSV in the first year of life may vary in severity from mild to life-threatening or even fatal. Although essentially all first RSV infections are symptomatic, the vast majority have an uncomplicated course. The morbidity and mortality are greatest in the very young infant and in children with underlying diseases, especially those affecting the cardiac, pulmonary, and immunologic systems. Apnea is also a frequent manifestation of RSV infection, especially in premature infants and those in the first several months of life. RSV is a major cause of tracheobronchitis in preschool-age children and occasionally may be manifest as croup. Close to half of primary infections are manifest as lower respiratory tract disease and the other half are manifest as upper respiratory tract infections and otitis media.

RSV causes frequent and repetitive infections throughout life. In children approximately 3 years of age or older, these infections are most often expressed as upper respiratory tract infections, otitis media, and tracheobronchitis. RSV is commonly associated with recurrent wheezing and may sometimes present as a febrile, influenza-like syndrome. Adults may manifest recurrent RSV infection as bronchitis, wheezing, febrile upper respiratory tract infection, a cold, or with little in the way of symptoms. These mild

226

infections are more apt to occur in those with recent or frequent exposure to children with RSV infections, such as staff in child care centers. Such mild infections may nevertheless be a source of spread of RSV.

ETIOLOGIC AGENT

RSV is an enveloped RNA virus of medium size that is currently classified in the family Paramyxoviridae and in the genus Pneumovirus. RSV strains are divided into two major groups, A and B. These groups are based mostly on the antigenic variations in the two major surface glycoproteins, the F or fusion protein and the G or attachment protein. The F protein is relatively well conserved and thus antigenically similar among strains A and B. The major antigenic differences occur in the largest surface glycoprotein, the G protein. The immunologic, clinical, and epidemiologic importance of strain variation is currently unclear but may contribute to the frequency of repetitive RSV infections within a short time, even within the same season.

EPIDEMIOLOGY

Source of the Organism.   RSV is highly contagious and spread from person to person. In the normal host, the presence of the virus in the secretions indicates an acute infection. Repetitive infections may occasionally be asymptomatic, but carriage or latent infection does not occur.

High-Risk Populations.   The major risk factor for acquisition and severity of RSV infection is young age. RSV tends to occur in annual winter outbreaks; many children acquire RSV infection during the first outbreak they experience, and essentially all children experience RSV infection by 3 years of age. In day care settings studies have shown that during the first year of life the infection rate is close to 100%, and about half will have lower respiratory tract disease. Even in the second and third year of life in child care settings two thirds to three fourths of the children will become infected with RSV. Within families the rate of infection is slightly lower but is still high. Approximately two thirds of the infants in the first year of life cared for at home have been shown to acquire RSV infection, and an even higher percentage have been shown to acquire RSV in the second year. During the third and fourth year of life one third to one half of children will become infected each year.

Children at risk for the most severe and complicated disease from RSV are those with cardiopulmonary disease, especially congenital heart disease with pulmonary hypertension and bronchopulmonary dysplasia, compromised immunity, and multiple congenital anomalies or neurologic diseases. Older children with hyperreactive airway disease may have exacerbations of wheezing and more prolonged illness.

Mode of Spread. RSV is spread by direct contact with infectious secretions. This appears to be primarily by large-particle aerosols from infected individuals within close proximity and from contact with infectious secretions contaminating the environment. In this latter mode of spread, infectious secretions on surfaces, toys, clothes, and other objects are transmitted by touching, with subsequent inoculation of the virus occurring when the eyes or nose is touched. The virus may remain infectious on surfaces and skin from one-half hour to more than a day, depending on the temperature, humidity, and type of surface.

Incubation Period. The incubation period most frequently appears to be 5 to 7 days but may occasionally be as short as 3 days.

DIAGNOSIS

The season, age, and clinical presentation, especially bronchiolitis, allow a presumptive diagnosis in many infants. Specific diagnosis may be made by viral isolation from respiratory secretions, which usually requires 3 to 7 days, or by a rapid diagnostic test for antigen in respiratory secretions. A variety of commercial antigen detection tests are currently available, most of which employ monoclonal antibodies in an immunofluorescent or enzyme-linked immunosorbent assay technique. Serologic diagnosis is generally impractical and insensitive.

THERAPY

Most children with RSV infection do well with supportive therapy. In hospitalized children with severe disease or with high-risk conditions, ribavirin may be used in addition to careful monitoring and supportive care.

INFECTIOUS PERIOD

The period of infectivity correlates with the shedding of the virus in the nasopharyngeal secretions. In young infants this is most frequently 1 to 2 weeks but may occasionally be 3 weeks or longer. In older children and adults, shedding of the virus more frequently occurs for 3 to 7 days.

INFECTION CONTROL

Vaccine.   None.

Exclusion from Child Care or Preschool Attendance.   Because of the ubiquitous and prevalent nature of RSV during a winter community outbreak and because the clinical presentation may be variable and not distinguishable from a mild cold of many other agents, preventing an infected child from attending a child care or preschool setting is impractical in most instances. Furthermore, children may be highly infectious just prior to the onset of symptoms. For those children known to have RSV infection, particularly with lower respiratory tract infection, the best guideline for return to the child care setting is when the child is clinically well enough to be able to attend and participate in the usual activities.

Recommendations for Other Children.   Studies have shown that once one child in a child care or preschool setting is infected, spread of infection is rapid and inevitable. The risk of infection is so high for young children in or out of the day care setting during a community outbreak that recommendations for other children in a center once a child has become infected are of little value.

Recommendations for Personnel.   Personnel in a child care center or preschool may frequently become infected with RSV, which most often is manifest as an upper respiratory tract infection, and they may serve as disseminators of the infection to others in the center. The most effective infection control method is good and constant handwashing since the primary mode of spread is by direct contact with infectious secretions which may remain contagious on skin and environmental surfaces for some time.

Parental Advice.   If parents request information, they should be informed about the prevalence and contagiousness of RSV among young children in any setting during a community outbreak of RSV infection. They should understand that all children acquire RSV infection in the first few years of life, and if the child is over 1 year of age or has been in the day care center through a previous RSV epidemic, the child is highly likely to have already experienced RSV infection. Thus, if their child acquires a respiratory infection, they should treat it as any other respiratory illness and seek the advice of their private physician.

49

Rhinoviruses
(Common Cold)

RONALD B. TURNER, M.D.

CLINICAL MANIFESTATIONS

The rhinoviruses are an important cause of the common cold. The symptoms of rhinovirus colds are limited to the upper respiratory tract in most people; fever, myalgia, and malaise are uncommon. Gastrointestinal symptoms are not associated with rhinovirus infections. The first symptom noted by many individuals is a mild sore throat. This is soon followed by development of nasal stuffiness and rhinorrhea. About one third of rhinovirus illnesses are associated with cough. Symptoms reach a peak after 1 to 2 days of illness and usually resolve within 1 week.

Although rhinovirus infection is usually minor and self-limited, a small proportion of infected individuals will have complications. Otitis media due to either the rhinovirus itself or a secondary bacterial infection occurs in approximately 3% of rhinovirus colds. Sinusitis may also complicate the viral infection. Lower respiratory symptoms, especially exacerbations of asthma, are reported in about 1% of these infections.

ETIOLOGIC AGENT

The rhinoviruses are members of the family Picornaviridae, which also includes the enteroviruses. This family is composed of small (approximately 25 nm) nonenveloped RNA viruses. The rhinoviruses are distinguished from the enteroviruses by their inactivation by exposure to acid. There are more than 100 different serotypes of rhinovirus. Serotype-specific antibody generally protects against infection, although the degree of protection is dependent upon the size of the inoculum received.

EPIDEMIOLOGY

Source of the Organism. Infection with the rhinoviruses is acquired exclusively from other infected individuals. There is no animal host for this virus. The virus can survive on inanimate objects for several hours, and contaminated objects can presumably serve as a source of infection.

High-Risk Populations. There is no population that is known to be at increased risk of infection with the rhinoviruses. Patients with asthma may be at risk of more severe illness if infection with rhinovirus occurs.

Mode of Spread. Spread of rhinovirus infection has been demonstrated to occur by direct contact, via fomites, and in aerosols. The relative importance of these different routes of spread in the natural setting is not known.

Incubation Period. The incubation period for rhinovirus infection is 1 to 2 days.

DIAGNOSIS

Rhinovirus illnesses are generally mild, and specific etiologic diagnosis is not generally attempted. Laboratory diagnosis is accomplished by isolation of the organism in cell culture. Optimal conditions for cell culture require that the specimen be incubated at 33° C on a roller drum. There are no reliable antigen detection methods for rhinovirus, and serologic diagnosis is generally not attempted because of the large number of distinct serotypes.

THERAPY

There are no anti-infective therapies of proven benefit for treatment of rhinovirus infections. Cold symptoms can be palliated with decongestants. Topical adrenergic agents are generally most efficacious. Antihistamines have a modest effect on the runny nose associated with colds; however, drowsiness is a frequent side effect.

INFECTIOUS PERIOD

Infected individuals may shed virus in nasal secretions for as long as 3 weeks. Transmission is most likely when nasal symptoms are present.

INFECTION CONTROL

Vaccine.   None available.

Exclusion from Child Care or Preschool Attendance.   Exclusion of rhinovirus-infected children from child care settings is not indicated.

Recommendations for Other Children.   Transmission of infection may be reduced by frequent handwashing.

Recommendations for Personnel.   Transmission of infection may be reduced by frequent handwashing.

Parental Advice.   No special measures are indicated.

50

Roseola
(Exanthema Subitum)

MARY ANNE JACKSON, M.D.

CLINICAL MANIFESTATIONS

Roseola (also called exanthema subitum) is the most common acute febrile exanthem of children ages 6 months to 2 years. In typical cases, high sustained fever is present and lasts for 3 to 5 days. Irritability, malaise, and runny nose may be present during this time, but usually, despite the high fever, most children are alert and playful. A red throat with small lesions on the palate or tonsils and lymphadenopathy involving the occipital, cervical, and posterior auricular chains may be the only other pertinent findings. Children with roseola may have eyelid swelling that gives them a "sleepy" or "droopy" appearance. Many clinicians believe this is a classic pre-rash finding.

The exanthem or rash phase of roseola generally occurs coincident with the disappearance of fever. Pale rose-pink macules measuring 2 to 5 mm are surrounded by a white halo and scattered over the neck and trunk, sparing the face and extremities. The rash lasts 24 to 48 hours, and a total clinical course of 5 to 7 days is typical.

High fever without localizing signs occurs frequently in primary infection. Febrile seizures occur in approximately 10% of these cases. In rare instances, encephalitis has been noted.

Fever, hepatitis, pneumonia, and bone marrow suppression have been reported in compromised hosts in whom reactivation has occurred.

ETIOLOGIC AGENT

Both human herpesviruses type 6 and type 7 have been detected in children with roseola. At times, roseola-like illness has been associated with other viruses including enteroviruses (most commonly ECHO 16 virus), adenoviruses, and parvovirus.

EPIDEMIOLOGY

Source of the Organism.   The human is the only known host for roseola.

High-Risk Populations.   Reactivated disease has been reported in immunocompromised hosts.

Mode of Spread.   Unknown.

Incubation Period.   5 to 15 days.

DIAGNOSIS

The major requirement in establishing the diagnosis of roseola is to document the fever, defervescence, and the rash pattern of the disease. Assays for antigen and antibody detection and urine isolation from peripheral blood are available only in research settings at this time.

THERAPY

Treatment is supportive. Febrile seizures and other neurologic manifestations of roseola may require further evaluation and other diagnostic studies.

INFECTIOUS PERIOD

The period of communicability is unknown.

INFECTION CONTROL

Vaccine.   None available.

Exclusion from Child Care or Preschool Attendance.   Generally speaking, children with febrile exanthems should not return to a child care or preschool setting until their rash is gone and they are well.

Recommendations for Other Children.   No contact prophylaxis is necessary.

Recommendations for Personnel.   No special recommendations are necessary for child care personnel.

Parental Advice.   Cases usually occur sporadically throughout the year. Occasionally, outbreaks have been reported, but parents can be reassured as to the benign nature of this infection. There is no known risk to pregnant women, and infection in children less than 3 months or children over 4 years of age is uncommon.

51

Rotavirus

THERESA A. SCHLAGER, M.D.

CLINICAL MANIFESTATIONS

Rotavirus infection is the most common cause of gastroenteritis occurring in the winter among infants and young children in the United States. The clinical features of rotavirus infection vary from asymptomatic fecal shedding of the virus to severe vomiting and diarrhea associated with circulatory collapse. Symptomatic illness usually is manifested by vomiting and low-grade fever followed by watery, nonbloody diarrhea. Vomiting and dehydration occur more frequently with rotavirus infection than with other causes of gastroenteritis. Diarrhea typically lasts between 3 and 8 days but may be prolonged in immunocompromised children. Respiratory symptoms are associated with rotavirus, but the virus has not been isolated from respiratory secretions. The overall course of rotavirus infection ordinarily is self-limited and without sequelae if appropriate therapy for dehydration is provided.

ETIOLOGIC AGENT

Rotaviruses are RNA viruses: five distinct antigenic groups (A to E) have been described, and group A is the major cause of infantile diarrhea. Rotavirus appears to cause disease by invading and altering (morphologically and functionally) small bowel mucosal cells, resulting in malabsorption and diarrhea.

EPIDEMIOLOGY

Source of the Organism. Rotavirus is one of the most common causes of diarrhea in the child care center for children younger than

3 years of age and represents a source of infection for parents and child care providers. Although symptomatic disease in adults is unusual, asymptomatic shedding of the virus by adults can be a source of infection. Animals are known to have rotavirus diarrheal disease, but animal-to-human transmission has not been documented under natural conditions.

High-Risk Populations.   The peak age for symptomatic rotavirus infection is 6 to 24 months. The disease is highly contagious, and contact with infected patients in the 6- to 24-month age group constitutes the greatest risk factor for disease acquisition. The immunocompromised child is at risk for developing chronic diarrhea.

Mode of Spread.   Fecal-oral spread is the most common mode of spread, but contaminated fomites may also transmit rotavirus.

Incubation Period.   1 to 3 days.

DIAGNOSIS

The diagnosis is usually made presumptively on clinical grounds. Watery diarrhea in a child 6 to 24 months of age, occurring in the winter months in the United States and associated with vomiting and dehydration, is most likely due to rotavirus infection. The absence of fecal leukocytes and blood along with a negative stool culture for bacterial pathogens is indirectly supportive of a rotavirus etiology.

Although a specific diagnosis is usually not necessary in sporadic cases, it may be useful in outbreaks, in isolating hospitalized patients, and in epidemiologic studies. Electron microscopy (EM) and immunoassays such as the enzyme-linked immunosorbent assay (ELISA) are the most reliable techniques for detection of rotavirus. Limited clinical access to an electron microscope has restricted the use of this method to major centers. Several easy-to-use commercial kits utilizing ELISA technology have made possible the early and accurate diagnosis of rotavirus infection by hospital laboratories. The sensitivity of ELISA tests is equal to that of EM. False-positive tests, however, have been reported.

Stool specimens from the first 4 days of illness have the highest yield for rotavirus diagnosis by ELISA and electron microscopy. This period usually correlates with the highest degree of shedding of the virus. In some patients, rotavirus may be shed for as long as 3 weeks, thereby permitting a diagnosis well after the initial onset of diarrhea. Presence of rotavirus in feces usually correlates with acute diarrhea caused by this pathogen.

THERAPY

No specific antiviral therapy is available. Adequate fluid replacement is the mainstay of treatment. Most patients can be managed appropriately with oral rehydration, but infants with marked dehydration may require hospitalization for aggressive fluid and electrolyte repletion. The routine use of oral immunoglobulin for rotavirus gastroenteritis is not currently recommended. However, in immunodeficient children with chronic rotavirus infection, orally administered rotavirus-specific immunoglobulin preparations may ablate shedding or ameliorate disease.

INFECTIOUS PERIOD

The infectious period is usually less than 1 week, paralleling diarrhea that usually ceases in 4 to 5 days. However, immunocompromised patients may excrete the virus for months.

INFECTION CONTROL

Vaccine.   Live, attenuated orally administered vaccines are currently being evaluated for safety and efficacy.

Exclusion from Child Care or Preschool Attendance.   The infected child should be kept out of the child care or preschool setting as long as diarrhea or vomiting is present.

Recommendations for Other Children.   Routine testing for rotavirus of case contacts within a child care center or preschool is not recommended. Washing of children's hands on arrival at the center, after a diaper change or use of the toilet, and before meals and snacks should be consistently practiced. Use of liquid soap in a dispenser along with disposable paper towels is recommended. Shared surfaces and toys should be disinfected on a daily basis with a freshly prepared solution of commercially available cleanser (detergents, disinfectant detergents, or chemical germicides).

Recommendations for Personnel.   Symptomatic staff members should not attend the center until fever, diarrhea, or vomiting ceases. Without failure, staff members should practice careful hand-washing (10 seconds with soap and warm running water) upon arrival at the center, after changing a child's diaper, after using or providing assistance to a child using the toilet, and before food handling. Disinfecting diaper-changing surfaces along with proper disposal is recommended.

Parental Advice.   A child care center or preschool should notify parents of children who have been in direct contact with a child who has diarrhea. Parents should contact their physician for advice if their child develops diarrhea.

52

Rubella
(German Measles)

GREGORY F. HAYDEN, M.D.

CLINICAL MANIFESTATIONS

Rubella (German measles) is commonly inapparent and unrecognized. When clinical illness occurs, it is generally benign and is manifested by rash and lymphadenopathy with mild constitutional symptoms. The pink maculopapular rash appears first on the face and then spreads downward and peripherally. The usual duration of rash is 2 to 5 days, leading to the lay term, "3-day measles." The illness is often more severe among adolescents and adults whose illness may begin with a prodrome of fever, malaise, headache, and respiratory symptoms. Arthralgia and arthritis may occur, especially in adult women. Rare complications include thrombocytopenic purpura and encephalitis.

In contrast to the usually mild nature of postnatal rubella, gestational rubella can be devastating to the developing fetus. Virtually every organ system can be affected, but especially the eyes, heart, and central nervous system. The clinical expression of congenital rubella depends on the timing of infection, with the risk of major anomalies being greatest during the first trimester.

ETIOLOGIC AGENT

Rubella is a spherical, enveloped, RNA-containing virus that is classified as a rubivirus in the togavirus family. Only one serologic type is recognized.

EPIDEMIOLOGY

Source of the Organism.   The human is the only known natural host and source of infection.

High-Risk Populations.   Rubella is uncommon in the first several months of life, but after this age, unvaccinated children remain at high risk of developing rubella if exposed.

Mode of Spread.   Transmission is via respiratory droplets or direct contact with an infected patient.

Incubation Period.   The incubation period is usually 16 to 18 days but can range from 14 to 21 days.

DIAGNOSIS

The clinical diagnosis of postnatal rubella can be confirmed by using virologic or serologic methods. Rubella virus can be isolated from the nose, throat, and other sites, but viral culture is relatively expensive and not universally available. Several serologic techniques are available, including hemagglutination inhibition (HI), complement fixation (CF), and enzyme-linked immunosorbent assay (ELISA). A significant rise in titer between acute and convalescent serum specimens is diagnostic of rubella infection. (For HI and CF tests, this is usually a fourfold or greater rise in titer; for ELISA methods, see the manufacturer's instructions for interpretation of a significant change.) The presence of rubella-specific immunoglobulin M (IgM) antibodies also suggests recent postnatal infection. A suspected or confirmed diagnosis of rubella should be reported immediately to the local health department.

THERAPY

No specific therapy is currently available.

INFECTIOUS PERIOD

The period of maximum communicability occurs from up to 5 days before rash onset until 5 to 7 days after rash onset. More rarely, virus has been detected in the nasopharynx as long as 7 days before and 14 days after rash onset.

INFECTION CONTROL

Vaccine.   Live, attenuated rubella virus vaccine should be given routinely to children after the first birthday, and is usually administered at 12 to 15 months of age as a part of the combined measles-mumps-rubella (MMR) vaccine. The cornerstone of rubella prevention in child care centers and preschools should be the vigilant insistence that all children 15 months of age or older have received rubella vaccine as a prerequisite for attending the center. There is no evidence for any difference in efficacy when rubella vaccine is administered at 12 versus 15 months of age. A single dose confers long-lasting immunity to more than 95% of vaccinees, but a second dose of MMR vaccine is recommended at 4 to 12 years of age.

Contraindications to live rubella vaccination include immunodeficiency, pregnancy, and recent administration of an immune globulin preparation or blood products. Children with minor illnesses, with or without fever, may be vaccinated. MMR vaccine is recommended for children infected with the human immunodeficiency virus (HIV), even those whose infections have become symptomatic.

Exclusion from Child Care or Preschool Attendance.   Children with postnatal rubella should be excluded from child care or preschool for 7 days after rash onset. Since patients are often contagious before rash onset, however, and since inapparent infections can be communicable, attempts to control spread by means of isolation are commonly ineffective.

Children with congenital rubella should be considered contagious until they are 1 year old, unless nasopharyngeal and urine cultures prove negative for rubella.

Recommendations for Other Children.   The first step is to verify that other children attending the center have already been immunized against rubella in accordance with established center policy. Children with documented previous immunization against rubella are highly unlikely to develop illness and may continue to attend the center. The management of unvaccinated children is more complex. Live rubella vaccine is not known to prevent illness when given after exposure, but it will at least protect against subsequent exposures if the child is not already incubating wild rubella infection. Immunization of a child who is incubating natural rubella is not known to be harmful. For unvaccinated children who have reached their first birthday, vaccination can therefore be recommended. Parents must understand, however, that the vaccine may not block the progression of incubating rubella, so that they will not wrongly blame the vaccine for rubella illness that develops after vaccination.

For infants younger than 1 year of age, vaccination is a less attractive option because the likelihood of seroconversion is believed to be lower. Although limited data suggest that it can potentially prevent or modify infection in exposed susceptibles, immunoglobulin is not generally recommended in this instance because of its expense, its questionable efficacy, and the usually mild clinical course of rubella in young children.

Recommendations for Personnel.   Ideally, all staff members should provide a documented history of immunization or serologic evidence of immunity at the time of employment. Strict adherence to such a policy will reduce or eliminate the needless disruption that can arise among personnel when rubella is diagnosed in a child attending the center. If appropriate preparations have not been made before such a case occurs, the first step is to determine whether any staff members are susceptible to rubella. This determination is particularly crucial for any personnel who may possibly be pregnant. Documented history of previous rubella immunization on or after the first birthday strongly suggests immunity to rubella. The detection of antibody by a properly performed test before or at the time of exposure provides strong evidence that the individual is immune and not at risk for developing rubella. If antibody is not detectable immediately after an exposure to rubella, additional blood testing will be necessary to determine whether infection has occurred. A pregnant woman exposed to rubella should consult her obstetrician immediately to discuss and evaluate the possible implications of this exposure. In most instances, the woman will already be immune to rubella and can be reassured that the exposure poses little or no risk to her developing fetus.

Parental Advice.   Parents should be advised that a suspected (or confirmed) case of rubella has occurred in a child at the center. They should be advised that the risk to their child is minimal so long as he or she has already received rubella vaccine. Parents of unimmunized children should be advised to seek medical advice immediately concerning the prompt vaccination of children over 1 year of age and concerning the potential risk their child may pose to susceptible pregnant contacts. Parents should also be urged to verify their own immunity status as well as the immunization status of any older children, especially adolescents, who do not attend the center and to seek vaccination as appropriate. A mother who is pregnant should discuss this possible exposure with her obstetrician.

53

Rubeola
(Measles)

CAROLINE BREESE HALL, M.D.

CLINICAL MANIFESTATIONS

The onset of rubeola is usually marked by fever followed by the "three C's"—coryza, conjunctivitis, and cough. These signs peak after about 3 to 4 days at the time the rash first appears. The typical morbilliform eruption starts on the head, around the hairline, and progresses to the feet over 3 days, changing from discrete maculopapular lesions to a confluent rash. About 2 days prior to the onset of the rash the characteristic Koplik spots may appear on the buccal mucosa. Once the rash appears, the respiratory signs and fever tend to abate. The rash fades over the subsequent several days, leaving a brown stain and then a generalized desquamation that has the appearance of bran. The course of classic measles generally resolves over a 10-day period, but the cough may persist. Bronchitis, otitis, and pneumonia may complicate the course of rubeola.

Clinical variants of classical measles include modified measles, atypical measles, and vaccine measles. Modified measles is a mild form of measles with a shortened course occurring in patients who possess some measles antibody, such as those who have received gammaglobulin, occasionally in infants with passive maternal antibody, and possibly in those with waning immunity from vaccination. Atypical measles is a severe and clinically unusual form of measles occurring in patients who have previously received inactivated measles vaccine, which ceased to be marketed after 1968. After exposure to the wild virus these patients developed a high fever and unusual exanthem which could be petechial, vesicular, nodular, or urticarial, as well as macular-papular. Pulmonary infiltrates, with a nodular appearance, also may complicate the course. Fortunately, with time and widespread use of live vaccine, this atypical disease is no longer seen. Vaccine measles is the mild illness that appears in some children following administration of the live attenuated vaccine. A mild rash and fever may appear approximately a week after immunization.

Acute encephalitis may be associated with measles in approximately 0.1% of cases. Subacute sclerosing panencephalitis is a late complication of measles occurring in approximately 1 in 100,000 cases.

ETIOLOGIC AGENT

Measles virus is classified as a paramyxovirus. It is an RNA-enveloped virus possessing six major proteins: NP, the nucleocapsid that contains the viral genomic RNA and the structural proteins associated with the nucleocapsid and RNA polymerase activity; associated with the envelope are the surface glycoproteins H, the hemagglutinin, F, the fusion protein, and M, an internal membrane protein. Measles is a relatively large (120 to 250 nm in diameter) and spherical virus related to canine distemper virus and rinderpest virus.

EPIDEMIOLOGY

Source of the Organism.   Measles is spread from person to person, and humans are the only source of the virus, although monkeys may be infected with measles.

High-Risk Populations.   Measles is highly contagious, and anyone who does not possess specific measles antibody is at high risk of acquiring infection. Infants, pregnant women, adults, and those with underlying diseases, especially immunocompromising conditions, including HIV, tend to be at increased risk for severe and complicated disease.

Mode of Spread.   Measles is spread by contact with secretions of infected persons. Infectious secretions may be spread by large-particle droplets, requiring close contact, or by small-particle aerosols that may allow rapid and distant transmission of the virus. Direct contact with infectious secretions also may occur via contact with contaminated surfaces or objects. Inoculation appears to occur through the nasopharynx and possibly the conjunctiva.

Incubation Period.   The incubation period is usually 10 to 12 days.

DIAGNOSIS

Diagnosis is often made clinically in the classical case. Confirmation of the diagnosis of measles may be made by a number of rapid antigen tests, which are usually much more readily available than viral isolation by fluorescent antibody techniques. Serologic diagnosis may be made early by identification of immunoglobulin M (IgM) measles antibody by rapid assays, such as enzyme-linked immunosorbent assay (ELISA). Acute and convalescent sera may be tested for rises to specific antibody by hemagglutination-inhibition (HI), complement fixation (CF), and neutralizing antibody techniques, as well as by ELISA for immunoglobulin G (IgG) antibody.

THERAPY

Measles is usually a self-limited disease, and therapy is mainly supportive. The antiviral drug, ribavirin, has been shown in vitro to have activity against measles virus. In controlled studies in children in other countries, oral ribavirin therapy has appeared to shorten the course of the disease. In the United States, aerosolized ribavirin has been used for severe measles pneumonia, but the experience is anecdotal, and the drug is not approved for this use.

Antibiotics should be used only for proven bacterial complications of measles, such as otitis media.

INFECTIOUS PERIOD

Measles is considered to be contagious from the onset of symptoms through the first day of the rash. Measles appears to be most infectious during the catarrhal stage when diagnosis is most difficult. Once the rash appears, the communicability of the disease rapidly declines.

INFECTION CONTROL

Vaccine.   The live, further-attenuated (Moraten strain) measles vaccine is recommended routinely for all children. Because of the sharp increase in the number of measles cases in recent years, particularly in preschool-age children and children over the ages of 10 years, two doses of measles vaccine for routine immunization are recommended. The initial immunization should be given at 12 to 15 months of age. The second immunization should be given by age 12 years, and in some states may be required at school entry. In epidemic situations the initial immunization may be given to children as young as 6 months of age.

Exclusion from Child Care or Preschool Attendance.   A child with a known or suspected case of measles should be excluded from the child care or preschool setting until 5 days after the onset of the rash.

Recommendations for Other Children.   In a child care center or preschool in which measles has occurred, a program of revaccination with MMR is recommended. Unvaccinated children who are 6 months of age or older also should receive the live measles vaccine. If the vaccine is given within 72 hours of exposure, it may give protection against infection. Immunoglobulin can be administered to unvaccinated children within 6 days of exposure (0.25 mL/kg). If the immunoglobulin is given, live measles vaccine must be delayed for 3 months.

Recommendations for Personnel.   Since susceptible adults are at risk for severe measles infection, it is essential that personnel exposed in a child care or preschool setting know their immunization status, preferably at the time of employment. Although recommendations specific for this setting do not exist, the recommendations for those in medical facilities and for young adults in the college setting are that at the time of employment or enrollment they must have proof of immunity or proof of having had two doses of vaccine. Similar recommendations would seem advisable for personnel in the child care setting who were born after 1956. Once measles has been introduced into the child care or preschool setting, all adults who do not have clear proof of having had measles or of having received two doses of the vaccine should be immunized, especially if born after 1956.

Parental Advice.   Parents of children attending a child care center or preschool in which measles has occurred should be immediately notified and the recommendations, as stated above for their children, should be given to them in written form, and they should be urged to consult their physician immediately. The importance and urgency of this should be stressed, and the contagiousness of measles emphasized. The parents should also understand that children who are susceptible and those who do not comply with the above recommendations will have to be excluded from child care or preschool until the risk of the spread of measles is over, which may mean 4 weeks from the time of the onset of the last case.

54

Salmonella

JOHN D. NELSON, M.D.

CLINICAL MANIFESTATIONS

Diseases caused by *Salmonella* can be classified into four categories: typhoid fever, enteric fever, diarrheal disease, and focal infection.

Typhoid fever is a multisystem illness that may or may not be associated with diarrhea. Enteric fever is the syndrome of diarrhea and high fever often associated with bacteremia. Following bacteremia, which may or may not be symptomatic, *Salmonella* organisms can localize in virtually any organ of the body and cause focal infection. The most common are meningitis, skeletal infections, urinary tract infections, and gallbladder disease.

Gastrointestinal syndromes take several forms. The most common is a mild to moderately severe diarrhea with mushy or soupy consistency of the stools without abdominal pain, tenesmus, or systemic symptoms. There is no fever or low-grade fever. The illness resolves spontaneously within a few days. When heavily contaminated food is ingested, a food poisoning syndrome ensues that is characterized principally by repeated vomiting for a few hours. On occasion, *Salmonella* causes colitis with a dysentery syndrome identical to that seen with *Shigella*. Finally, a failure-to-thrive syndrome occurs in some young infants who have indolent *Salmonella* enteritis without frank diarrhea.

ETIOLOGIC AGENT

Typhoid fever syndrome is caused by *Salmonella typhi, S. paratyphi A, S. paratyphi B,* or *S. cholesae-suis.* The other illnesses are caused by any one of several hundred named species of *Salmonella* that sometimes are referred to collectively as *S. enteritidis*. *S. typhimurium* is the most common species causing gastroenteritis. *Salmonella* organisms are Gram-negative enteric bacilli.

EPIDEMIOLOGY

Source of the Organism.   In typhoid fever the human is the principal reservoir of infection, whereas in other *Salmonella* infections domestic animals, especially chickens, are the reservoir. Pet turtles were a common source of infection until laws were enacted to control the problem.

High-Risk Populations.   Immunocompromised persons are susceptible to infection after ingesting small numbers of salmonellae that would not cause disease in healthy individuals.

Mode of Spread.   Person-to-person spread can occur, but this mode is very unusual except in the case of immunocompromised individuals. The usual source of infection is contaminated food. Eggs and products containing eggs are especially high-risk foods. Because normal individuals are resistant to small numbers of salmonellae, improper cooking and storage of contaminated foods under conditions that promote growth of the organism are important epidemiologic factors. There have been numerous epidemics of *Salmonella* infection from common source-contaminated foods. Person-to-person spread has not been a major problem in child care centers.

Incubation Period.   The incubation period is from 6 to 72 hours for gastroenteritis and from 7 to 14 days for typhoid fever.

DIAGNOSIS

Diagnosis of gastroenteritis is by culture of feces. In typhoid fever the organism can be cultured from blood, bone marrow, urine, or feces. Serologic tests for agglutinins to O and H antigens of *S. typhi* are helpful if the titer is greater than 1:160 and a fourfold or greater change in titer occurs between acute and convalescent serum specimens.

THERAPY

Fluid and electrolyte therapy are given as needed. Antibiotic therapy is given for typhoid fever for 2 weeks. Antibiotics that are effective when the organism is susceptible in vitro are chloramphenicol, ampicillin (intravenously), amoxicillin, trimethoprim-sulfamethoxazole (intravenously or orally), ceftriaxone, cefoperazone, and ciprofloxacin (for adults). Bacteremia and focal infections caused by nontyphoid fever strains of *Salmonella* are treated with the same antibiotics. The usual case of *Salmonella* gastroenteritis is not treated with antibiotics; exceptions are immunocompromised persons, those with chronic inflammatory bowel disease, those with dysentery, and young infants with a failure-to-thrive syndrome.

INFECTIOUS PERIOD

Asymptomatic individuals with *Salmonella* colonization often excrete the organisms for many months; this is particularly true of young infants. *Salmonella* infection in child care centers and preschools has not been a problem, probably because the infectious dose of organisms is high.

INFECTION CONTROL

Vaccine.   The typhoid vaccine available in the United States is heat-phenol-inactivated and has modest efficacy. It is given to family members of a typhoid carrier, selected travelers to endemic areas, selected laboratory workers, and military personnel. (An acetone-inactivated vaccine of better efficacy is given to the military.)

Exclusion from Child Care or Preschool Attendance.   Children should be excluded from child care or preschool attendance until the diarrhea ceases.

Recommendations for Other Children.   There is no action indicated for other children in the child care or preschool setting once one child is known to be infected. Other children with diarrhea should be seen by their physician.

Recommendations for Personnel.   There is no action indicated for personnel in the child care or preschool setting once a child is known to be infected. If more than one case occurs, public health providers should assist in screening food handlers and potentially infected personnel. Personnel who are typhoid carriers are not permitted to work in child care facilities.

Parental Advice.   Parents should be advised that spread of *Salmonella* is extremely unlikely in the child care or preschool setting. If diarrheal symptoms arise, the child should be examined, and the stool cultured, by their health care provider.

55

Scabies

DAVID A. WHITING, M.D.

CLINICAL MANIFESTATIONS

Scabies causes a severe itch that is usually worse at night. Burrows and vesicles are indicative of mite infestation. Burrows are 5 to 15 mm long and often are curved or S-shaped. They usually occur on wrist flexures, on the ulnar border of the hand, and in fingerwebs. They also involve the elbows, anterior axillary folds, nipples, genitalia, natal cleft, and buttocks. Nodular lesions that contain mites sometimes occur, especially on the buttocks and genitalia. Secondary lesions with small urticarial papules and excoriations and crusts may occur on the abdomen, thighs, and buttocks.

In infants, bullous lesions can occur on the palms and soles. Secondary infection is common, due to group A *Streptococcus pyogenes* or *Staphylococcus aureus*. Nodules can be very persistent. Lesions are rare on the scalp and usually only occur in infants.

ETIOLOGIC AGENT

Scabies is caused by *Sarcoptes scabiei* var. *hominis*. This is a white, hemispherical mite with four pairs of short legs. The average size of the female is 0.4 to 0.3 mm.

EPIDEMIOLOGY

Source of the Organism. The human body is the only known source of this mite.

High-Risk Populations. Populations at high risk of infection are those in congested housing with overcrowded sleeping quarters.

Scabies can be widespread in immunosuppressed individuals or in mentally defective patients who do not scratch.

Mode of Spread.   Spread is from human to human. The mite can only survive up to a few days off the human body, so spread by bedding and clothing is rare.

Incubation Period.   The incubation period from egg to adult is 14 to 17 days.

DIAGNOSIS

Definitive diagnosis depends on the microscopic demonstration of a scabies mite from a burrow on the skin. Supporting evidence is provided by an intense pruritic dermatosis affecting the wrists, finger-webs, elbows, axillary folds, nipples, buttocks, and genitalia, or palms and soles in infants, and by a history of contact with other cases.

THERAPY

Outpatient therapy is adequate.

The traditional treatment is 1% lindane lotion applied from the neck to the toes for 6 to 8 hours. It can be applied to older children and adults for 8 to 12 hours and to small children for a maximum of 6 hours. Due to possible toxicity to the central nervous system, it should not be used in infants, nor in very sick children, nor in children with inflamed and secondarily infected skin. The treatment should not be repeated in less than 7 days, the 1% strength of lindane should not be exceeded, and as little as possible should be used. A safer and more effective treatment for all ages is 5% permethrin topical cream (Elimite), applied once from head to foot, for 8 to 14 hours. Another safe treatment for small children is 3% to 10% sulfur in Eucerin applied to the whole body from the neck to the toes for three successive nights. Normal laundering of clothes and bedding in a domestic washing machine and dryer is all that is required after treatment.

INFECTIOUS PERIOD

The condition is infectious as long as living mites are present on the patient.

INFECTION CONTROL

Vaccine.   None available.

Exclusion from Child Care or Preschool Attendance.   The child should be isolated for 24 hours after adequate treatment.

Recommendations for Other Children.   Once one child is infected, it is recommended that all children in the center be treated as though infected.

Recommendations for Personnel.   Treatment is recommended for all personnel in the center.

Parental Advice.   Parents and family contacts of an affected child should be treated.

56

Shigella

JOHN D. NELSON, M.D.

CLINICAL MANIFESTATIONS

The principal illness caused by *Shigella* species is diarrhea. Rare manifestations are bacteremia, conjunctivitis, pneumonia, skeletal infections, meningitis, urinary tract infection, hemolytic-uremic syndrome, and vaginitis.

There are three clinical syndromes of diarrheal disease caused by *Shigella*. The first is the classic bacillary dysentery syndrome manifested by low-grade or moderate fever, cramping abdominal pain, tenesmus, and frequent small-volume stools containing mucus, pus, and sometimes blood. Untreated with antibiotics, it persists for a week or longer.

The second syndrome is the small bowel diarrheal illness. It is characterized by the abrupt onset of high fever, sometimes associated with a convulsion, vomiting one or two times, and large-volume explosive watery stools. There is spontaneous cure in 24 to 72 hours.

The third syndrome is the small bowel illness just described progressing to dysentery. During the watery diarrhea phase, one can predict this sequence if pus cells are seen in microscopic examination of the stool.

ETIOLOGIC AGENT

Shigella is a Gram-negative enteric bacillus whose only natural host is the human. There are four species. *S. flexneri* is most common in developing countries, while *S. sonnei* predominates in developed countries. *S. dysenteriae* is uncommon but produces virulent disease often complicated by hemolytic-uremic syndrome. *S. boydii* is rare. There are several serotypes of each of the species except *S. sonnei.*

EPIDEMIOLOGY

Source of the Organism. Humans. There are no animal reservoirs of *Shigella* infection.

High-Risk Populations. Crowded, unsanitary conditions and lack of refrigeration for food are risk factors. Child day care populations are a particularly high-risk group. Incidence of disease is also high in institutions for individuals with mental retardation or other disabilities. Sexual transmission can occur, especially with oral-anal contact.

Mode of Spread. Spread is from person to person by the fecal-oral route either directly or indirectly through contaminated food or fluids. *Shigella* organisms are easily spread by direct fecal-oral contact because the number of organisms needed to produce disease is small. Rodents, flies, and cockroaches have been implicated in the mechanical transfer of organisms. The chronic carrier state is unusual except in malnourished individuals.

Incubation Period. The interval from ingestion of organisms to onset of symptoms is usually 12 to 48 hours but can be as long as 7 days.

DIAGNOSIS

The diagnosis is based on culture of the organism from feces. There is no rapid antigen detection test available, and there are no useful serologic tests.

THERAPY

Antibiotic therapy of the dysenteric form of illness is effective in shortening the period of morbidity and of infectivity. Antibiotic resistance is common in *Shigella* organisms, so in vitro susceptibility testing is important. Trimethoprim-sulfamethoxazole is most commonly used; other drugs effective when the strain is susceptible in vitro are ampicillin, chloramphenicol, tetracycline, nalidixic acid, and fluoroquinolones. The latter are not approved for use in children.

The duration of antibiotic therapy is 5 days. Fluid and electrolyte therapy is accomplished with oral rehydration solutions or intravenous fluids. Severe abdominal pain is relieved with antispasmodics, but these drugs should not be used repeatedly because they prolong the duration of diarrhea.

INFECTIOUS PERIOD

Shigella cannot be recovered in stool cultures 1 to 4 days (average, 2 days) after start of antibiotic therapy. Untreated patients carry the organism for 7 to 30 days and rarely longer than that.

INFECTION CONTROL

Vaccine.   There have been many candidate vaccines tested, but no vaccine is available for use.

Exclusion from Child Care or Preschool Attendance.   The child should not attend child care or preschool until completion of 5 days of antibiotics or until two successive stool cultures are negative.

Recommendations for Other Children and Personnel.   No action is required for a single case. If there are multiple cases, stool cultures should be obtained on all children and personnel to identify and treat infected individuals. Handwashing practices should be reviewed and improved when necessary.

Parental Advice.   Other family members are at risk of becoming infected from children. If diarrhea develops, parents should inform their physician that their child has shigellosis.

57

Staphylococcus
(Impetigo, Boils, Cellulitis, Osteomyelitis, Endocarditis)

RICHARD F. JACOBS, M.D.

CLINICAL MANIFESTATIONS

Staphylococcal infections are commonly associated with diseases of the skin (bullous impetigo, furuncles, or boils), bones and joints (osteomyelitis, septic arthritis), pneumonia, and endocarditis. They cause a wide variety of localized suppurative (pus-producing) diseases but also may cause sepsis or toxin-mediated diseases (toxic shock syndrome, staphylococcal scalded skin syndrome) or food poisoning. The most common infection in child care centers and preschools involves the skin and varies from impetigo to furuncles (subcutaneous abscess), folliculitis (hair follicles), cellulitis, and wound infections. Staphylococci are also a frequent cause of pyogenic lymphadenitis seen most commonly in the cervical area in children. Respiratory tract infections including otitis media, sinusitis, and mastoiditis have variable involvement by staphylococci, but this organism can cause severe extensive pneumonia.

Staphylococci are the most common cause of osteomyelitis and septic arthritis in children and should be suspected in children with a limp and fever, refusal to walk, and swollen extremities or joints and in younger children with fever and irritability but no other obvious source of infection. Staphylococcal food poisoning is characterized by the abrupt onset of severe cramps, vomiting, and diarrhea. The short incubation (30 minutes to 7 hours), short duration of illness, epidemiology, and lack of fever help distinguish it from the other causes of food poisoning. Staphylococcal toxic shock syndrome is an acute febrile illness with myalgias, vomiting, diarrhea, pharyngitis, rash (diffuse macular erythroderma with desquamation), and mucous membrane–conjunctival redness. Syncope (orthostatic or dizziness) due to hypoperfusion or hypotension complete the criteria.

ETIOLOGIC AGENT

Staphylococcus aureus is a Gram-positive coccus that appears in grape-like clusters that grow on most bacteriologic media and produce an enzyme, coagulase, which is important in tissue breakdown and pus formation. The organisms multiply aerobically and anaerobically, are resistant to heating (up to 122° F), drying, and high salt concentrations and can survive indefinitely on surfaces, in clothing, and on fomites. *S. aureus* is one of three staphylococcal species.

EPIDEMIOLOGY

Source of the Organism.   Staphylococci are ubiquitous and are found on most environmental surfaces. The human is a common source of staphylococci via the anterior nares (airborne spread), skin, and infected sites; therefore, staphylococcal carriers can spread the organism.

High-Risk Populations.   Newborns, immunodeficient children, and children with recent surgical placement of indwelling devices (ventriculoperitoneal shunts) are high-risk populations. Crowding, poor hygiene, or inadequate infection control measures are predisposing factors.

Mode of Spread.   Multiple routes: contact with infected persons, contact with asymptomatic carriers, airborne spread, and contact through contaminated objects.

Incubation Period.   Usually 1 to 10 days for skin and soft tissue infections. Other staphylococcal infections may have an incubation period from days to weeks.

DIAGNOSIS

The presence of purulent drainage, bullous lesions, or bone/joint infections should make staphylococcal infection very likely. Gram-stain smears of material from suppurative lesions can provide a presumptive diagnosis. Culture of infected material remains the confirmatory test.

THERAPY

The severity, extent of involvement, organ system involvement, and age of the child dictate the necessity for hospitalization and parenteral antibiotic therapy. For superficial infections, aggressive local care and topical antibiotics may be sufficient. Abscesses should be surgically drained. The mainstay of antistaphylococcal therapy remains antibiotics. Most mild to moderate staphylococcal infections can be treated with 7 to 10 days of oral antibiotics. The site of infection in serious staphylococcal disease (pneumonia, endocarditis) dictates the duration of intravenous therapy.

INFECTIOUS PERIOD

Patients with draining staphylococcal lesions should be isolated (avoidance) for 48 hours from starting effective therapy and until the active drainage has diminished.

INFECTION CONTROL

Vaccine.   None available.

Exclusion from Child Care or Preschool Attendance.   The child with staphylococcal infection should not attend child care or preschool for at least 48 hours after the initiation of appropriate antibiotics and until drainage of infected material has stopped or diminished to the point that barrier protection is effective.

Recommendations for Other Children.   The best recommendation is prevention of spread. This includes proper disinfection procedures, good handwashing, avoidance of drainage, improved hygiene, and reduced crowding. Children with any sign of early staphylococcal infection should be referred to their pediatrician. In situations of multiple cases (outbreak), all infected children should be referred to their pediatrician, and consideration of temporary closure of the facility should be discussed until the infections are controlled. Good handwashing is critical in an outbreak situation.

Recommendations for Personnel.   The involved personnel should implement contact isolation, improved handwashing, and early recognition and treatment of infected children. No routine cultures or antibiotic therapy (oral or topical) is indicated for contacts unless an epidemic occurs.

Parental Advice.   Parents should institute close observation for early signs of staphylococcal infection with aggressive recognition and treatment. Symptomatic children or relatively asymptomatic children with clinical evidence of staphylococcal disease should be taken to their local pediatrician for diagnosis and therapy.

58

Streptococcus
(Cellulitis, Impetigo, Pharyngitis)

RICHARD F. JACOBS, M.D.

CLINICAL MANIFESTATIONS

The most common illnesses associated with group A beta hemolytic streptococci (GABS) are pharyngitis and impetigo. Pharyngitis varies greatly in severity from subclinical (30 to 50%) to severe with high fever, nausea, vomiting, and collapse (less than 10%). The onset is acute with sore throat, fever, headache, or abdominal pain. The pharynx and tonsils usually appear red, swollen with exudate (50 to 90%) and palate petechiae. Exudate usually appears around day 2, is whitish-yellow, and appears early as discrete patches with progression to confluence. Swollen, tender cervical lymph nodes are found in 40 to 60% of cases. Clinical manifestations usually subside spontaneously in 3 to 5 days unless suppurative complications (peritonsillar abscess) occur. Nonsuppurative complications may occur in approximately 10 days (nephritis) to 18 days (acute rheumatic fever). An infantile form (children less than 2 years of age) may occur with GABS and is more prolonged with persistent nasal discharge, fever, and lymphadenopathy. Scarlet fever represents a manifestation of GABS with a red papular rash on the trunk, spreading peripherally within several hours to days. The typical "sandpaper" rash fades on pressure, usually desquamates, has petechiae in joint folds (Pastia's lines), and is associated with a strawberry tongue and red swollen lips.

A scarlatiniform rash also may be associated with the most common cutaneous manifestation of GABS, impetigo. It usually appears within 10 days of GABS infection. Impetigo patients are usually afebrile and asymptomatic. The lesions most commonly occur over excoriated areas, such as insect bites, where GABS is introduced into normal skin. The skin lesions usually start as superficial vesicles and erythematous pustules and progress to thick yellowish crusted lesions that last from days to several weeks. Secondary infection with staphylococci is common and may lead to purulent pustules or cellulitis. Nephritis is the most common nonsuppurative complication and has a latent period of around 3 weeks. This type of superficial pyoderma may complicate abnormal skin (eczema) or follow trauma or burns.

Other infections associated with GABS include more serious skin infections (cellulitis, erysipelas), otitis media, sinusitis, and pneumonia.

ETIOLOGIC AGENT

GABS are Gram-positive cocci that form chains that produce clear hemolysis (beta) on blood agar plates. Presumptive differentiation from other streptococci can be provided by GABS sensitivity (inhibition) to a bacitracin disc on blood agar. More than 80 different types of GABS are known. They are separated on the basis of different serologically distinct surface proteins, M proteins. Some GABS strains are known to be rheumatogenic and cause outbreaks of acute rheumatic fever.

EPIDEMIOLOGY

Source of the Organism. Upper respiratory tract and skin lesions are the most common source of GABS. Contaminated food or milk have caused some outbreaks, and anal carriage has been linked to several hospital outbreaks.

High-Risk Populations. Crowding, poor hygiene, and improper handling of infected children are associated with the greatest risk of transmission and predisposition to GABS disease. Children with diagnosed acute rheumatic fever are a high-risk population for acquisition and recurrences.

Mode of Spread. Close contact with an infected individual by direct projection of large respiratory droplets (not aerosols) or physical transfer of respiratory secretions or infected skin lesions.

Incubation Period.   Streptococcal pharyngitis: 12 hours to 4 days. Streptococcal impetigo: few days to several weeks (usually around 10 days).

DIAGNOSIS

The clinical appearance and epidemiology should provide the care-taker with a high degree of suspicion. Culture of the tonsillopha-ryngeal bed or infected skin lesions with the isolation of GABS is confirmatory. Due to the time frame for this procedure, a number of rapid detection kits for identifying GABS pharyngitis in minutes to hours have been developed. Caution should be used in interpreting negative tests for purposes of treatment in areas where rheumatic fever is a problem. Cultures should be obtained on these cases to confirm a negative rapid test. Serologic tests (blood antibody test) may be helpful retrospectively.

THERAPY

The therapy for GABS pharyngitis is antibiotics, with penicillin the drug of choice. It is usually given as a single intramuscular injection of long-acting penicillin or oral penicillin three or four times a day for 10 full days. Erythromycin given four times a day is the regimen of choice for penicillin-allergic children. For GABS impetigo, local care with abrasive cleansing of lesions is effective. Oral penicillin may be beneficial in children with numerous lesions. Hospitaliza-tion is only required for suppurative (peritonsillar abscess, cellulitis, erysipelas) or nonsuppurative complications.

INFECTIOUS PERIOD

The period of maximal infectivity is in the acute phase of the illness with most secondary cases occurring within 2 weeks of acquisition.

INFECTION CONTROL

Vaccine.   None available.

Exclusion from Child Care or Preschool Attendance.   At least until 24 hours after appropriate therapy is started and they are afebrile.

Recommendations for Other Children.   The best current control measure is prompt recognition and treatment of GABS infections.

Contacts with recent or current clinical evidence of GABS infection should be cultured and treated if culture-positive, to reduce transmission and nonsuppurative complications. Siblings do have a higher acquisition rate (approximately 25%; 50% in epidemics).

Recommendations for Personnel.   In nonepidemic situations, symptomatic personnel should be cultured and treated if positive. Screening asymptomatic children or personnel, especially in nonepidemic situations, is not warranted. In epidemics or in family situations in which a child has acute rheumatic fever, selective cultures of contacts may be warranted.

Parental Advice.   If the child becomes symptomatic, he or she should be taken to the local pediatrician for culture and treatment if positive. If the child has a previous diagnosis of acute rheumatic fever and a history of close contact with a proven GABS patient, he or she should be taken to the local pediatrician for culture and initiation of prophylactic antibiotics to prevent recurrences of rheumatic fever.

59

Syphilis

THOMAS A. BELL, M.D., M.P.H.

CLINICAL MANIFESTATIONS

The manifestations of syphilis are myriad. In adults, primary syphilis infection is accompanied by a painless chancre at the site of inoculation, of which the host may be unaware.

The secondary stage has diverse manifestations that include a generalized exanthem that may affect the palms and soles, malaise, alopecia, condylomata lata, mucous patches, generalized lymphadenopathy, and mild neurologic symptoms. In pregnant women, syphilis often causes miscarriage.

Congenital infection has an even greater variety of stigmata. They include a vesicular or bullous exanthem, a papulosquamous eruption, condylomata lata, mucoid nasal discharge ("snuffles"), mucous patches, osteochondritis, anemia, pneumonia, hepatitis, and meningovasculitis.

Tertiary syphilis involves damage to the heart and central nervous system.

Nonvenereal syphilis occurs in some developing countries but not in the United States. It may resemble infection with the closely related treponeme that causes yaws.

ETIOLOGIC AGENT

Treponema pallidum is a spirochete that is difficult to study because it cannot be propagated in vitro. Numerous antigenic variants may exist.

EPIDEMIOLOGY

Source of the Organism.   In adults, coitus is the only important means of transmission. In theory, *T. pallidum* may be spread non-venereally by contact with infected blood or mucocutaneous lesions of congenital or secondary syphilis.

Newborns may acquire the organism from the mothers, either during delivery or, more rarely, while still in utero. In older children, acquisition is almost exclusively sexual.

High-Risk Populations.   Syphilis in pregnant women is usually associated with youth, poverty, and psychosocial problems. Older children with syphilis tend to come from similar backgrounds because they promulgate sexual abuse by infected persons.

Mode of Spread.   In adults, almost all spread is venereal. However, the organism may be transmitted in blood, and lesions of secondary syphilis, such as mucous patches of the mouth and condylomata lata, are also infectious, as they are in children with congenital syphilis. In practice, such nonvenereal transmission is rare except in developing countries with endemic nonvenereal syphilis.

Incubation Period.   The incubation period of venereal syphilis is 10 to 90 days.

DIAGNOSIS

The primary means of diagnosis is by the Venereal Disease Research Laboratory (VDRL) serologic test, which, if positive, requires confirmation with a more specific "treponemal test." Diagnosis in the newborn is more complicated because maternal antibody acquired transplacentally may obscure the infant's immune response for several months. Confirmation of cerebrospinal infection requires lumbar puncture to obtain specimens and is indicated in the evaluation of congenital syphilis. Organisms in chancres, condylomata lata, mucous patches, and the infected nasal secretions of newborns may be visualized with dark-field microscopy.

THERAPY

The treatment of choice is intramuscular benzathine penicillin. One dose of 2.4 million units is usually sufficient for the primary stage, but three doses given at weekly intervals are required for later stages. Infants require either injections of aqueous procaine penicillin, 25,000 units/kg/dose intramuscularly twice daily for 10 days, or aqueous crystalline penicillin G, 25,000 units/kg/dose intravenously twice daily for 10 days. Hospitalization is required for intravenous therapy of congenital syphilis and is usually indicated for intramuscular therapy. It also may be indicated for management of sexually abused children. For the treatment of persons allergic to penicillin, desensitization should be attempted. Erythromycin and tetracyclines (only for older children) may be used if desensitization is unsuccessful.

INFECTIOUS PERIOD

The infected person is no longer contagious within hours of receiving effective treatment. Without therapy, the period of contagiousness may last for months.

INFECTION CONTROL

Vaccine.   None available.

Exclusion from Child Care or Preschool Attendance.   The child may return to day care the day after being given effective treatment.

Recommendations for Other Children.   The risk of nonsexual transmission to other children is low but real. If the child was infected elsewhere, no further measures for control of infection are necessary after the child has been treated, but the child may be subject to emotional and behavioral problems.

Recommendations for Personnel.   The risk of transmission to personnel is low but real.

Parental Advice.   If the infection was not acquired at the child care center or preschool, other parents should not be informed because the infection is stigmatizing and the risk of transmission is negligible. Detection of the infection may have forensic implications for the child care center or preschool.

60

Tinea capitis, corporis, cruris, and pedis
(Ringworm, Athlete's Foot, Jock Itch)

DAVID A. WHITING, M.D.

CLINICAL MANIFESTATIONS

Tinea capitis: This condition causes partial hair loss. Patches vary from well-circumscribed, round lesions to vague and irregular areas of hair thinning that are difficult to detect. Redness and scaling may be present and can range from mild to severe. In the United States, affected hairs are generally broken off flush with the scalp and appear as black dots, due to infection by *Trichophyton tonsurans,* but occasionally are grayish-white and are broken off 1 to 3 mm above the skin surface, due to *Microsporum canis* infection. Inflammatory types of scalp ringworm sometimes cause fluctuant, boggy, purulent masses associated with hair loss, a so-called kerion infection. The sex incidence of tinea capitis is equal. Tinea capitis peaks at age 5 and usually disappears at puberty, although black-dot ringworm and favus can affect adults.

Tinea corporis: This condition usually starts as small, reddish, itchy, scaly macules that gradually expand outward, clearing in the middle, forming annular lesions with scaly margins and clear centers. Sometimes, new lesions form in the middle of an expanding lesion and spread outward to cause concentric rings. The lesions are usually single but, if multiple, are often unilateral or at least asymmetrical.

Tinea cruris: This condition is rare before puberty. It causes itchy, reddish, and scaly lesions in the groin and on the adjacent thighs, and may extend around the anus onto the buttocks, with advancing scaly borders and central clearing. Some types of tinea cruris, especially those due to *Trichophyton rubrum*, may produce large, circinate lesions around the genitalia.

Tinea pedis: This condition is also rare before puberty. There are three types, namely, the interdigital, the vesicular, and the moccasin. The interdigital type usually starts in the lateral toe webs and spreads medially, and the vesicular type generally affects the instep. The lesions are usually unilateral and asymmetrical, except for the moccasin type of tinea pedis in which both feet are affected by a diffuse, scaling rash. Tinea pedis is aggravated by heat and sweating.

ETIOLOGIC AGENT

Tinea infections are caused by one or more of the dermatophytes, which are imperfect fungi (phylum Deuteromycetes) belonging to genera *Trichophyton*, *Microsporum*, and *Epidermophyton*. Infection is confined to keratin, the dead horn of skin, hair, and nails. At present, 39 species of dermatophytes are recognized in humans: 21 in the genus *Trichophyton*, 16 in the genus *Microsporum*, and 2 in the genus *Epidermophyton*. Almost all human infections are caused by 16 species, only 5 of which are common in the United States, namely, *Trichophyton rubrum*, *T. tonsurans*, *T. mentagrophytes*, *Epidermophyton floccosum*, and *Microsporum canis*. Infrequent causes of disease are *T. schoenleinii*, *T. violaceum*, *T. verrucosum*, *T. megninii*, *T. terrestre*, *M. audouinii*, *M. distortum*, *M. gypseum*, *M. ferrugineum*, *M. nanum*, or *M. fulvum*.

EPIDEMIOLOGY

Source of the Organism.   Anthropophilic (human): *T. tonsurans*, *M. audouinii*, *T. rubrum*, *E. floccosum*. Zoophilic (animals): *M. canis*, *T. mentagrophytes*, and *T. verrucosum*. Geophilic (soil): *M. gypseum*. Patterns of infection in tinea capitis: small-spore ectothrix: *M. audouinii*, *M. canis*, and *M. ferrugineum;* large-spore ectothrix: *T. mentagrophytes* (*interdigitale*), *T. verrucosum*, and *T. megninii;* endothrix: *T. tonsurans*, *T. violaceum*, *T. soudanense*, *T. gourvilii*, and *T. yaoundei*. Favic pattern in hair (no spores): *T. schoenleinii*.

High-Risk Populations.   Children especially, aged 2 to 20 years. Overcrowding with head-to-head contact predisposes to tinea capitis. Contact with cattle and horses can result in animal ringworm.

Mode of Spread.   Tinea is spread by direct contact with humans, animals, or soil or by indirect contact with contaminated combs, brushes, headgear, towels, pillows, bedding, or clothing.

Incubation Period.   It takes 3 to 5 days for microscopic infection and 2 to 3 weeks for clinical manifestations to develop. The condition can spread for 3 to 4 months, and then after a refractory period, spontaneous regression may occur.

DIAGNOSIS

The diagnosis is made on the clinical appearance, positive Wood's light in some cases of tinea capitis, microscopic demonstration of fungal hyphae in potassium hydroxide preparations of skin, hair, and nails, and fungal culture.

THERAPY

All treatment is managed on an outpatient basis.

Tinea capitis: The preferred treatment is griseofulvin taken orally in a dose of 10 to 15 mg/kg body weight for 6 to 12 weeks. Second-choice therapy is ketoconazole, 3.3 to 6.6 mg/kg body weight for 6 to 12 weeks. Itraconazole is also effective. To prevent cross infection, clip the affected hairs and shampoo with selenium sulfide 2.5% twice weekly, or apply a topical antifungal preparation, as for tinea corporis, daily.

Tinea corporis: Topical clotrimazole (Lotrimin), econazole (Spectazole), ketoconazole (Nizoral), miconazole nitrate (Monistat-Derm), oxiconazole (Oxistat), sulconazole (Exelderm), naftifine (Naftin), or ciclopirox olamine (Loprox) can be used once or twice daily. A salicylic acid and benzoic acid combination (Antinea) can be used. In severe cases, oral griseofulvin (see above) can be used for 2 to 4 weeks.

Tinea pedis: In the inflammatory stage, soaks with Burow's solution or potassium permanganate solution can be used. The fungal infection can be treated topically as for tinea corporis, and undecylenate powder (Desenex) can be sprinkled in the socks. Oral griseofulvin may be necessary (see above).

Tinea cruris: Topical antifungal therapy as for tinea corporis. In addition, oral griseofulvin may be necessary in extensive cases.

INFECTIOUS PERIOD

The patient is infectious as long as organisms can be found invading the tissue on potassium hydroxide examination or culture. Tinea capitis may persist from 3 months to several years. Tinea corporis may persist or recur for many years, as may tinea cruris or tinea pedis.

INFECTION CONTROL

Vaccine.   None available.

Exclusion from Child Care or Preschool Attendance.   No isolation needed after effective treatment is started.

Recommendations for Other Children.   Watch for development of infection and treat if necessary.

Recommendations for Personnel.   Watch for development of infection and treat if necessary.

Parental Advice.   Parents should be notified that there has been a case or cases of tinea in the center. They should watch for the development of infection and seek medical attention for diagnosis and therapy as necessary.

61

Toxocara

ANDREA J. RUFF, M.D.

CLINICAL MANIFESTATIONS

The clinical manifestations of toxocariasis depend on the size of the infecting dose of larvae. Individuals who ingest small numbers of larvae may remain asymptomatic, while those ingesting large numbers may develop visceral larva migrans. Characteristic findings in visceral larva migrans include fever, hepatomegaly, eosinophilia, and hypergammaglobulinemia. A cough, wheezing, and pulmonary infiltrates also may be present, and, rarely, myocarditis or encephalitis may develop. *Toxocara* larvae may invade the eye, producing retinal granulomas or endophthalmitis and occasionally resulting in blindness. Visceral and ocular larva migrans are rarely observed concurrently.

ETIOLOGIC AGENT

Toxocariasis is caused by *Toxocara canis* and *Toxocara cati,* common roundworms of dogs and cats; the majority of cases in this country are due to *T. canis.* Less often, visceral larva migrans can be caused by infection with other helminths. Dogs and cats are commonly infected by *Toxocara* spp., with most having acquired the infection early in life. Infected animals harbor adult worms that pass eggs in the feces. After several weeks of embryonation in soil, infective larvae develop within the eggs. Humans acquire toxocariasis by ingesting embryonated eggs that hatch in the small intestine, releasing larvae. After penetrating the intestinal wall, the larvae begin to migrate throughout host tissues. The larvae cannot complete their normal development in humans, and therefore they do not mature into adult worms capable of passing eggs in human feces. After a variable period of migration, the larvae within a human host will eventually die.

EPIDEMIOLOGY

Source of the Organism.   *Toxocara* infections occur in both temperate and tropical areas, being most prevalent where dogs are common and hygiene is poor. Eggs passed in dog and cat feces become infective in approximately 3 weeks and may persist in the environment for months. Parks and playgrounds are often heavily contaminated, providing a ready source of infective eggs. Ingestion of even small amounts of dirt may result in the transmission of relatively large numbers of eggs.

High-Risk Populations.   Children are at higher risk of acquiring toxocariasis because they are more likely to eat dirt and to contaminate their hands and food with soil.

Mode of Spread.   Humans acquire *Toxocara* infections by ingesting soil containing infective eggs. Transmission is generally the result of geophagia in young children and of exposure to hands or possibly food contaminated with infective eggs in older children. Since humans do not pass *Toxocara* eggs in their feces, person-to-person transmission of the infection does not occur.

Incubation Period.   The time interval between acquisition of infection and the development of visceral larva migrans appears to be quite variable, ranging from days to months. Although not well-established, the incubation period prior to the development of ocular larva migrans appears to be longer, ranging from months to years.

DIAGNOSIS

Visceral larva migrans should be considered in any child with a history of geophagia or exposure to dogs who presents with hypereosinophilia and hypergammaglobulinemia. Elevated titers of isohemagglutinins to the A and B blood group antigens are also often present in toxocariasis. The diagnosis can be confirmed by demonstration of larvae in a liver biopsy; however, the larvae may be difficult to find, and a negative liver biopsy does not rule out the diagnosis. An enzyme-linked immunosorbent assay, available at the Centers for Disease Control, can be used to establish a serologic diagnosis.

THERAPY

To date, no controlled studies have proven the effectiveness of any therapeutic regimen against toxocariasis. However, treatment with either diethylcarbamazine or thiabendazole has been reported to decrease symptoms in some patients. Mebendazole has also been used to treat toxocariasis and appears to be associated with fewer adverse effects. All of these drugs are considered investigational for this condition by the U.S. Food and Drug Administration. Corticosteroids have also been used in individuals with significant involvement of the heart or central nervous system. Optimal therapy for ocular larva migrans has not been well-established; past approaches have included the use of antihelminthic agents and corticosteroids.

INFECTIOUS PERIOD

Humans with toxocariasis are not infectious.

INFECTION CONTROL

Vaccine.   None available.

Exclusion from Child Care or Preschool Attendance.   A child with toxocariasis cannot transmit the infection to other individuals and therefore does not need to be kept out of any child care or preschool setting.

Recommendations for Other Children.   Other children in the center will acquire toxocariasis only if they ingest soil containing infective eggs. Given the high prevalence of infective eggs in most communities, children should not be allowed to eat dirt, and good hygiene should be enforced.

Recommendations for Personnel.   Personnel should minimize their exposure to infective *Toxocara* eggs by maintaining good hygienic practices. They should also attempt to diminish children's exposure by not letting them eat dirt and by covering play areas such as sandboxes in order to prevent animals from defecating in them.

Parental Advice.   Parents should be reassured that a child with toxocariasis will not transmit the infection to their own children. The mode of spread should be explained to them, emphasizing the need to keep their children from eating dirt and to properly dispose of cat and dog feces. Pet owners should be encouraged to seek expert advice from a veterinarian regarding treatment of puppies and kittens with appropriate antihelminthics to avoid exposing their children to *Toxocara.*

62

Trichuris trichiura
(Whipworm)

ANDREA J. RUFF, M.D.

CLINICAL MANIFESTATIONS

The clinical manifestations associated with *Trichuris trichiura* infections depend on the intensity and duration of the infection and on the age of the host. Light infections are generally asymptomatic. Heavy infections, most often seen in young children, may be associated with a diffuse colitis, chronic diarrhea, and rectal prolapse.

ETIOLOGIC AGENT

T. trichiura is an intestinal nematode also known as the human whipworm. Humans acquire trichuriasis by ingesting infective-stage ova derived from human feces. The eggs hatch in the small intestine, and the larvae mature into adult worms located primarily in the cecum and ascending colon. Female worms produce eggs that are passed in the feces; if exposed to favorable conditions of soil, moisture, and temperature, the eggs embryonate, developing into infective-stage ova within 11 to 30 days. Eggs that have not embryonated are not infective.

EPIDEMIOLOGY

Source of the Organism. Although *T. trichiura* infections are found worldwide, they are most prevalent in the tropics, particularly in overcrowded communities with poor sanitation. Infective-stage eggs are found in soil contaminated with human feces, and infection may result from direct ingestion of soil or indirectly through contaminated hands, utensils or food.

High-Risk Populations.   In areas where *T. trichiura* is endemic, children are often infected by the time they are 2 years old, and reinfection is common. Infection of young children is often a consequence of geophagia, whereas older children and adults are more likely to be infected through indirect contamination.

Mode of Spread.   Transmission occurs through ingestion of infective eggs. Since *T. trichiura* eggs are not infective until after they have embryonated in the soil, person-to-person transmission of the infection does not occur.

Incubation Period.   The interval between the acquisition of *T. trichiura* and the passage of eggs in the feces is approximately 90 days. The time from infection to the development of symptoms has not been well-established.

DIAGNOSIS

The diagnosis can be made fairly easily by microscopic stool examination with detection of the characteristic eggs. In symptomatic individuals it may be important to quantitate the intensity of the worm burden, since significant symptoms are rarely associated with light *T. trichiura* infections and may indicate the presence of other pathogenic processes. Adult worms may be seen on proctoscopy or during rectal prolapse in heavy infections.

THERAPY

In countries where trichuriasis is endemic and where reinfection is common, light infections are often untreated. However, in this country, *T. trichiura* infections are generally treated with mebendazole given in an oral dose of 100 mg twice daily for 3 days. Although mebendazole appears to be fairly effective with low toxicity, data regarding its use in children younger than 2 years are limited.

INFECTIOUS PERIOD

If untreated, trichuriasis may persist for many years.

INFECTION CONTROL

Vaccine.   None available.

Exclusion from Child Care or Preschool Attendance.   Children with trichuriasis do not need to be isolated or kept out of any child care setting. Human-to-human transmission does not appear to occur, and *T. trichiura* eggs are not immediately infectious when passed in feces.

Recommendations for Other Children.   Other children in the center will become infected with *T. trichiura* only if they ingest eggs that have embryonated after several weeks in the soil. If fecal contamination of the environment is a problem in the center, children must be kept from ingesting infected dirt either directly or indirectly through contaminated hands or food.

Recommendations for Personnel.   Inadvertent contamination of food, utensils, and hands with soil containing infective eggs should be avoided. Personnel should maintain good handwashing practices and ensure the appropriate disposal of fecal material.

Parental Advice.   The mode of spread should be explained to parents, reassuring them that person-to-person transmission does not occur. In *T. trichiura* endemic areas, the need to discourage geophagia among young children and to encourage good hygiene among older children should be emphasized to parents.

63

Tuberculosis

JANE D. SIEGEL, M.D.

CLINICAL MANIFESTATIONS

Approximately 40 to 50% of infections in infants less than 1 year of age, and 80 to 90% of infections in older children will cause no recognizable symptoms or merely a low-grade fever. This is referred to as "tuberculous infection." Symptomatic disease may develop within a few weeks of the initial infection or many years later when the body's normal immune system becomes suppressed either by another disease process or by chemotherapeutic agents used to treat the disease (e.g., human immunodeficiency virus infection, leukemia, tumors, bone marrow, or organ transplant). The presence of active disease in one or more organs is referred to as "tuberculosis." Overall, only 5 to 15% of patients with tuberculous infection will become ill with tuberculosis. Pulmonary disease is the most common manifestation of tuberculous infection. Children with primary pulmonary tuberculosis have fever, cough, poor appetite, weight loss, and occasionally wheezing. Enlarged hilar and sometimes paratracheal lymph nodes and small focal or lobar infiltrates are present on chest x-ray. Some children may have persistent fever, weight loss, and night sweats without a cough, but pulmonary infiltrates are present on chest x-ray. Infants and young children usually do not have cavitary lesions observed in adolescents and adults. Infection of the cervical lymph nodes (scrofula) is another early form of disease caused by *Mycobacterium tuberculosis.*

Less frequently, the mycobacteria may spread from the original site of infection in the lungs through the lymphatic system and bloodstream to other organs and cause "extrapulmonary" tuberculosis. The clinical picture that results is determined by host susceptibility and by the quantity of mycobacteria that are released. The most serious complications of tuberculous infection are miliary tuberculosis and meningitis, both of which occur at 3 to 6 months following the initial infection. The onset of miliary disease may be insidious or abrupt with a rapid progression of respiratory symptoms and multiple organ involvement. The chest x-ray pattern of uniform distribution throughout both lung fields is diagnostic. Meningitis develops in approximately 1 of every 300 primary infections. Children 4 months to 6 years of age are at greatest risk for this complication. There is a high case fatality rate, and many serious neurologic sequelae occur in the survivors if tuberculous meningitis is not recognized and treated early. The case fatality rate increases with the more advanced stages of disease at the time of initiation of antituberculous therapy. Other sites of disease that may occur at least 7 to 12 months after initial infection include bones and joints, most notably the vertebrae (Pott's disease), kidneys, genital tract, eyes, and skin. Delayed recognition and treatment of these later complications may lead to chronic failure to gain weight and to deformities. These more extensive types of disease can be prevented by treatment of asymptomatic tuberculous infection or early pulmonary disease.

ETIOLOGIC AGENT

The agent that causes tuberculosis is *M. tuberculosis*, often referred to as "M. TB" or the "tubercle bacillus." This mycobacterium is identified presumptively during light microscopic examination of body fluids that have been stained with special dyes by its "acid-fast" character and appearance as a red rod. This organism is slow-growing and requires up to 6 weeks of incubation on traditional culture media before it can be isolated and identified definitively by its biochemical reactions. Automated systems (e.g., Bactec) may allow isolation after only 1 to 2 weeks of incubation. Several different strains of *M. tuberculosis* have been distinguished by bacteriophage typing. There are reports of the presence of two distinct phage types in the same individual. Isolation of the infecting organism is important to allow in vitro susceptibility testing. During the 1980s, the rate of resistance to isoniazid (INH) had been approximately 7% in the

United States overall but may be as high as 13 to 60% in patients who come from areas of the world (e.g., Mexico, Southeast Asia) where tuberculosis is endemic and antituberculous drugs are given frequently for an inadequate length of time. However, since 1990, multiple drug resistance has become a major concern in the United States. Nationally, 14.4% of strains were resistant to at least one drug and 3.3% were resistant to both INH and rifampin, the most effective medicines available. In 1992, a survey in New York City found these numbers to be 33% resistant to one drug and 19% resistant to both INH and rifampin. Case fatality rates of 70 to 90% have been associated with United States outbreaks of multiply drug-resistant disease. Within each patient, there are several different populations of organisms. Because of the varying rates of multiplication and conditions of pH, nutrient supply, etc., a combination of two or more drugs is required for effective treatment.

EPIDEMIOLOGY

Source of the Organism.   The reservoir of *M. tuberculosis* for the child is the infected adult. Continued close contact of children with untreated adults in poorly ventilated rooms provides the greatest opportunity for transmission of infection. Although *Mycobacterium bovis* may cause disease in animals, it causes infection and illness in humans in the United States very rarely. Dogs are susceptible to the human type of tubercle bacillus, but there is little evidence to support a role for dogs in the transmission of tuberculous infection to children.

High-Risk Populations.   The following factors are associated with an increased risk of development of active tuberculosis: (a) age (less than 5 years, adolescence, elderly), (b) immunosuppression associated with primary disease or chemotherapy, (c) poor nutrition, (d) weight loss, (e) poorly controlled diabetes mellitus, (f) chronic renal failure, (g) silicosis, (h) intravenous drug use, (i) ethnic groups with high rates of endemic tuberculosis (e.g., Southeast Asians, Hispanics, Haitians, Indians, and Alaskan Eskimos), (j) the homeless, and (k) health care workers. The most important risk factor for the development of active tuberculosis is the presence of human immunodeficiency virus (HIV) infection and acquired immunodeficiency syndrome (AIDS). There is a nearly 200-fold increase in the risk of active disease in patients with far advanced AIDS.

Children younger than 5 years of age and especially infants in the first year of life have a reduced ability to limit spread of the initial tuberculous infection to other organs. Hormonal changes associated with puberty result in poor healing of the primary focus of infection, and waning immunity of the elderly who have been infected years previously accounts for their characteristic patterns of slowly progressive disease with cavitary lesions. The reactivation of earlier tuberculous infection in young urban males with AIDS as well as recent acquisition of infection, the influx into the U.S. of foreign-born individuals with undiagnosed tuberculosis and the decline in resources to support TB control programs explain the 20% increase in the number of cases of tuberculosis in the U.S. from 1985 to 1992. The 8.7% decrease in reported cases from 1992 to 1994 reflect the impact of federal funds to support directly observed therapy programs that ensure high treatment completion rates and cures. Active tuberculosis occurs early in the course of AIDS and may be the illness that leads to the diagnosis of AIDS in many adults.

Mode of Spread.   Tuberculous infection is spread primarily by airborne droplet nuclei. Although repeated direct exposure to infected individuals is usually necessary, it has been shown that sharing a common air supply with a highly infective individual may be sufficient. Only 4 to 5% of individuals with active tuberculosis transmit infection to their close household contacts, and 1% are considered "dangerous disseminators" because they transmit infection to their remote as well as close contacts. The risk factors most highly associated with transmission of infection are as follows: high concentration of organisms characteristic of cavitary lesions in adults, prolonged duration and proximity of exposure, increased frequency of cough, failure to cover mouth and nose when coughing and sneezing, aerosolization of infected body fluids and inadequate ventilation system of buildings. Of note, infants and young children are not routinely considered infective because they do not have cavitary lesions and are unable to generate a forceful cough; their sputum is usually swallowed rather than expelled and aerosolized. **In any child care or preschool setting, the visiting family members and friends who may have undiagnosed active tuberculosis are more likely to infect other children than is the young child who has been diagnosed and is on appropriate therapy.**

Since 1990, there have been several outbreaks of multiply drug-resistant tuberculosis within hospitals or correctional facilities involving highly compromised adults (usually HIV infected with highly contagious disease in poorly ventilated areas). Preschool-aged children have not been implicated in the transmission of tuberculosis. There are, in fact, few reports of transmission of tuberculosis in the child care or preschool setting. When it has occurred, spread was from adult to child rather than the usual child-to-child or child-to-adult route associated with diarrhea and viral respiratory infections in the child care center or preschool. Contact investigation of either the adult index case or the ill child identified several infected children within two separate day care homes.

Rarely, mycobacterial organisms present in purulent material that is draining from either an infected lymph node or bone could be transmitted to another individual either by direct contact or via hand carriage of a caretaker.

Incubation Period.   The incubation period from the time the mycobacteria enter the body to the time that the individual develops a positive skin test (cutaneous hypersensitivity) may vary from 2 to 10 weeks. The onset of tuberculin hypersensitivity may be accompanied by fever lasting for 1 to 3 weeks.

DIAGNOSIS

Standardized tuberculin skin testing is indicated to confirm a diagnosis of tuberculosis in the presence of one or more of the following conditions: (a) history of contact with an individual with active tuberculosis, (b) contact with immigrants from an endemic area, and (c) clinical and/or x-ray findings compatible with tuberculosis. Multiple puncture devices (Tine, Mono-Vacc, Aplitest) are no longer utilized for screening because of their inaccuracy. The intradermal (Mantoux) test where the exact dose of antigen, i.e., 5 tuberculin units (TU), is known and the size of the reactions can be interpreted reliably is now recommended by the Centers for Disease Control and Prevention, the American Thoracic Society, and the American Academy of Pediatrics. All tuberculin skin tests must be read by a health care professional at 48 to 72 hours after placement. Reactions occurring within the first 24 hours are not significant. A skin test is considered positive if there are 10 mm or more of induration at 48 to 72 hours. In close contacts of infective patients a skin test reaction of 5 mm or more of induration is considered positive. A 5-TU purified protein derivative (PPD) skin test that results in 10 mm or more of induration in an individual who has previously received bacillus Calmette-Guérin (BCG) vaccine is indicative of tuberculous infection. Any person with a positive skin test requires a chest x-ray and physician evaluation. Routine skin testing in low-risk groups or communities with a low prevalence of tuberculosis is not recommended.

Underlying conditions may suppress the skin test reaction; therefore, if the diagnosis of tuberculosis is strongly suspected, other methods of diagnosis must be pursued. Microscopic demonstration of *M. tuberculosis* in sputum, gastric aspirates, or other body fluids or tissues and isolation in culture are the definitive diagnostic techniques. Occasionally, skin test results are equivocal and must be repeated in 3 months.

THERAPY

All children with asymptomatic tuberculous infection or uncomplicated primary pulmonary tuberculosis are treated with oral antituberculous medications and do not require hospitalization. For asymptomatic infection, a single drug, INH, is given daily for 9 months. When there is evidence of active disease, a three-drug regimen, INH, rifampin, and pyrazinamide, is prescribed for 2 months and then INH and rifampin are continued for at least another 4 months to complete a minimum of 6 months of therapy. These medications are given daily for the first 4 to 8 weeks. Because the mycobacteria are so slow-growing, the medications may be given twice a week for the remaining 7 to 8 months of the course. Twice-a-week regimens are particularly advantageous for those families in whom compliance cannot be assured, since it is then feasible for school, child care, or public health workers actually to administer the medications. Direct observation of patients taking their medications is recommended for those families who are likely to be noncompliant.

In the presence of extensive disease (e.g., severe pulmonary involvement, miliary tuberculosis, meningitis, bone infection) or suspected drug resistance, a minimum of four antituberculous drugs is prescribed. Such children usually require hospitalization at least for the first several days or weeks of the illness. Once the disease process has been controlled, therapy may be completed as an out-patient. The course of therapy may be extended to 12 to 18 months, depending on the clinical response and the susceptibility of the or-ganisms to the drugs used. In cases of multiple drug resistance, other antituberculous medications, such as amikacin, streptomycin, ethambutol, and ethionamide, may be added to make up a 4- to 6-drug regimen. The addition of Ofloxacin is indicated for treatment of the multiply drug-resistant strains associated with the recent out-breaks in United States urban areas. Of all these antituberculosis medications, only amikacin and streptomycin cannot be given orally. Surgical drainage of localized infection may be required most frequently with bone or joint involvement. A prescribed course of therapy must be completed in order to prevent relapse or dissemi-nated disease. Young infants with asymptomatic tuberculous infec-tion are at great risk of developing meningitis or miliary tuberculo-sis if incompletely treated.

INFECTIOUS PERIOD

Children with asymptomatic or noncavitary lung disease are not in-fectious. Adolescents and adults with cavitary disease are infec-tious until effective antituberculous therapy has been initiated, the cough has decreased, and there is a diminishing number of organ-isms identified on acid-fast stains of their sputum. Infectivity de-creases dramatically after just a few days of appropriate therapy and only rarely persists beyond 1 to 2 weeks. Because of the threat of multiply drug-resistant tuberculosis, high-risk patients are con-sidered infective until there are *no* organisms seen on acid-fast stains of their sputum.

INFECTION CONTROL

Screening Prior to Entry.   Child care workers should be screened with a tuberculin skin test (preferably intracutaneous) prior to em-ployment. In the day home setting, *all* household members must be included for screening even if some individuals will not be caring for the children directly. Any person with a positive skin test requires a chest x-ray and physician evaluation. If a staff member with active tuberculosis is identified, he or she should be reported to the public health department, treated, and excluded from the child care center or preschool until no longer considered infective by the supervising physician. A complete contact investigation must be performed.

It is preferable to screen children at age 12 to 15 months with a tuberculin skin test. If, however, in very-low-risk areas, this practice is deferred, certainly any individual child from a high-risk group must be screened before enrollment. A positive skin test requires complete physician evaluation, chest x-ray, and contact investigation of the family before the child is admitted to the day care center. Routine screening every 1 to 2 years is recommended for children in high-risk settings.

Vaccine.   The BCG vaccines are derived from an attenuated strain of *M. bovis* and are effective in preventing serious disease resulting from tuberculous infection. These vaccines are used routinely in all newborns only in areas of the world where disease rates are excessive and surveillance and treatment of infected individuals are not possible. In the United States, the only candidates for BCG vaccine are young infants who will have repeated exposures to persistently untreated infective adults. This vaccine is given within the first few days of life.

Exclusion from Child Care or Preschool Attendance.   Infants and children with tuberculosis may attend the child care setting as long as they are receiving appropriate chemotherapy according to a carefully formulated plan. The normal level of activities may be resumed once symptoms have disappeared. Infants and children with draining wounds require a physician's statement that the drainage is no longer infective. The most important control measure is the limitation of exposure of other day care children to adolescent and adult household contacts of children with tuberculous infection until the contact investigation of the family has been completed and all individuals with active tuberculosis are on appropriate chemotherapy and judged to be noninfective.

Recommendations for Other Children.   The public health department should be notified and will assist in completing the contact investigation. Extent of exposure of the other children to the source adult case will determine extent of screening:

1. If the source adult is a child care worker or a family member who has had regular contact with the children, the exposure is high-risk, similar to that of household contacts. All children less than 6 years of age are skin-tested, have a chest x-ray performed,

and begin INH preventive therapy. Any child with a negative skin test is retested at 10 to 12 weeks. If the test remains negative, the initial chest x-ray was negative, and the child is well, INH is discontinued. If either the first or second skin test is positive, INH is continued for 9 months. Children 6 years or older do not require INH preventive therapy in the absence of an initial positive skin test.

2. If the source adult is a household contact of the infected child and has had limited or no exposure to the other children in the center, the risk of infection is minimal. All children are skin-tested initially. Children with positive skin tests receive chest x-ray and INH for 9 months. Repeated skin testing at 10 to 12 weeks for those children who are initially negative is not recommended unless other family members with regular exposure to the child care center or other child care center attendees were discovered to have active tuberculosis during the contact investigation.

3. Alternative preventive drugs will be considered if the index case is infected with a multiply drug-resistant strain of *M. tuberculosis.*

Recommendations for Personnel.   As for the children, the extent of contact with the source adult determines the extent of screening that is recommended. If there has been frequent exposure to the source adult, initial skin testing is performed and, if negative, repeated at 10 to 12 weeks. Initiation of INH preventive therapy for adults with a negative initial skin test is indicated only for individuals who have impaired immunity. Pregnant women are evaluated as healthy adults and are treated only when definite infection has been demonstrated. If extent of exposure to the source adult is unclear, a single skin testing is recommended.

Parental Advice.   The parents must be informed of the situation and educated concerning the projected risks to their children. It is most effective to prepare a written statement in collaboration with the public health department or a physician who serves in an advisory role for the child care center or preschool, in addition to holding a group meeting. It is important to provide reassurance and education that will correct the common misconceptions that people have about tuberculosis. When the source adult is a family member who has had minimal or no contact with the other children and is not a teacher or child care worker, it should be emphasized that skin testing is a conservative precaution and the risk of infection in the children is minimal. New enrollees should not be accepted until the tuberculin status of all adult child care workers has been determined.

64

Varicella-Zoster Virus
(Chickenpox, Shingles)

ANNE A. GERSHON, M.D.

CLINICAL MANIFESTATIONS

Varicella (chickenpox) is the primary infection with varicella-zoster virus (VZV). It usually occurs in children younger than 10 years of age, although it may develop in older children and even adults. Symptoms include a rash that begins with maculopapular lesions that rapidly progress to vesicles, pustules, and crusts. The lesions are most concentrated on the trunk, face, and scalp. They are intensely pruritic. The illness is often accompanied by fever and lasts for about 5 days. Subclinical varicella is believed to occur in about 5% of cases. The major complication in otherwise-healthy persons is bacterial superinfection of the skin. The disease is usually benign in children, unless they are immunocompromised. In severe cases the lesions may number in the thousands and become hemorrhagic. Primary varicella pneumonia is a serious complication in such patients. Generally, the extent of the skin rash is a good indication of the mildness or severity of a case of varicella; the more severe the illness, the greater the number of skin lesions. The average child with chickenpox develops 250 to 500 vesicles over about 5 days.

Zoster is a secondary infection with VZV. It occurs only in persons who have experienced a previous episode of either clinical or subclinical varicella. The virus becomes latent in sensory ganglia during varicella and may remain latent for months to years. The virus infects a dermatomal area of skin, resulting in a unilateral localized vesicular eruption that may be painful. Zoster is most common in immunocompromised patients and the elderly, although children may manifest it. Children seem to be at increased risk if, while they were in utero, their mothers had varicella or they had varicella before 1 year of age. Zoster in childhood is usually a mild self-limited illness, unless the child is immunocompromised.

ETIOLOGIC AGENT

VZV is a herpesvirus closely related to herpes simplex viruses, cytomegalovirus, and Epstein-Barr virus (EBV). There is only one serotype. There is no cross-protection among these agents although there are some shared antigens. All of the herpesviruses become latent after primary infection and may later reactivate. VZV and herpes simplex viruses become latent in sensory ganglia.

EPIDEMIOLOGY

Source of the Organism.   The major sources of the virus are the respiratory tract and the skin lesions of both varicella and zoster, which, when moist, are full of infectious virions. Presumably, virions become aerosolized when patients scratch the skin lesions. Although it is almost impossible to culture VZV from respiratory secretions, the respiratory tract is also probably a source of infectious virus, and children are believed to be at least somewhat contagious to others 1 to 2 days before developing the varicella rash. Varicella is extremely contagious, but zoster is less so. In both instances, varicella is transmitted to others.

High-Risk Populations.   Individuals who have not previously been infected with VZV and who therefore have no antibodies or cell-mediated immunity to VZV are at risk to develop varicella following exposure to someone with either varicella or zoster. Second attacks of varicella are unusual, and if they occur, they are likely to be mild. Subclinical re-infection of persons who have had varicella is common following subsequent exposure.

Patients with defects in cellular immunity are at additional risk to develop severe varicella if they have not had the infection previously. Newborn infants whose mothers have the onset of varicella between 5 days before and 2 days after delivery are also at high risk to develop severe varicella. They should be given passive immunization and/or antiviral therapy (see Therapy).

Mode of Spread.   The virus is spread by the airborne route. Varicella is not spread by fomites but requires person-to-person contact. In family settings the attack rate among susceptibles is 80 to 90%. Transmission after less intimate exposures (such as in school) is less predictable. The disease is not transmissible until 1 to 2 days prior to development of rash, and it remains transmissible until skin lesions have crusted.

Incubation Period.   10 to 21 days.

DIAGNOSIS

The diagnosis of both varicella and zoster can usually be made on clinical grounds, based on the history of contact and the nature and distribution of the rash. When the rash is not characteristic of varicella, a scraping of a skin lesion can be obtained for staining with commercially available fluorescein-labeled monoclonal antibody to VZV, and the diagnosis made within a few hours. Skin lesions may also be cultured for the presence of virus. Acute and convalescent antibody titers for VZV antibodies may also be obtained, but the diagnosis cannot be made for at least 7 to 10 days after the onset of illness by this method. The diagnosis of zoster can be made on similar grounds. There is no need to elicit a history of contact with someone with VZV, however, since zoster is the result of reactivation of latent infection.

THERAPY

Double-blind placebo-controlled studies of oral administration of acyclovir (ACV) to children and adolescents within 24 hours after onset of the rash of varicella have indicated that this therapy shortens the course of the illness by about a day. The dose is 20 mg/kg (maximum, 800 mg/dose) four times a day for 5 days. The American Academy of Pediatrics has published recommendations for use of ACV in children with chickenpox. One approach is to administer it to children over age 12 years and to secondary household cases that are predictably more severe than the primary case in a family. It is not recommended that ACV be given to try to prevent varicella from developing if an exposure has been recognized.

Immunocompromised children with no history of varicella should be given varicella-zoster immune globulin (VZIG) within 3 (maximum,

5) days of a close exposure to someone with either varicella or zoster. Infants born to women with the onset of varicella 5 days before delivery to 2 days after delivery should also receive VZIG.

Children who develop severe varicella should be treated with intravenous ACV, 1500 mg/m^2/day, for 7 to 10 days. Immunocompromised children who develop varicella and have not received either VZIG or varicella vaccine (see below) should also be treated with intravenous ACV as early in the illness as possible, even if the disease is mild and there are few skin lesions, mainly to prevent the development of varicella pneumonia.

Usually, zoster in children does not require therapy, since it is a self-limited illness. Exceptions include zoster of the ophthalmic division of the trigeminal nerve and zoster in an immunocompromised child. Each case requires individualization. Dosages are as for treatment of varicella.

INFECTIOUS PERIOD

Patients with varicella and zoster are infectious to others until all the skin lesions have crusted; usually this occurs within 5 to 7 days, but it may be longer in immunosuppressed patients.

INFECTION CONTROL

Vaccine.   A live attenuated varicella vaccine (Oka strain) was licensed by the FDA for use in all children over the age of 12 months and for adults who are susceptible to chickenpox, in March 1995. It is recommended by both the American Academy of Pediatrics and the Centers for Disease Control that vaccine be routinely given to varicella-susceptibles. Children should be immunized on the basis of a negative history; individuals older than 21 years should be serologically tested for antibodies to VZV if they have no history of disease before vaccination. Most adults with no history of varicella are, in fact, immune. Since the vaccine cannot be given to pregnant women, and since it is recommended that women not become pregnant until at least 3 months after a dose of varicella vaccine, it is particularly important to determine if women of childbearing age with no history of varicella have detectable antibodies. Administration of vaccine inadvertently to persons who are immune to varicella, however, is not harmful.

Exclusion from Child Care or Preschool Attendance.   Children with acute natural (wild-type) varicella should not attend day care or preschool until all the lesions have crusted. This usually leads to exclusion for about 5 to 7 days. The rare child with zoster can attend day care or preschool if the skin lesions are on the trunk and can be fully covered with a sterile dressing and clothing. (Children who were immunized may develop a rash during the 6 weeks following immunization. Only 5% of vaccinated children develop a rash, and most of these rashes consist of only a few lesions that resemble insect bites. Although these children with rash may potentially transmit vaccine-type VZV to others, when there are less than 10 skin lesions transmission of vaccine-type virus is highly unlikely. Since the vaccine-associated rash can theoretically be transmitted much like zoster, the lesions should be covered or the child should not attend day care for the 2 to 3 days that the lesions are present.) It should be remembered, however, that until there is universal use of varicella vaccine with resultant little circulation of wild-type VZV, some children with apparent vaccine-associated rashes may actually be in the early stages of natural varicella that was in the incubation period when they were immunized. It should also be kept in mind that transmission of vaccine-type virus is less dangerous than transmission of wild-type VZV. It appears that the vaccine-type virus is less able to result in transmission and when transmission occurs the resultant illness is a very modified form of varicella due to the attenuated nature of the vaccine-type virus. Clinical reversion to virulence has not been observed. In general, these recommendations also apply to adults who have recently been immunized. It is strongly recommended that day care and preschool facilities prospectively develop their own policies for potential management of vaccinated children and adults; these will need to be modified periodically as the vaccine is more widely implemented. Routine use of varicella vaccine should prevent much disease in child day care settings. In addition to the theoretical potential for transmission of vaccine-type VZV, there is also potential for vaccinees to transmit wild-type virus to others months to years after vaccination. Breakthrough infections can occur after exposure to the natural virus. However, only about 1% of immunized children will develop a mild case of breakthrough varicella annually, after being immunized with the currently licensed vaccine.

Recommendations for Other Children. VZIG is recommended only for immunocompromised children at high risk to develop severe varicella. "Regular" immune globulin is not useful unless given in massive doses, and its use is therefore strongly discouraged.

Recommendations for Personnel. Adults who have never had varicella should be immunized before being exposed to VZV. Adults (and children who have already reached the 13th birthday) should be given two doses of vaccine 4 to 8 weeks apart. This will result in a seroconversion (measured by the latex agglutination assay for VZV antibodies) in about 90% of adults. Those who do not seroconvert after two doses may be given a third dose and be retested for development of antibodies. Adults who fail to seroconvert after three doses of vaccine are unlikely to respond to a fourth dose and must be regarded as varicella-susceptible. Adults who seroconvert after two doses can be expected to be protected against varicella. About 70% will achieve complete protection; the remaining 30% will develop modified varicella with an average of 50 skin lesions and rapid recovery. About 10% of adult seroconverters lose detectable antibodies within several years after varicella; those that do are among the 30% who are at risk to develop breakthrough varicella. It is possible for physicians to arrange for testing of VZV lesions to determine whether they are due to wild- or vaccine-type VZV. Adult vaccinees who remain seropositive are highly unlikely to develop breakthrough varicella following exposure to the wild-type virus. Varicella-susceptible pregnant women who develop wild-type chickenpox in the first or second trimester of pregnancy have a 2% risk of delivering a child with the characteristic constellation of birth defects (skin, nervous system, and eyes) of the congenital varicella syndrome. This syndrome has not been observed to be caused by the vaccine-type virus, although at present there is little information on this subject. Presumably the attenuated vaccine-type virus poses less of a risk.

Parental Advice. Parents should be notified of the occurrence of varicella in an attendee or staff member in case there is a varicella-susceptible pregnant woman or immunocompromised person in the family.

65

Yersinia

WILLIAM J. RODRIGUEZ M.D., PH.D., AND BARBARA A. JANTAUSCH, M.D.

CLINICAL MANIFESTATIONS

Yersinia pestis is responsible for human plague. *Yersinia enterocolitica* and *Yersinia pseudotuberculosis* cause gastrointestinal illness that is collectively called yersiniosis. *Y. enterocolitica* primarily causes diarrhea, nausea, and fever and also can cause mesenteric adenitis. It is the cause of large epidemics of enteritis. Children with *Y. enterocolitica* infections may have fever to 40° C with bloody diarrhea, nausea, vomiting, and colicky abdominal pain. Stools may be watery but are more often mucoid. Illness may last from a few days to 1 month, but it usually is present for less than 10 days. Infection may be asymptomatic. *Y. pseudotuberculosis* causes abdominal pain and mesenteric adenitis. It also can be responsible for a pseudoappendicitis syndrome, prompting appendectomy that in most cases yields a normal appendix and suppurative mesenteric lymph nodes.

Extraintestinal manifestations of *Yersinia* infections include arthritis, erythema nodosum, Reiter's syndrome, thrombocytopenia, bacteremia, and meningitis. Asymptomatic infections occur rarely.

ETIOLOGIC AGENT

Yersinia is an enteric nonlactose-fermenting Gram-negative coccobacillus belonging to the family *Enterobacteriaceae*. The genus *Yersinia* contains three species: *Y. pestis*, *Y. pseudotuberculosis*, and *Y. enterocolitica*. *Y. pseudotuberculosis* has 7 serogroups distinguished on the basis of somatic O antigen; *Y. enterocolitica* has 34 distinguishable

O serotypes, with O:3 being the most common and O:3, O:5, O:8, and O:9 causing the majority of human disease.

EPIDEMIOLOGY

Source of the Organism.   Primary reservoirs for *Yersinia* are contaminated food and water and animal carriers, specifically, dogs, cats (especially those who have stayed in animal shelters), pigs, cows, goats, horses, rabbits, squirrels, domestic fowl, and fish. A recognized cause of yersiniosis in young infants is contact with an adult who has handled pork intestines (chitterlings).

High-Risk Populations.   Children with hemolytic conditions such as those leading to increased storage of iron may be at high risk, as are those on immunosuppressive therapy. Nosocomial transmission of *Y. enterocolita* has been reported.

Mode of Spread.   Food or water contaminated by feces or urine from animals is probably the main mode of spread; others include the fecal-oral route and person-to-person transmission. The organism is able to survive in refrigerated milk.

Incubation Period.   The incubation period is 2 to 11 days, with an average of 5 days, but may extend up to 3 weeks.

DIAGNOSIS

Y. enterocolitica may be isolated from stool cultures by using enteric media with incubation at room temperature to facilitate growth. "Cold enrichment" by inoculation of broth cultures and incubation at 4° to 6°C for a few weeks may enhance recovery of organisms, but it is usually too time-consuming to be considered practical in an acute clinical situation. *Y. pseudotuberculosis* is rarely recovered from stool cultures; in cases of mesenteric adenitis it has been grown from infected lymph nodes. In disseminated infection, *Yersinia* can be readily recovered from standard media such as blood agar, which supports the growth of Gram-negative organisms. A fourfold rise in antibody titer specific against the offending serotype could be diagnostic.

THERAPY

Despite the fact that antibiotic therapy has not proven to be definitively effective in *Y. enterocolitica* enterocolitis, we would recommend the use of effective oral antimicrobial agents (as determined by antibiogram) in symptomatic patients. *Y. enterocolitica* is usually sensitive to aminoglycosides, third-generation cephalosporins, chloramphenicol, and trimethoprim-sulfamethoxazole. For those older than 9 years tetracyclines could be used if susceptible. Treatment of enteric disease without invasion should be with absorbable antimicrobials for 5 to 7 days.

INFECTIOUS PERIOD

Y. enterocolitica has been recovered from the stool 4 to 79 days (average, 27 days) after symptoms have resolved and as long as 6 weeks despite antimicrobial exposure.

INFECTION CONTROL

Vaccine.   None available.

Exclusion from Child Care or Preschool Attendance.   Although the period of communicability is unknown, it seems reasonable to keep the child out of the center while symptomatic.

Recommendations for Other Children.   Children should avoid contact with feces. Other children in the setting who become symptomatic with diarrhea should be removed from the setting and have their stools cultured for *Yersinia.*

Recommendations for Personnel.   Personnel who become symptomatic should remain at home and have their stools cultured for *Yersinia.* All personnel should practice good handwashing. Diapers should be disposed of properly, and separate diaper and food preparation areas provided. Toys that the infected child played with should be disinfected. New children should not be enrolled during an outbreak.

Parental Advice.   Parents should observe their child for symptoms of enteritis. Symptomatic children should be removed from day care, seen by their pediatrician, and have their stools cultured. The physician should be informed of what is going on at the child care center or preschool.

Index

Page numbers followed by "t" denote tables.